YOUR AURA
YOUR CHAKRAS

ALSO BY KARLA McLAREN

BOOKS
*Rebuilding the Garden: Healing the Spiritual Wounds
of Childhood Sexual Assault*

Further Into the Garden: Discovering Your Chakras

AUDIOTAPES
Healing Your Auras & Chakras: Accessing Your Energetic Wisdom

Healing for Healers: How to Give Without Giving it All Away

YOUR AURA & YOUR CHAKRAS

THE OWNER'S MANUAL

Karla McLaren

SAMUEL WEISER, INC.
York Beach, Maine

First published in 1998 by
Samuel Weiser, Inc.
P. O. Box 612
York Beach, ME 03910-0612

Library of Congress Cataloging-in-Publication Data

McLaren, Karla.
    Your aura and your chakras : the owner's manual / Karla McLaren.
        p.   cm.
    Includes bibliographical references and index.
    ISBN 1-57863-047-9 (alk. paper)
    1. Aura.   2. Chakras.   I. Title.
BF1389.A8M35   1998
133.8'92—dc21   98-22486
                                                          CIP

Cover design by Kath Christensen

Typeset in 11 point Berkeley

Printed in U.S.A.

EB

05 04 03 02 01 00 99
  10 9 8 7 6 5 4 3 2

The paper used in this publication meets all the minimum requirements
of the American National Standard for Permanence of Paper for Printed
Library Materials Z39.48.1984.

Beyond sculptures and symphonies,
beyond great works and masterpieces,
is the greater, finer art of molding a conscious life.
Genius appears everywhere, but never so magnificently
as in a life well lived.

—*Karla McLaren*

CONTENTS

ACKNOWLEDGMENTS

I would like to thank my many teachers. My parents taught me to live effectively in the tension between the opposites. My brothers and sisters adored and challenged me, and made me smarter, faster, funnier, and kinder than I ever would have been without them. My mother continues to offer (but only when I ask) encyclopedic information about health, spirituality, art, and integrity. Mary Figueroa taught me to shine without excuses or apologies. Bruce Hyde modeled renown coupled with tenderness and dignity. Sarah Stone knew I was a writer before I did. She is my touchstone.

Marshall, Quinta, Brocke, and Kyia Lever provided me with moral and spiritual discipline, and an unintended education about the dangers inherent in spiritual leadership and group pursuits. Lewis Bostwick, Michael Tamura, and Pat McAnaney taught me about the limits and responsibilities of psychic power. My spirit guides persist in teaching me about the difference between knowledge and wisdom. And my many students and allies teach me everything else.

The people at Samuel Weiser continue to teach me about precision, clarity, and commitment. Kath Christensen helps me balance (beautifully, I might add) art and commerce. My son's patience (and lack of it) helps me balance the writing life with real life. My incomparable husband, Tino, embodies and inspires compassion, integrity, and emotional genius in every moment. I am blessed.

INTRODUCTION

Working knowledge of the aura and the chakras has long been the exclusive domain of psychics and mystics. This is understandable in a culture that exiles spirituality to the outer fringes, but it is unfortunate. At present, psychics and mystics hold all of our spirituality, while the rest of us knock around in a world bereft of meaning.

Without a personal connection to our own spirituality and to God, most of us live in a netherworld, however pretty or moneyed it might be. We place our spiritual communication skills in the hands of churches and clergy, or shamans and mystics, and miss out on the greatest and most evolutionary adventure of all: the search for personal relevance, individual destiny, and a rich, meaningful path.

Without personal meaning, life is only a shadow of what might be. Deep devotion to a certain pre-existing spiritual path can bring meaning to some, but it can't work for everyone. One simple look at the many splinter factions of any given religion will make this clear.

Even Christianity, that supposed bulwark of all religions, has more splinters, fighting factions, strange offshoots, and fundamentalist ideologies than can be counted. The only common thread is a devotion to Jesus the Christ, though his appearance and demeanor change startlingly from one Christian sect to the next. It is much the same in any religious tradition.

The only thing religions have in common is a belief in a higher intelligence and a wish to share (often forcibly) that belief with others. Most religions do not support independent thought, nor do they allow their followers an autonomous connection to God. They wouldn't be religions if they did; they'd be philosophical societies.

Welcome to my philosophical society. The rules are pretty simple. I trust your abilities and your intelligence; I trust in

God and Jesus, but I do so in my own way. I also trust in Lao Tse, Krishna, Buddha (in his peppier moments), Allah, Horus and Osiris, and Kurt Vonnegut, Jr.

I am fatigued with the New Age and its focus on money, power, and perfect health. I prefer to live in the actual world, where I am a child of God, but not God himself. My work with psychic healing tools is not a way to gain power and perfection. It is my way to clear out my mind and psyche so I can receive healthy guidance, and not waste God's time on problems I can handle myself.

This isn't the place to find a new religion, more power, more money, or perfect health, but if you're looking for some new ideas, or help on your path back to your excellent, messy, meaningful, real life, then you're a part of my philosophical society, and I'm a part of yours.

PART I

THE BASICS

GETTING STARTED

You won't need fantastic psychic power or vision to become a competent self-healer; all you'll need is simple, in-the-body, grounded awareness. If you are already a psychic and you've come to this book to increase your abilities, please know this: there is no ability higher than the ability to know yourself.

I have known too many gifted psychics whose lives went nowhere; I have seen and known the tragedy of using spiritual gifts on others *instead* of on the self. I have also found that truly well and integrated people are the best healers of all, though their healing is usually hidden in perfectly timed phone calls, searching questions, and loving gifts. The best healers don't swoop in and remove all discomfort; they simply assist people in healing themselves. The best healers remind you of your personal connection to God, or to the creative energies of the universe. They won't stand above you, god-like, and block your view of the divine.

Don't fall for the idea that some other human is more spiritual than you are, and don't try to wield spiritual power over others. Healing is not a self-aggrandizing event or a sideshow. Healing is a process of awareness, intention, and discovery. This work is *not* about channeling, past-life readings, precognition, fortune-telling, or external psychic power. This work is about getting into the meat of your life; it's about dealing with the issues you brought here, and the issues you've created. This work is about getting you grounded.

A real healer can heal because he has done, and continues to do, his own work. He works with his own health or lack of it. He is honest with himself and he is honest with others. His healing is not a bag of tricks or pills, but a collection of awareness techniques and supportive stances. He attains these through study—both of his healing modality and of his own life. He attains healing status by maintaining his inner life *and* his healing practice.

Your first job—before you learn to heal, before you learn to read your aura and chakras—is to create a place from which to read and heal. You will need to clear a space in your busy life and your busy mind. If you don't, you'll be coming at this information as a dabbler, and not as a serious student. You won't come away with knowledge; you'll only have facts.

Consider alchemy, which is the fabled ability to turn base metals into gold. The very idea is exciting. Imagine having that kind of power! But no one does. The reason isn't that alchemy is impossible, but that the steps to becoming an alchemist are arduous and time-consuming. In times past, an aspiring alchemist had to learn all the arts of herbalism and magic, fire-making and divining, reading, writing, dead languages, and more. As you can well imagine, none of this drudgery was tolerable to people who just wanted gold, gold, gold!

Somewhere along the way, the few alchemists who accepted the drudgery and "made the cut" became less interested in gold, and more interested in the learning itself. The gold fever dissipated as the soul discovered more tangible wealth. Perhaps the ability to transform metal was achieved, perhaps not. The role of the alchemist in society, however, was always gained through his or her vast and deep knowledge. The flashier magic tricks played only a minor (though memorable) role.

If you'd like to be a Merlin without doing any work, I'm sure you'll find a teacher or a book to help you. I'm not that teacher, and this isn't that book. Feel free to skip ahead to the sections on flashy aura and chakra readings, but know that the flash only comes after the work, and then, the flash turns to light and awareness. The path of the competent psychic reader is one of work, study, self-appraisal, more self-appraisal, more study, and more work. It's good work, if you can get it.

AND NOW, THE WARNING: Change is wonderful and change is vital, but most living systems will resist change. This resistance, this *stasis*, is also wonderful and vital. Both are needed in a healthy body, a healthy family, a healthy community, and a healthy society. However, because we are a people trained to look at one thing *or* the other, and very seldom both, we objectify change and stasis as good or bad, depending on our situation.

We love it when our bodies utilize stasis and continue to function and maintain their weight when we forget to eat, sleep, and care for ourselves—but we hate it when they utilize stasis and won't drop weight when it's time to get into summer clothes. Conversely, we love changes when they benefit us, and hate them when they don't. We aren't trained to take the long view—to see change and stasis as equal parts in a perfect and healthy continuum.

This book will change your life, which means that your life and the people in it may attempt to utilize stasis in order to keep you from changing. Though your people may drive you out of your mind, and their stay-as-you-are tactics may feel unsafe and unsettling, stasis just *is*. When people slow you down and question you and threaten you and get in the way of your change, it means they consider you a part of their universe. By stifling you, they are protecting you, their universe, and the status quo. This pull toward stasis is a sign of a working (though not necessarily healthy) system that is being disrupted by your steps toward consciousness.

Depending on your environment, stasis may come at you as concern, interruptions and increased attention from others, or criticism and derision to bring your self-worth back to a manageable low. All interference needs to be addressed either verbally, or through the separation techniques included in this book, such as *destroying images* and *burning contracts* (see pages 56 and 77). You must understand however, that interfering people are only trying to help you live up to the relationships you have worked with, fought for, and agreed upon together.

When we enter into relationships, we often create energetic contracts that state which behaviors are acceptable, who does what to whom, how we will all look and react, and so on. These unconscious contracts create a shape and a container for the relationship. Even in healthy relationships, the freedom to make sudden change is rarely a part of such contracts. When people make changes, their contractual partners may feel a right to re-examine those unconscious contracts and force compliance in whatever way they can. This is not a bad thing in itself. It just *is*. Often, people who won't allow change are simply trying to protect a position and a relationship that was agreed upon over time—whether the parties were consciously aware of it or not. It is immeasurably helpful to remember this fact when working through this book.

In this book, there are a very large number of separation and safety tools to help you make your vital changes without pulling a huge blob of stasis down onto your life. It is important to realize, however, that stasis is an irreplaceable aspect of any natural system. Once your healing tools are a part of you, and your system accepts new ideas like grounding and centering, reading your chakras, and healing your aura, these tools will become a part of your new stasis. You won't have to consciously ground and heal yourself every day. These techniques and abilities will become a part of your life; they won't feel foreign or threatening. Soon, any threats to your newfound healing abilities will pull that blob of protective stasis over your aura and your grounding. Then, you'll know you've moved to a new place in consciousness.

As you move on in consciousness, you will most likely move on in your relationships as well. This can be lonely and frightening if you don't realize what's happening. As I made my changes, I became disconnected from my entire nuclear family. I now have a group of friends and relations who are my spiritual family. The energy of stasis helped me realize that I was losing something that had importance, but the energy of change helped me to know that I was moving on to something closer to my real self. Both change and stasis are necessary in any real forward movement.

As you move onward, your old ways of living will call to you. Sometimes, they will scream. If you can recognize these calls as stasis energy and thank them for protecting you, you will move on more gracefully. If the calls for stasis come from the people in your life, no matter how painfully loud the calls are, you can see them as love and safety offerings of one kind or another. If you can see the concern behind the calls and address them from that knowledge, instead of from a knee-jerk peevishness, you will not only move on more gracefully, you will bring light into the lives of those around you.

It's important to note, as you make these changes, how other people attempt to maintain the status quo. You may be very surprised, in the weeks and months ahead, at who supports you with concern and attention and who hinders you with violence and shame. Your circle of friends may change in startling ways as your energy changes. You will soon reach a new stasis, however, and create a new contractual foundation for your life and relationships. The key here is to remove yourself from people who try to maintain stasis at the cost of your health and sanity.

If you are in an abusive environment, or if you want to stay in an abusive relationship (to people, to work or living arrangements, or to drugs), I would ask you to put this book down immediately and stop right here.

This work will navigate you out of unworkable situations. You will begin to break away from old patterns. You will shake up your world. If you're ready to move on, this shake-up is excellent. If you want to stay where you are, and you are being abused or are abusing yourself, this work will create terrible upheavals. When shake-ups happen, your lack of resolve will turn them into full-scale, inescapable dramas—instead of interesting detours on your journey home.

The real warning is this: don't go any further if you want to stay where you are. It is a very dangerous thing to undertake a spiritual journey if you have no intention of ever getting anywhere. Please, if you want to stay put, accept my regards and *put this book down*. There are many paths besides this one. You have the time to honor stasis in your own present-day world. Your change may need to come later.

However, if you're ready to go on, turn the page and let's get started.

A Room
of Your Own

Our very first step in becoming competent intuitive readers is to create a safe and quiet place from which to read. Many therapies and meditation systems help people create mental sanctuaries. We'll go one step further and create this sanctuary within your body, within the present time, and within your actual life. We'll create a room inside your head.

The room in your head is a private and unreachable place that does not depend on others or on physical surroundings for its peacefulness. It doesn't even require quiet or large blocks of time. It is a place where privacy is always available, inside your body. The room in your head can help to anchor your consciousness in your body by giving you a way to control what goes on inside it.

For many people, being inside the body will be a new sensation. Most of us spend our time in the past, in the future, in conflicts, and in what-ifs. This first tool gives us a chance to gather our awareness and begin to integrate.

CREATING THE ROOM IN YOUR HEAD

Here's how to make the room: draw an imaginary line straight backward from the top of your nose to the back of your head. Now draw another line from the top of your right ear to the top of your left ear (see figure 1, page 10). The point where these two lines intersect will be the center of your room. Make sure

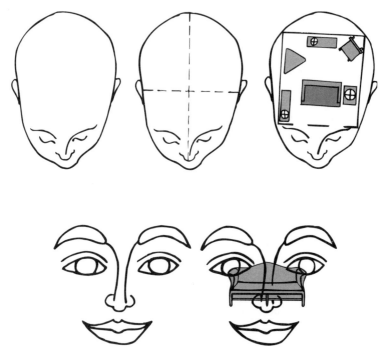

Figure 1. Creating the room in your head.

that the floor of your room is centered low in your head, at about the middle of your nose, and not any higher. If it's centered higher, you could experience dizziness (see the Troubleshooting Guide, page 268 for an explanation).

Create four walls, a floor, and a ceiling—all inside your head. In the front of the room, there will be two windows (your eyes) with a door between them. Hang a *Do Not Disturb* sign outside this door while you work.

Now comes the fun part. Decorate this room in any style you like, but remember that this is your sanctuary. Don't fill it with noise and bustle, or make it inviting to anyone else. Other people are absolutely not allowed in this room. Bring in art and pillows, a hot tub or a fireplace, and perhaps a totem animal or two. Make your room into an Egyptian temple, a crystal cave, an Old English castle library, or a Mesopotamian pavilion. Do not replicate a room that exists in your life already; instead, make this room your fantasy destination.

Create a luxurious, comfortable seat for yourself (and no one else) right in front of the windows of your eyes, and imagine looking out at your very favorite nature scene. With this scene before you, you can have a sense of peace and a connection to nature that won't depend on your surroundings. Even in the middle of a traffic jam, you can be looking out on a garden or a forest, or on a desert at moonrise.

When your room is ready, take your seat in it and practice looking out from behind your eyes. Try staying in your room for a minute or so, but don't worry if you can't just yet. It can take a little practice to actually stay in your body. I've had my room for almost twenty years now, and sometimes I stay out for days or weeks at a time. When I notice this, I don't smack myself, I just get back in. I'm always reminded, however, that I never do my best work during these totally out-of-body times.

One very easy way to tell if you're not in your room is to bring your hand toward your face and press the top of your nose with your fingers. If you feel your attention being moved back into your head, you probably weren't there to begin with. Another quick way to check in is to notice whether you can see your nose and your eyelashes without focusing on them. If your awareness is centered behind your eyes, your nose and your lashes will always be within your field of view.

Keep working at staying behind your eyes and in your room. If you don't want to be there at all, change the decor or the configuration until you are comfortable. Check in with yourself throughout the day to see how your room or your feelings about it have changed. Don't hesitate to redecorate, and remember that this room can be as opulent or fantastical as you like. It won't cost you anything!

※

Most people have heard that it is best to "Be Here Now." I have heard over and over again that the only real power lives in the present—that the past is a memory and the future a dream.

None of it clicked for me, however, until I got into my body (I left my body during a childhood assault; see my book, *Rebuilding the Garden* [Columbia, CA: Laughing Tree Press, 1997]). The room in my head anchored me to the real world because it gave me, for the first time that I could consciously remember, a place to be alone, in control, and at peace. One of my students describes this room as the control center. I agree with that description. Being in your room feels like being in the cockpit of an airplane, in a lookout tower, or on a throne. There's a lot of quiet power inside our bodies.

As for the "Be Here Now" theory, each of us lives in a vessel that can only be here now. Our bodies cannot live in the past; they cannot travel to the future; they can only exist in each moment. If we climb into our bodies and sit behind our eyes, we will live in the moment. It's as simple as that. Since all power exists in the present moment, living in our bodies will give us the power we need to live and grow and heal.

❋

If creating your room is difficult, it is perfectly acceptable to just pretend to do so. Creating the room in your head may be the first conscious contact you've had with your body for a while. As such, your body will usually have a great deal to say to you about this pain here, and that person there, and these emotions, and so on. This chatter will fade, and the technique called *grounding* (see next section) will help your body to calm down. For now, it is perfectly sufficient to establish the space behind your eyes, fill it with things you adore, make yourself a comfortable chair, and look out on your favorite nature scene for as long as you can manage.

I must stress that being in the center of your head should not feel natural to you yet. We're not taught to center ourselves, and the focal point of our consciousness could be just about anywhere. If you're a good athlete or mathematician, your consciousness may hover somewhere above and in front of your head, but it could also be behind your head or beside your shoulder. It is natural and healthy for your consciousness to drift around. It should drift whenever it likes, but you should also have an aware connection to it. You should be able to call it to attention when you need to.

Your consciousness already knows how to change its focus and its location. You already have a reading and writing focus, an art or music focus, a cooking and eating focus, a just-before-bed focus, a balancing focus, etc. Your consciousness already knows how to move and how to stand still. This exercise of creating a meditative focus can be simplified if you realize that you are merely creating a new center for your consciousness to visit.

You should not try to force your consciousness to stay in the center of your head at all times of the day. This would not only be unnatural and unhealthy, it would be impossible. Your consciousness must be allowed to move as it wishes, until you need to center yourself for meditation. Then it should be able to gather itself behind your eyes as you work. As an aid, you can simply press your fingers on the top of your nose and usher your awareness back into your room. It's not cheating; I do it all the time. When I'm done with my meditation, I let my conscious focus go wherever it likes. It knows what it's doing.

Take your time and create your room (cave, grotto, throne room, turret, tent, or whatever) even if you can't get into your head at all. Create a foundation. It gets easier.

GETTING GROUNDED

Creating the room in your head is a gentle way to say hello to your body. Your body needs more than a greeting from you, however, if it is to live in peace. Grounding and connecting yourself to the Earth is the next step.

People can connect with their bodies and the Earth in many ways: through touch and body work, through eating, through being out in nature or in water, through contact with animals, and through healthy sex. I call the process of getting in the body and connecting to the present and the Earth *grounding*. It is a very simple process that most people do naturally throughout the course of each day.

If you've ever been light-headed from hunger and then felt a sigh of contentment as you fed your body the perfect meal, you've experienced grounding. If you've ever melted into the back rub you got from a trusted person at the end of a stress-filled week, you've experienced grounding. Anything that brings you back to the present and back to a sense of pleasure and release is grounding.

People who are not grounded tend to be unfocused, unsettled, stress-filled and stressful, and heavily invested in controlling everything around them. People who are naturally grounded are generally earthy, centered, and at home in their bodies. The act of grounding tends to center and focus people, because it calms their bodies down and creates a warm and peaceful place in which to live. Controlling others becomes unnecessary, because grounding gives the body a way to control itself, release pent-up energy and emotions, and cleanse itself on a moment-by-moment basis. Try it and see.

CREATING YOUR FIRST GROUNDING CORD

Here's how to ground yourself: sit upright in a straight-backed chair with your arms and legs uncrossed and your feet flat on the floor. Get into the room in your head if you can. Place your right hand on your belly just above your pubic bone, and your left hand behind you at the very base of your tailbone.

Keep your eyes open if you can, stay centered, and envision a circular energy center inside your pelvis, right between your hands. (If you know about the chakra system, you'll recognize this center as your first chakra, shown in figure 2, page 16.) This center is usually envisioned as a disk three to five inches in diameter. This disk faces forward, with colored energy swirling visibly inside it (the color should be red).

This firmly anchored disk of energy resides within your body at all times. This energy center has been present since before you were born. It has a constant and unlimited supply of energy, and its primary function is to feed and serve you.

Stay in your head, envisioning the energy swirling inside this chakra, and see a cord or a tube of this same energy moving straight downward. The cord can be the same diameter as your chakra, or slightly smaller. It may help to envision a brightly colored, plumbing-pipe-sized grounding tube. Visualize your chakra as firmly anchored inside your body, and see the cord moving downward out of your genitals, through your chair, and into the floor beneath you.

Know that there is an unlimited amount of energy available to create your cord. You are not draining your first chakra, you're simply redirecting some of its inexhaustible energy down toward the center of the planet. Keep breathing, stay in the room in your head if you can, and relax. See your grounding cord moving further downward, through the foundation of the building you are in, into the layers of the ground below you, and on down to the center of the planet, however that may look to you.

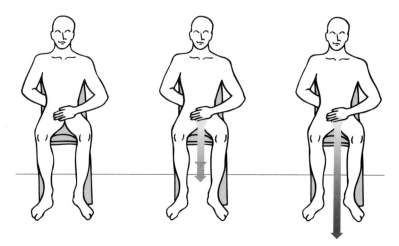

Figure 2. Creating your first grounding cord.

Are you still inside your head, or did you go swooping down to the center of the planet? You don't need to follow your cord around. Stay in the room in your head and direct your grounding cord through visualization. Your cord will obey you.

When your cord reaches the center of the planet, anchor it there so it is firmly attached. You can envision your cord as a long chain with an actual anchor, as a tree with roots that wrap around the center of the planet, as a waterfall with a constant, unwavering downward flow, as an electrical cord you can plug in to the center of the planet, or as any image that works for you.

Feel the strong connection between the center of your gravity (your pelvis) and the center of the planet's gravity, and feel the solid attachments at either end. Call your full birth-name down your cord three times, or see your name written all over the energy that swirls through it. This is your first grounding cord!

When you feel comfortable with being in your head and being grounded, destroy your cord. Drop it out, throw it away, burn it, or make it vanish. Use whatever method you like, just get rid of it. Let it go completely. You made it and you can make it go away. Let it go. Do it now.

Why? Because the world of spiritual information and communication has been either deified or devalued for too long. When people first start to work with energy, they tend to become unbalanced. Many believe that dead relatives will appear, or God will yell at them. Nonsense. This is just you working with your own energy in your own body. That's all. I remind you that we have no language and no context in this culture to explore the spirit. Chakra is an East Indian word; we don't even have the concept in the West! Consequently, when Western minds explore the spirit, a whole Pandora's box of hooey and fear tends to erupt.

Separate yourself from all that reactive, uneducated fear of the spirit. Remind yourself that you are in charge of your energy and your energy creations. Your energy tools belong to you. If they aren't perfect, or the right color, or the right size, you can destroy them and start over. You are in charge here. You can destroy anything you create (with full impunity) and start all over again. You are in charge.

Now ground yourself again in any way you like. If you can ground yourself standing up, without placing your hands on your first chakra, do it! Choose a bright color for your cord; it doesn't have to be red, even though your first chakra is. Let your cord have movement and liveliness, and let it know you're in charge. Call your name down your new grounding cord.

There are only a few rules about creating your grounding cord: it should be securely anchored at both ends; there should be a constant downward flow, so it can be used as a cleansing tool; and the outside edges of the tube or cord should be rounded, without any holes, tears, or breaks to leak energy or confuse it. Beyond that, its size, color, and anchoring system are yours to create.

Get up and move around. Jump. Run. Lie down. Does your grounding cord come with you and move easily? If not, drop it out of your body. I like to snip off a not-quite-right cord with imaginary scissors and let it fall down to the center of the planet. Create a new cord with a better flow, or attach wheels to the one you have, if you don't want to get rid of it. Remember to call your name down each new cord you create.

If you are having real trouble with grounding, don't worry. At this moment, all you need to do is keep an open mind. Your mind is wonderful at maintaining a conceptual reality until your body can catch up and create physical reality. Relax and read. You will be able to ground soon enough. It took me months to get grounded, but I was very stubborn and no one knew how to stop my assault-centered dissociation. You're luckier than I was, because this book has all sorts of grounding-helpers for you. Stay in your head and keep working.

GROUNDING OUT ATTITUDES

When you're ready, sit down again and try this first grounding exercise. Get in your head and establish your grounding cord. Relax yourself, stay grounded, and bring forward some small recent event that annoyed you. Think about it until you get a vivid picture of the way you felt when that annoying thing happened. See if you can really work yourself into that feeling of annoyance again.

Now, speed up the downward flow in your grounding cord. Take the whole experience of annoyance (which you just called into your body out of nothingness), wrap it into a ball, and drop it down the center of your grounding cord. Watch as this ball of annoyance drops away.

Stay in the room in your head and let your grounding cord vacuum the annoyance out of your body. Feel the tenseness leave your stomach, feel the chatter leave your head; feel the annoyance leave your body. Feel the cleansing whoosh as these attitudes drain away from you, leaving you with a million choices about how to feel right now.

As the energy of your annoyance travels downward to the center of the planet, watch as it loses its annoying character and becomes simple, clean energy again. Notice that annoyance is something *you* attached to this energy. You could have used the same energy to laugh, to cry, to act, or to sleep, but you chose to be annoyed.

Watch your annoyance fall away. Watch it until you can see it as neutral, all-purpose energy again. When the energy reaches the bottom of your cord and the center of the planet, allow it to exit your grounding cord all shiny and clean. Let it go back to wherever it belongs. Notice how big this ball of energy is. In other words, check out how much energy and attention you diverted from living and healing yourself to become annoyed. Consider, as you let this one simple situation go, that you have choices about what you do with your energy. Feel the difference inside you now that you are free of just one episode of annoyance. Perhaps you feel lighter and freer, perhaps not. That depends on how much you like to use annoyance in your life.

If you miss your annoyance, if you're not done with it yet, know that the energy will come back to you cleansed and ready to help you create a whole new level of supersonic mega-annoyance! Remember, you're in charge. You get to choose how you use your energy.

You may notice, as you sit in your head and watch this cleansed energy leave your grounding cord, that the energy flies away from you completely and disappears. Congratulations! You have just grounded out *someone else's energy*.

What does that mean, *someone else's energy*? All of us routinely pick up and nurture messages, attitudes, and ideologies that do not belong to us and are not growth-enhancing. These are examples of having someone else's energy inside us. The ideas can be as trivial as "Don't talk with your mouth full," or as deep as "People won't love you until you're perfect." These ideas and messages can be something you learned in your family (getting sad or angry in certain triggering situations), something you learned in your gender identification ("Nice girls don't . . . , Real men never. . . "), or something you picked up from your peers (including everyone's best friend, the media).

Part of the process of grounding and cleansing your energy is finding out which stances and attitudes you take in life are authentic, and which are artificial. Whatever the idea, if it is not comfortable or healing in your present-day life, it needs to be grounded out and examined from a more neutral, objective viewpoint. If the message or attitude or idea is yours, its energy will return once you've grounded and cleansed it. If the message belongs to someone else, it will return to that person, cleansed of your involvement.

When you ground, you remove your attachments to your behaviors and free up energy for new attitudes (if you so desire). You also perform a service for others by cleansing the messages and stances you borrowed from them. Before you give the energy back to its rightful owner, you take responsibility for your agreement with their viewpoint. This is a spiritually responsible way to separate yourself from the thoughts, needs, and ideas of others.

In every moment of every day, you need fresh, present-time, examined responses to the world around you. When your grounding cord is on and running, your body and your emotions will have a way to cleanse themselves in every moment. You can begin to see yourself as an unlimited being, unhampered by past behaviors, past actions, or old messages that trap you like a fly in amber. When you are grounded, the silent strength and power you feel will remind you that you are the cause, and not the effect, of your busy life.

By now, students of the martial arts have recognized the grounding cord as a form of *Chi* energy. In most martial arts, students are first taught to stand correctly and balance themselves before they are ever allowed to jump and kick. In order to balance, students are taught to run the Chi inside their pelvic girdle downward, and to center themselves in their bodies and on their center of gravity. Running the Chi creates the warrior stance, with the legs firmly planted, the body relaxed, and the awareness finely tuned. The warrior stance in most martial arts is not aggressive and defiant, but watchful—aware of strengths and weaknesses. The martial-arts warrior stands firm, with all weapons sheathed, ready for anything that might come along, but not asking for a fight.

Grounding creates this same sort of preparedness in spiritual seekers like yourself. Your grounding helps you to stand firm within your own life and psyche by keeping you centered and connected to the earth and to the present. You can now stand firm and steadily use your grounding cord to remove the thoughts and attitudes that unsettle you and distract you from your power and your life.

GROUNDING OUT MESSAGES

Get into your head and check your grounding. If there is any flimsiness to your cord, get rid of it and make yourself a new cord in a day-glo color. Call your name down your cord again and try another grounding exercise. This time, let's get rid of something bigger than an annoyance reaction. Let's send a whole message down the cord and away from us.

Choose an easy message at first, like a stereotypical parental rule or a television idea about how your gender should behave. This message can be in words or feelings, sensations or pictures. However you experience this message, get a complete sense of it before you let it go. As you let your grounding cord have this message, check and see if you feel like calling it back. If you feel a sense of loss, you may not be through with this message yet. Let it go anyway. When the message has been cleansed and finally flies out the bottom of your grounding cord, try to see where it's headed.

If you can't see any of this, don't worry. I'm not a visual psychic either. I just postulate and know that energy work is occurring by being aware of how my body feels. When I let energy go, my ears will pop, or my breathing will deepen and my body will relax. You can use your imagination and your bodily senses to guide you. Your body doesn't lie.

Watch or sense where the energy of your released message is headed. If the message shoots off easily, you're done with it. If it comes right back to you, it's a message you still need or believe. If the message comes back, study it. Now that you've grounded out its "other-people," "other-time" identity, you can take a look at it from the present, on your own terms. Perhaps the message makes sense to you on some deep level. If so, feel free to reintegrate it (now that it's clean) into your present-day life.

If, in the next moments or days, this message doesn't feel right, go ahead and ground it out again. Remind yourself that, if you picked up this message somewhere in your travels, you have every right and all the power to drop it back off again. You are in charge. When messages touch a chord in you, feel free to keep them, but ground out their "past-time," "other-people's" energy before you store them away.

Here's an example: Your father is a great cook. Not just good, but great. You like to cook, but it's hard for you to do so without thinking of his specific way of sharpening knives, wiping surfaces, and measuring herbs. You find you can't experiment with flavors because your father, who isn't even in the house, wouldn't like your ideas. So you tell yourself you weren't really hungry anyway, or you end up creating an inedibly spicy meal just to prove you can.

If you get into the room in your head and ground out your father's cooking rules and attitudes, you'll see that you don't need to live up to them. You don't need to be like him to love him. You can keep the organized and conscious aspects of his cooking, but you can send him a nice clean ball of his own intense energy. You can learn to own the spirit of food preparation without needing to live your father's life. Or, you can continue to fight his memory. It's up to you.

Know that messages are just noise and ideas we've attached to energy. They're not laws handed down from God. Only our focused attention can give a message life in our hearts and minds, and only our conscious release can turn the message back into the nothingness it is. Ground the messages you live with every day. If the messages are hogwash, don't let them back in. Remember that you have the right to individuate and choose your own personal way to respond to the world, no matter what anyone else says or does.

※

Individuation is a life-long process of finding the meaning of your own existence, irrespective of anyone else's needs, wants, and demands. The early focus of individuation is not in finding who you are, but in learning who you are not.

Removing foreign messages and attitudes is a primary step in creating a quiet space where your authentic, spiritual self can come alive. By freeing you of thoughts, feelings, and behaviors that cause discomfort, grounding can make your individuation possible. With the knowledge that you can and do control your response to the inner and outer world, you will fit much more easily into the world as it truly is. You will not need to expend energy controlling the world around you, because your energy will be focused on being clear and authentic in each moment.

Grounding connects you to the earth and gives you a constant support system; it gives you constant opportunities to dislodge old messages, old ideas, and old ways of living. Grounding makes the work of individuation easier, because it throws the focus inside, on you and you alone, right here and right now. Grounding helps your spirit rest in your body safely and easily. When that happens, you will always "Be Here Now."

GROUNDING OUT PAIN

Grounding, you will soon find, is useful in many situations. Try this exercise the next time you have an ache or a pain. Get in your head and make sure that your regular grounding cord is in place. When you are comfortable with your main grounding cord, create a second grounding cord directly in the center of your discomfort. Allow the cord to grow from within the energy of the pain and to travel downward to the center of the planet.

Instead of anchoring this second grounding cord inside your body, let it drain the painful energy away from you, like a rope unraveling off the edge of a table and finally falling off altogether. Notice how attached you are to this pain as it leaves your body, how much energy you gave over to it, and how you feel about living without it.

Remember that pain, physical or emotional, is only a signal. It is not an entity in itself that needs to be feared, escaped from, or drugged into submission. Pain is a signal that something is wrong. If you had no pain, you wouldn't be aware of danger in your environment or illness in your body. Without pain, you would traipse blindly into things that could cause you real damage. Pain alerts you to danger and illness, and it alerts you quite suddenly, with no subtlety or subterfuge. Pain doesn't play games, and neither should you.

You're not supposed to pretend to adore pain, and bargain with it, and imagine that it feels wonderful so it will magically disappear. That's not the shift required. You need only listen respectfully to your body, review your emotional attachment to the idea of suffering, and focus your healing attention (or the attention of your doctor/healer) on the painful area.

Grounding is an excellent way to address pain, because it lets your body know that you're home and aware, that you're listening, and that you're acting on its messages. As you continue with your energy work, you'll be surprised to see how many aches and pains your body manifests just to get your attention back inside you and centered on the present. You can identify this kind of pain very easily—it goes away when you ground it, as if by magic!

❋

Keep your main grounding cord attached and running at all times. In the beginning, it's good to get into your head and check your cord at least twice each day. You don't have to find a quiet room. Just sit or stand still for a moment, get into the room in your head, and ground yourself. It should only take you a few seconds. If your grounding cord is flimsy or unreal, let it go and make a new one. Change your cord every day, if you like. It doesn't cost anything, and it can be fun to coordinate your cord with your attitude or your outfit.

Stay grounded while you drive, eat, sleep, and exercise. Check into your grounding when you're at work, at a movie, or in the middle of a fight. Work on your grounding when you're sick, when you're balancing your checkbook, when you're cooking, when you're dancing, and when you make love. If you need some help, you can ground yourself in the shower by training the flow of water on your back or pelvis and following the downward movement in your mind. If this doesn't help and you still cannot ground at all, skip ahead to the section on the first chakra on page 151. Understanding the functions and dysfunctions of the first chakra should make grounding much easier.

There are more grounding skills, rules, and ideas in the section called Advanced Techniques (page 101). Please feel free to skip forward, but beware of confusing yourself with too much input. It is perfectly normal, and even expected, to have difficulties with grounding at first. If things get difficult, get into the room in your head and ground immediately. The more you ground, the easier it gets, because your body becomes clearer and cleaner each time you do it. Soon, you'll be clear enough to remain grounded without constant attention.

If you find yourself exerting heavy effort, groaning and straining to ground and stay in your head, you haven't gotten it at all! Energy work takes application, *not* effort. Energy work is created out of gossamer and magic and willingness. It doesn't require blood and sweat. If you are exerting a lot of effort, stop. Relax. Lighten up. Read through the grounding exercises again, and have some fun with your energy.

THE BASIC GROUNDING RULE

A note before we go on: If grounding works wonders for you, that's great! I'm sure you think it would work wonders for other people in your life, and it *would,* if they grounded themselves. But grounding other people is not okay at all.

Don't forget, grounding is a healing. And it's the height of bad spiritual etiquette to heal anyone without asking. Moreover, your personal grounding cord won't work for anyone else. You'd be putting the energy of your healing and your answers into the lives of others. Bad manners. No one but you needs to learn *your* lessons and experience *your* grounding!

If you know someone who is crying out for grounding, let them borrow your book for a few days. Teach them what you know, but do not ground them! Do not make yourself responsible for other people's spiritual growth. It won't work. Take care of yourself, please.

Defining
Your Aura

The setting of proper boundaries is the major premise of all psychological methods, and a major point of contention and discussion in all relationships. Yet the procedure for setting boundaries is unsure, unscientific, and usually ineffective.

When people do not have reasonable boundaries, their lives don't flow properly. Their inner lives are usually a jumble of unmet needs and unrealized dreams, while their outer lives are filled with overwork, or desperately important social causes. Because they do not know where they begin and end, these people will take personal responsibility for almost anything, from their friends' emotional states, to the state of the environment. They find definition in how much they affect others, not in how effective they are in their own lives.

People without boundaries will often use weight to create boundaries: too much weight so they can take up more space and protect themselves, or too little weight so they can prove their self-control and disappear into nothingness. Such people may also use physical security or neatness to exert control and create boundaries. None of these false boundaries work.

People without boundaries are often extremely active in and concerned about health, the environment, politics, business, or finance. These are not bad activities in and of themselves. Excessive focus on these exterior activities, however, helps to define hyperactive and boundary-impaired people. I call them *runaway healers*.

Runaway healers differ from regular healers in very important ways. Runaway healers are often phenomenally good at what they do. A close look at their inner lives, however, reveals emptiness and chaos. All of their energy pours out of them and into the things and people they heal; they make no time for themselves.

A good test for identifying runaway healers is to ask them what they do for themselves—how they rest and nurture themselves. Regular healers will rattle off a list, after a small hesitation. Runaway healers will be rendered speechless, or will start to drone on about their *selfless mission.*

Selfless is exactly right. Runaway healers attempt to deal with their pain by "de-selfing" themselves, by becoming unimportant footnotes in their own lives. By constantly healing others and ignoring their own needs, these people are trying to remove themselves from their inner chaos, even if they become ill or die in the process. In healing others or going up against social injustice, such people are at least trying to keep their healing energy flowing, but, because they don't have or understand boundaries (and are probably heading toward physical or mental illness themselves), their healing attention can be damaging to others.

Runaway healers cannot let other people sit with their own pain. If they could, they might have to sit with their own, God forbid. They will often whisk away blockages and difficulties before their "heal-ees" have learned the lessons tied into their personal discomfort. Runaway healers mean well, but they usually create unworkable dependencies because they need to heal, they have to heal, and they can't let others or the world simply *be.* They've always got to be finding new missions and new injustices, usually by starting with *your* life and all its difficulties.

The basic force behind runaway healing seems to be a compulsion to rid the world of suffering, but it is really a compulsion to rid these healers of the memory of their own pain. Because of this, runaway-healing work tends to come from a very driven and stressful place, where the healer's very self-image is inextricably tied to their healing ability. Forget their needs, their health, their homes, and their finances; they're on a mission! This mission is a sad thing to watch. Because runaway healers always burn themselves out, mentally or physically, they will have to stop healing, sooner or later. At that inevitable moment, runaway healers are disconsolate. Without their mission, what do they have? What can they do? How can they survive?

If runaway healers can stop themselves before their inevitable breakdown and focus their incredible energies in their own lives, they can turn their decay around quite swiftly. When they discover their boundaries and begin to work with their own pain, they can generally accept the pain of others; they can then stop interfering—I mean *healing*. The first step is to stop them from healing others—stop them completely—because they are almost certainly unable to say no, unable to rest, and unable to accept nurturing.

Runaway healers' peace of mind will come, not from a world filled with justice and devoid of pain, but from an ability to deal with the inner issues that cause them to expend all their vital energy on anything but themselves. Such healers have to be able to create inner justice and personal relief from pain first. They must heal themselves and have a real, everyday connection to their own balance and wellness before they can help manifest peace and justice in the world at large.

Individuals with a strong sense of personal territory do not look for self-worth within the ability to heal others or to create external justice. They make sure they are well enough to offer competent help first. People who know where they begin and end do not use weight or lack of it for physical safety. Their physical and emotional boundaries do not compromise their health. They are not compulsive or excessively careless about their belongings, and they do not believe that their world needs to be locked up, or wired against intruders.

People with boundaries do not heal others unasked, because they are too busy living their own lives; they don't need to become co-dependently enmeshed in another's. People with boundaries heal others naturally, by example. People with boundaries are physically safe because they care for themselves, because they ground out their own distress, and because they place themselves in supportive environments. People with boundaries have a comfortable, spacious, spiritually defensible place they call home.

You have a God-given boundary system already in place—the aura. Although the aura has had some unfortunately wacky metaphysical connotations attached to it, it is simply the energetic boundary of your personal territory.

If you have ever felt, but not seen, someone looking at you, or coming up behind you, then you've had a physical experience of your aura's energy boundary. In its simplest form, your aura's energetic feelers can alert you when people enter your physical territory—whether you have visually detected them or not. With a little bit of practice and attention, your aura can also help to make you aware of your emotional and spiritual territory. When you have this awareness, the setting of proper boundaries will no longer be a mystery. You'll actually be able to see and feel your boundary as a real, useful, and practical entity.

Awareness of your aura and personal boundary system tends to grow with you as you move through childhood and adolescence, and away from the protection of your family. Further awareness usually comes when you have the experience of losing and then regaining your boundaries in relationships, jobs, higher schooling, and healthy sexual contact.

As we mature, we continually come up against new and novel experiences that prompt us to lower (or even drop) our boundaries. We gauge whether this new person, idea, or experience is worth changing ourselves or our viewpoint. With a suitable support network, most of us can come through these challenging and exhilarating moments with a stronger sense of who we are, and a stronger knowledge of how our newly examined and restored boundaries fit into the world around us.

Most of us, however, tend to lose contact with our boundaries, probably because they are not a normal topic in life or conversation ("Say, how's that aura?"). Most parenting and schooling techniques strive to exert external control of some sort on children, which leaves them with an uncertain self-boundary system. Self-direction, individuation, and private needs tend to be undervalued in our media-infected and group-centered society. Spoken or not, the imperative to fit in is intense. This creates a society of people who know the right things to own, the right clothes to wear, the right things to say, the right information to have, and so on. It doesn't create people with much connection to themselves.

Getting reacquainted with your aura will place you back inside your own life, which is where the center of healing, truth, spirituality, and your connection to God dwell.

HOW TO DEFINE YOUR AURA

Here's how to define and cleanse your aura. Ground yourself and get into the room in your head. Stand up and envision a large, oblong bubble completely surrounding you. Light the edges of this bubble with a very bright, even garish, neon color. See the bubble above your head, below your feet, behind you, in front of you, and on either side (see figure 3, page 32). The distance from your body to the lit-up edges of the bubble should be a consistent twenty-four to thirty inches (arm's-length is best).

Stay in your head and envision your grounding cord. Notice it growing out of your first chakra and flowing steadily and calmly downward. With your aura lit up like this, you can see your grounding cord and your aura boundary interact. They intersect at arm's-length, below your feet. Change the color of your grounding cord so that it matches your aura bubble, and be aware of the result. You may feel a shiver or a sense of release, which means that your aura is using your grounding cord to release some of its unwanted energy. Good!

Stay in your head and study your aura. You just defined its area and gave it a bright color, but is it getting bulgy or changing color? Is it pulling itself closer to you or disappearing in spots? Do you see holes or tears in it? Are parts of your body feeling uncomfortable? If so, congratulate yourself; you are receiving communications from your aura! If you perceive no changes, congratulate yourself, too: your aura wants to be in the present moment with you right now. In either case, don't worry about what you see. We'll study the aura in more detail later. Right now, we're ready to do some aura-cleansing work.

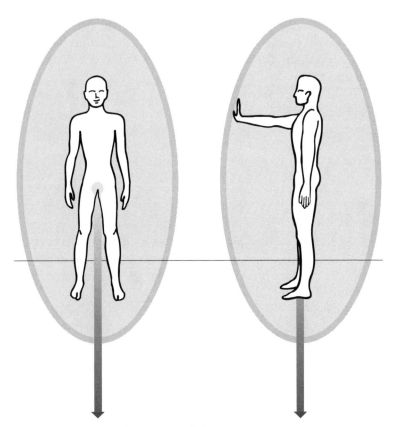

Figure 3. Defining your aura.

CLEANSING YOUR AURA

Here's how to cleanse your aura. Sit in a straight-backed chair with your feet flat on the floor, your arms uncrossed, and your hands upturned comfortably on your knees. Get grounded and in your head, and light up your aura bubble. Match the color of your grounding cord to the color of your aura.

Now, create another grounding cord—a very large tube this time—with its opening on the floor around your aura boundary. Make its edges the same color and circumference as your aura. See the edges of this aura-grounding cord surrounding and enveloping your aura boundary at floor-level (see figure 4), then drop it quickly to the center of the planet. Stay in your head and maintain your regular first-chakra cord. Know that your main cord will stay right where it belongs, no matter how many other grounding cords you create.

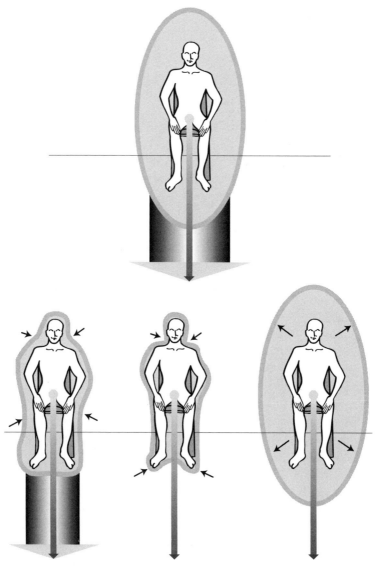

Figure 4. Cleansing your aura.

Envision your floor-level aura-grounding tube, and allow the energy stuck in your aura to flow down and out of it, just as the energy stuck in your body flows down and out of your first-chakra cord. Let the clogged energy fall down and away from your aura. You may feel globs of stress coming away from your head, shoulders, or stomach; your ears may pop or ring; you may get the shivers or feel hot and cold areas in and outside of your body; you may actually see people and events leaving your aura. Whatever happens, stay in your head and keep both grounding cords going.

Read through this next step before you go on. It's not complicated, but it is a bit tricky to explain, which is why I've included illustrations.

Slowly bring the edges of your aura in toward your body. As you do, notice all the old energy inside it being squeezed out and down through your aura-grounding tube. As you pull your aura inward, know that the circumference of your aura-grounding tube will shrink, along with your aura boundary. The end result should give you a feeling of being closely enveloped in your own brightly colored auric field.

Imagine the feeling of your aura all over your skin. Feel your aura boundary above your head, behind your back, under your feet, along your chest and abdomen, around your arms, behind your knees, and so on. Stay in the room in your head and get a sense of this bright color touching and enveloping your body. Know that there is no space or opening for old energy or information, because you've grounded everything out. Take a moment to become acquainted with your shiny clean aura.

When you have been able to feel your aura on your skin for about thirty seconds, thank your aura-grounding tube and drop it down and away from you. Stay in your head and keep your first-chakra cord attached.

Is your first-chakra grounding cord still the same color as your aura bubble? If not, change it so that they match one another. Your first-chakra cord may have changed color to do something else while you grounded your aura with that larger tube. This is great, but now you'll need your body's grounding cord to pay attention to directions for a few minutes.

When you've gotten a sense of being completely enveloped in your aura, expand your aura back to its normal dimension. You can pop it out; blow it up like a balloon; manually move it away from you; or simply imagine it at its normal size. As you expand your aura, fill it with a pastel wash of the color you chose for its boundary. For example: if you chose a neon yellow for your aura's boundary, you will create a pale wash of that yellow throughout your aura. The pale yellow will touch your skin and radiate above you, below you, behind you, in front of you, and on either side. Though your cleansed and resized aura boundary will not touch your skin, this light residue of its energy will. This connection will make it easier for you to be aware of the many ways your aura protects and envelops you. Connecting to your aura's boundary in this way will help you to be aware of its functions, its reactions, and its fluctuations.

When your aura is cleansed and back to its correct size, get up and move around. Your aura should move easily with you and maintain itself whether you stand, bend, sit, or jump. If your aura doesn't come with you or move easily, sit down, ground yourself, and get into your head again. Change or intensify the color of your aura boundary and see if that makes your aura any more mobile. If not, perform another aura cleansing, and your aura should become more fluid and flexible. Take a few minutes to move around with it, to sit inside it, and to get a sense of its energy completely surrounding and protecting you. Become acquainted with your aura. If you can't get any feel for it yet, don't worry. You will. For help, skip ahead to the section on The Gold Sun Healing (page 65).

Cleansing your aura and maintaining a conscious, present-time connection with it is as important as cleansing your body through grounding. The energy you store inside your body has to do with your feelings and ideas about yourself. Being able to ground, examine, and renew this interior energy helps you redefine your self-view. With grounding, you can actually move old attitudes and belief systems away from your inner life so they can't haunt you.

The energy you store inside your aura, on the other hand, has to do with your feelings about your place in the exterior world and about how others see you. If you communicate with your aura, you can begin to identify exterior messages. You can see how you have learned to act and react in the world around you. Both your inner and outer energy bodies benefit tremendously from these simple acts of conscious energy-cleansing. When your body and your aura rid themselves of messages, attitudes, ideas, and memories that do not serve them, both will begin to heal.

If you are not comfortable with your newly defined aura boundary, let it go and create a better one. Sit inside your new aura and, if it feels right to do so, say your full birth-name out loud, or see your name in writing throughout the fabric of your aura.

Check in with your aura periodically throughout the day. Your aura's boundary should be bright and evenly oblong, with no bulges, holes, or tears. Its edges should stay about an arm's length away from your body at all points. With the help of this information from you, your aura can take good care of itself. If you are receiving communications from your aura at this time (meaning that it shows you different colors, shapes, or distances than the ones you created for it), relax. You will get to aura reading soon enough.

In essence, you are, at this point, *telling* your aura how it should look, not asking how it feels. If you communicate this to your aura, it will most likely calm down and let you be in charge. If it continues to bombard you with images even after you make it clear that you are currently an aura-reading novice, then feel free to skip ahead to the section on Reading Your Aura (page 121).

Working with the energy of your aura is not quite like creating a grounding cord or a room in your head from scratch. Your aura has always been present, even if it has been totally ignored. What you are doing here is reacquainting yourself with your aura; you're reminding it how it should look and feel.

If you begin to maintain and heal your aura, it will become more real to you, and you can begin to read it. If it gets very big, it can mean you are trying too hard, taking on too many outer projects or too much responsibility, or not maintaining your distance from others. If your aura tucks itself closely around you, it may mean that you feel threatened or out of place. If your aura has holes or missing pieces, it can mean that you are losing your boundaries, or handing them over to others.

If you notice your aura changing, you can simply light it up and see it as whole, vital and boundary-enforcing. This quick aura-brightening (it takes less than a second) will often wake up your aura, which usually fixes itself right away.

When you are in contact with your aura, you may notice how much time you spend out of your body and ungrounded. This is okay. Congratulate yourself for noticing, and keep doing your cleansing work. You are becoming clearer with each passing moment, even if you don't feel very clear right now. Be easy on yourself, laugh a little, and keep working.

Each of these energy tools supports the others. For example, it is easier to ground if you're in the room in your head, easier to get into your head if your aura is defined, easier to define your aura if you're grounded, and so on. One or more of these energy tools may be impossible for you right now, but keep working with ease, relaxation, and silliness. Don't throw pointless visions of perfection at yourself. Perfection is for joyless drones who don't have any imagination. This work, on the other hand, is all about the imagination, which makes growth and change possible.

Growth and change don't look perfect. Sometimes this work is going to look and feel just terrible, and at other times you'll be the most competent and graceful being on the planet. Keep breathing and laughing and grounding, and it will all come together.

An aside: If you've read anything about the aura, you may be waiting for me to go into lengthy descriptions of all the colors and layers of the aura. Sorry, but I've never seen the point. Auras are living things that are in a constant state of change and flux and redefinition, not only in color, but in shape, size, completeness, and vibrancy.

I have learned to trust my own aura. As its loving owner, I clean it, redefine its shape, and heal it when it's hurt. I don't obsess on its thousand fluctuations, or peer and poke at all its layers. I believe in it and trust it to work. An abandoned aura needs more work at first, but it will right itself very quickly. Clearly, this is a book about reading the aura. It's much simpler, however, than most aura-work tomes I've seen. I've found that the simple act of listening intuitively to what my aura tells me can be the best reading/healing of all, no matter what all its layers and colors are doing at the moment.

*

Your meditation at this point should go like this: Sit, ground yourself, and call your full name down your cord. Get into your head and make sure your meditative sanctuary is still there. If you can't locate your room, envision a new one in any style you like.

When you're grounded and in the room in your head, light up your aura in a bright color and see your grounding cord intersecting with it. At this point, you can envision your aura boundary and your grounding cord in different colors if you like, but if your aura is indistinct or wavering, give it a much brighter color and match your grounding cord to that color. When you do this, your grounding cord will naturally help your aura center itself and dump off its excess energy. Also, brighter colors set better boundaries.

Don't worry about taxing your regular grounding cord with too much work. The first-chakra energy is boundless. It can do a hundred things at once and still make a flawless gourmet meal for twenty. Your grounding cord can do anything you ask of it.

Once you've developed your skills, your daily healing check-in can take less than thirty seconds. Sit, ground, get into the room in your head, light up your aura, and attend to any difficulties or incompleteness. That's it!

Protecting
Your Aura

I f you have done any metaphysical work before, you may have learned about the psychic protection systems called the Wall, the Mirror, or the White Light. These are barrier tools that some people use to protect themselves from others—and from any "evil" spirit energy that might come their way. I have found that these barriers tend to create more problems than they solve.

The Wall is an energy barrier that actually looks and feels like a wall of bricks. People who use the Wall are often rigid and inflexible in their dealings with the world. The Wall is erected as an impenetrable defense. Unfortunately, many beings love a challenge and will be drawn toward Wall people like moths to a flame. Though they truly want to be left alone, Wall people usually find themselves surrounded by off-center and manipulative people. Wall users do not realize that their defense system is riveting and/or insulting to others, who will try to break through just to prove they can.

Wall people rarely achieve the isolation they crave and are often heard to say: "How do these crazy people/jobs/relationships find me? Do I have a sign on my forehead or something?" Actually, since everyone is intuitive and completely able to perceive things like rude energy barriers, the Wall *can* be likened to a sign on the forehead that says, "Please bother me!"

The Mirror looks like its name and is a slightly less insulting barrier erected to send back the energy or attention coming toward its user. It is a way of saying: "Whatever you send to me belongs to you, so I won't become involved in your communications at all." The Mirror is only partially effective. While most people tire of having their communications come right back to them unchanged, some like to hang around and do their spiritual hair, as it were. Living behind a Mirror can be lonely, because very little gets through. It can also be annoying if the Mirror attracts spiritual narcissists who like to hang around the Mirror-user and gaze at themselves.

Like the Wall, the Mirror is dead and brittle. Neither one has any flow, and it's hard to invest them with any buoyancy or humor. Because of their rigidity, both interfere with the health and fluidity of the aura.

The White Light is another story altogether. The White Light is a brilliant white aura bubble used as an all-purpose protection system. This idea came from the world of spirit guides and guardian angels, whose energy usually appears as white or silver in an aura or a chakra. Though these kind beings are fascinating enough to warrant a whole book of their own, we will only touch on them briefly because of the enormity of the subject (which requires an understanding of the afterlife, reincarnation, the superconscious, soul mates, karma, and the Akashic records, among other topics).

Essentially, guides and angels are beings who agree to watch over us in our lives here on Earth. They often act as mediators between us and the information we desire, between us and God, and between our spirit and our immediate trauma. In times of transition or shock, spirit guides will often provide us with a protective screen of white or silver energy. This white security blanket is wonderfully healing, but it soon wears off, so that our own natural colors and energies can reassert themselves.

When people set up an all-purpose White Light barrier on their own (or worse, send it to others), thinking that if some white light is good, too much is better, a type of auric *rigor mortis* sets in. The aura becomes rigid and unhealthy from the strain of being compelled to maintain one color at all times. Soon enough, White Light people find themselves isolated from earthy energy, from their own energy, and from other people as well. Their spirit guides may even have a hard time contacting them, because the White Light's job is to keep everything out. Without any input, personal growth generally stops.

Don't misunderstand me; the White Light is very important. It's great for emergencies or illnesses, but it was never meant as an all-purpose tool. In my own meditations, I never use White Light anymore. I leave its application to the sole discretion of my spirit guides.

※

When people come to me for classes or healings with these types of boundaries, I focus immediately on the underlying fear they imply. Generally, people with a need for these boundaries believe strongly in evil and spiritual danger, and have probably experienced a great deal of both. I know I did, that is, until I began grounding and defining my aura. With the work we're learning now, I was able to get in touch with the projections I cherished—projections that helped me to live in a spirit world filled with evil and danger.

I was molested throughout my childhood by many people, starting around the age of two or three. I grew up very interested in horror and evil. When I got involved with spirituality at the age of ten, I fancied myself encountering evil on many levels. Though my spiritual teachers all belonged to the White Brotherhood, I felt there must therefore be a Dark Brotherhood against which I would always battle in some grand apocalyptic struggle.

In my inner travels, I used all the aforementioned protection systems and anything else I could find to keep all the "bad guys" away. Sometimes the magic worked, but most times, it didn't. I got myself into a lot of psychic emergencies. Thankfully, one of those emergencies landed me on the doorstep of a psychic study center. There, I finally saw that my belief in evil had very much more to do with my beliefs about my life than it had to do with reality.

I began to see that, because I didn't believe God could protect anyone (where was He during my assaults?), I lived in a world filled with unrelieved danger. Traveling alone, without knowledge or connections and armed with fear-based boundaries, I knocked around in the inner (and outer) world like an accident waiting to happen. I lived in constant, unconscious fear and drew fearful experiences to me like a magnet. I couldn't even recognize the positive, safe, and life-giving people and messages I encountered every day. I had no time for such lightheartedness; I was too busy ferreting out and destroying evil! I was going to heal the planet, even if I lost my mind or died in the attempt. I was on a mission!

Luckily, my mission was cut short by the skills I'm teaching you now. As I learned to ground and define and cleanse my energy, my defensive postures began to slip away. Nasty people and experiences didn't slam into me quite so often. I think that, because I was no longer involved in such fevered drama, it was less fun to bother me.

At first, I felt lost without all of the excitement and terror of seeing nasty spirits and being in constant danger. I was even bored! I persevered, however, because it seemed that the skills I was learning put me in a different spiritual category, one that gave me more room to breathe. From within my head and behind my aura, I could watch chaos without being compelled to become *one* with it.

I soon became very proficient at healing disturbed people. It was very simple for me, comfortable even, to get into the mindset of schizophrenia and visions and voices and paranoia. As a trained healer, I could use my new protection skills to get myself and my "healees" safely back out of the craziness and onto solid ground.

As I worked on myself and healed others of their terrors, I learned a very important lesson. I began to see that the beings I once called fearful, crazy, and evil were more pitiful than anything else. Just like me, they stored a deep well of sadness and an unimaginable sense of loss just under the surface of their fearfulness. I stopped reacting to the ways they tried to frighten and control me (creating fearsome apparitions, repeating words over and over, and threatening me), and found we had a great deal in common. I was able to see scary beings as lost, frightened children who needed to go home and feel safe. I addressed them from a similar place within myself. Evil became a quaint and simplistic concept when I began to understand the individuals trapped within its confines.

For a time, I did exorcisms and healed schizophrenics. With each tortured spirit I helped release, I was able to release more of my own fear of the spirit world. Today, I don't have much interest in that carnival type of psychic healing, but it certainly helped me then. These days, I spend all my intense healing and releasing energy in helping myself, and in helping others to learn to communicate with themselves.

I now know that each of us chooses to become good or evil; it's up to me to learn to identify the dark beings and to stay out of their way, inasmuch as I or anyone can. I learned that, if I pay attention to myself and my healing, I naturally move closer to God and farther from beings who are stuck in horror. Actually, when I finally began to tend to my inner life, I found that God and safety had been waiting there for me the whole time.

The protection systems I now use do not stem from a fear of other people or spirits, but from an understanding of their needs. When I need to distance myself from others, I do not imagine them as loathsome. I see them as having lost their way, or their God, just as I once did. When I erect huge, complicated, and fascinating boundaries, I don't really protect either of us. I just interrupt our journeys, draw attention to my own boundaries, and impede our healing. I've learned instead to gain distance from people by staying within my own body and behind my own aura.

When I sense an intrusion (to which my healthy aura alerts me by changing shape or color suddenly), or when people and situations begin to get to me, I don't get frightened or enraged as often as I once did. I use a protection symbol and mini-healing that moves people away from me in a powerful way, without fear or insult on either side. I send living, loving presents. I send flowers.

✳

The gift of flowers and plants has long been symbolic of love, respect, welcome, and recognition. Though other gifts have their meanings, none convey concern and attention more universally than living, healthy flowers and plants. Plants and flowers can be used to welcome a birth or mourn a death, to congratulate or console, and to signal affection, ardor, or friendship. They can even signal the end of a relationship. Because of the universal symbolism of flowers and greenery, they are perfect symbols to use in self-protection and communication with others.

In the everyday world, such living gifts are generally accepted as a symbol of concern and devotion. The same is true in the energetic or spiritual world. Because plants and flowers are unobtrusive and nonthreatening, their use does not require that you be in a fearful frame of mind; therefore, they will not draw fearful experiences to you. On the contrary, protection with flowers and plant life requires that the knee-jerk fear of others and the spirit realm be soothed and set aside.

The protection systems you create with lively, colorful plants are very, very simple—so simple that it's hard to believe that they can actually work. At first, I had a hard time replacing my formidable Walls and Mirrors and White Lights with wimpy little flowers, ferns, and trees. In a very short time, however, I learned to prefer my simple, effective garden-based tools to the old clunky boundaries I had once employed. My living, growing protection symbols were the key to moving away from terror.

The first living protection symbol you will create is called the Sentry. Its function is to stand in front of you, greet everyone you meet, and ground out energy that comes at you. It will stay with you at all times, guarding the outer edge of your aura. First, however, we'll get a little intuitive practice and do a mini-reading with our first creation—an imaginary rose.

YOUR FIRST READING ROSE

Here's how to create your first rose: Sit down, ground yourself, and get into the room in your head. Light up your aura and make sure it has a smooth, oblong shape. If not, ground it and perform an aura healing before you go on. Be aware of the connection between the edges of your aura boundary and your regular, first-chakra grounding cord. Should they be the same color today, or can they clash? You decide.

From behind your eyes and within your grounded body, look out at your aura boundary. It should be about an arm's length away from your face. See the edge clearly in your mind, and envision a large, long-stemmed rose just at the outside edge of your aura. See this imaginary rose's petals, leaves, and thorns. Note the color and the openness of its bud, and note which way the heart of the flower is facing. What you have just created is a graphic depiction of yourself as a spirit at this exact moment in time.

Study this rose for a moment. Because you will be using a rose like this one as a protection symbol, you will need to reconstruct it with a number of specific, protective attributes. For now, however, it's helpful to know what each part of this particular rose means, and what it says about you right now. Here are a few generalities about reading roses.

SIZE AND LENGTH

I asked you to create a large, long-stemmed rose, but I didn't give you any dimensions or illustrations, because I didn't want to taint this portion of the reading. I wanted you to use the first rose that came to mind, because this first rose is an excellent indicator of where you are right now as a spirit.

The total size of your rose correlates to the space you are willing to take up in the world. If your rose can fit comfortably between your nose and your navel, you have a normal, well-adjusted fit in your world. If your rose is much larger than that, you may need to look at the ways your energy or personality dominates the situations around you. A very large rose may mean it's time to move upward in your milieu, so that your talents and abilities do not stagnate in an unchallenging environment.

If your rose is much smaller than average, you are very likely in a world that inhibits your growth as a spirit. Your task is exactly the same as the task of a large-rosed person. It's time to evolve upward and outward. It's time to find people and interests that speak to your heart and create safety for you. Your surroundings are thwarting you.

The size and openness of your rosebud: These signify your ability or willingness to listen to your own spiritual information at this moment. The size of your bud relates to your spiritual capacity right now, while its openness relates to your actual use of your own information.

You can have a huge bud which is tightly closed, signifying tremendous spiritual capacity but an unwillingness to open up to it. You can have a tiny bud which is fully open, meaning that your life hasn't given you the spiritual support you need, and you are remaining as connected to your own information as you possibly can be.

If your rose is just a bud, you're beginning again, and probably clearing out a lot of garbage in your life before you open back up. If your rose is wide open, you're relying on your spiritual information, perhaps to the exclusion of the information in your physical life. Why? If your physical life is providing you with so little support, it may be time for a few changes—in diet or exercise, in career or relationships, or in the places where you live and work.

The length of your stem: This indicates your connection to the Earth and your physical life. It also relates to your grounding abilities at this moment. A very long stem means you are very grounded, but a very long stem attached to a tiny or tightly shut rosebud can mean that your spirit-to-body connection is skewed very heavily toward your body. This can imply a distrust or fear of the spiritual realm, or a lack of belief in God.

A very short stem points to an unwillingness to be grounded or in your body right now. A shortened stem can also signify a lack of physical exercise or proper nutrition and health care. Healthy, fit bodies tend to ground naturally.

As an inverse to the previous stem-flower connection, a very shortened stem attached to a large or very open rose can mean that the spirit-body connection is skewed very heavily toward your spirit at this moment. This often indicates an unrewarding, chaotic, or dangerous physical existence, one in which you don't want to have much part. If your rose looks like this, get grounded! You can't help your body if you aren't in it, and you can't make any useful changes if you don't live in your life. Get grounded and get moving!

COLOR

I have included a brief overview of the possible meanings of color in the section on Reading Your Aura (see page 121), but I have done so rather grudgingly. The experience of color is so tremendously subjective that I think it's just silly to say, "Red is anger." Red means so many things to so many different people; depending on the culture, red can signify almost anything.

Here's one small example. In our culture, black or dark colors signify mourning; in other cultures, white and vibrant colors do. In these cultures, our tasteful black funeral suit would be absolutely insulting. It's just not possible to elucidate all the meanings of color.

Shade and intensity of color, however, are entirely different matters, because they *can* indicate a level of emotional intensity or participation. If your rose is very light or pastel, that can signify a newness, a kind of soft uncertainty in your spirit right now. Deeper colors can signify vibrant certainty, and very dark colors can signify a level of stubbornness that goes beyond certainty into a harsh law-making attitude.

Swirls of colors can signify lots of action, or information from many levels, and sparkling colors can signify a great deal of spiritual information coming through (or moving along, if your spiritual information is being re-assessed and renewed right now). Beyond that, the significance of your rose's color is up to your interpretation.

DIRECTION AND AGE

Where do your petals face? If they are facing away from you, this may signify that you are looking for your answers in someone else's life. Right now, you're reading a book on spiritual growth, so your rose may be turned toward this book, or it may be facing upward, seeking information from your spiritual aspects. Your rose may be looking down at its stem if you need more grounding, or it may face you directly, seeking your next instructions.

How old is your rose? Is it brand new? If so, much of your spirit has been through change and growth in recent times. Is your rose old and wilting? This can mean that you have outgrown your old ways of living and being, but you can't quite let go yet, even though the old ways don't work any more. You can easily replace your old rose with a fresh new one, if you like, but wait until we're through studying it. This particular rose is showing you where you are as a spirit right now.

LEAVES AND THORNS

Leaves and thorns signify your current capacity for growth and your willingness to protect yourself, respectively. Don't be surprised if your stem is absolutely bare right now, because the capacity for growth and spiritual protection are aspects of which very few people are aware. Take a deep breath and ground yourself, and ask the stem of your rose to show you its leaves and thorns. It will.

Lots of leaves can denote a great capacity for growth, and a great need for it. Many leaves can mean that you are in, or are ready to start, a period of major growth and transition. Very few leaves doesn't necessarily mean you aren't growing or can't change; they may just mean that you are already doing so much for yourself that you've used up the leaves that were once there. No leaves means you don't believe in your capacity to grow, not that you haven't *got* the capacity.

Usually, a leafless stem shows up with a very light and unsure, or very dark and stubborn-colored rose. With light-colored roses, the lack of leaves is a lack of confidence in the self. In very dark-colored roses, the lack of leaves indicates a "can't teach an old dog new tricks" sort of belief. The belief systems that create this lack of leaves can be grounded out very easily.

The presence of thorns signifies your ability to protect yourself. Roses themselves have evolved thorns to keep people and animals from stripping each bush bare. When horticulturists breed domestic roses, however, they generally breed the thorns out as much as possible. If you've seen wild roses, you'll know that most are so covered with thorns that you have to handle them with gloves. Are you a wild rose, or have you been domesticated?

Lots of thorns of different sizes mean you have a nicely varied series of protection responses. Lots of thorns of one size mean you've only got one basic defense, but one with a lot of energy behind it. Very few thorns mean your protective energies are at an ebb, and no thorns mean you are at a loss right now as to how to protect yourself.

If you've got a very small number of very big thorns, it can mean that you are running out of energy to protect yourself, and perhaps starting to yell or lash out at people or situations that just won't go away. If you've got thorns that are hazy, or appear and disappear, your main protection right now is probably dissociation. Don't become alarmed if your self-protection systems aren't very effective. We'll fix them.

Now that you have looked at the rose that symbolizes your current condition, thank it for showing you how things are at this moment. Make sure you're still grounded, inside the room in your head, and behind your healthy aura. When you've thanked your rose, let it go. This can be done by having it vanish, by draining it away, by burning it, or the quickest method, by blowing it up. Know that you can always call up a reading rose for yourself, to get a quick look at your present-time condition. Just make sure your reading roses stay outside your aura, that you do not ground them, and that you make them disappear completely after you have read them.

Each time you create a reading rose for yourself, you may use the guidelines above to start off your reading, but then follow your own intuition, please. My guidelines are very general. You will soon have much to add to them.

After you've let your first reading rose go, you'll create a rose that will not be used as a reading tool, but as a protection tool. This new rose, which I call the Sentry, should be the healthiest, liveliest rose you can imagine. As you create this new rose, consciously invest it with any qualities your reading rose lacked. This is a healing in and of itself.

CREATING YOUR SENTRY

To make your first Sentry, make sure you're still in the room in your head and grounded, and that your aura is still lit up. You may sit or stand, whichever you prefer. From within your room in your grounded body, create a large, long-stemmed rose in a warm, vibrant color. Place this rose just outside the front edge of your aura (see figure 5). The rosebud should be fairly open and facing toward you. The flower should be directly in front of your face, and the stem should bear many healthy leaves and thorns and reach all the way to your first chakra. Envision this flower as very large (bigger than your face), and try to get a sense of hiding behind it, to some extent.

Greet your Sentry, and attach a grounding cord to its center (at the ovary, or the rosehip). See this grounding cord move down the stem, reach the floor, and travel down to the center of the planet. Stay in your head.

See both ends of your Sentry's grounding cord as stable and anchored, and call your name down it three times. Now, turn the face of the rose away from you, so it faces frontward, like a good sentry. Stand up and walk with your rose in place; get a sense of it preceding you wherever you go. It will act as your energy bodyguard.

Your Sentry will stay at the front edge of your aura at all times and act as a primary protection symbol for you. This rose is meant to replace the Wall, and other projections. Its function is to act as an intermediary between you and the people you encounter.

Though you may find a more suitable plant species for your Sentry in your own meditations, I chose the rose because it has

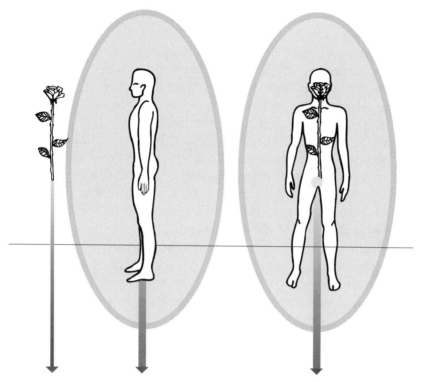

Figure 5. Creating your sentry.

something few other plants possess: a self-protection system. The thorns of the rose will, I hope, help to remind you that your sentry symbol exists to protect you and your aura. Other plants and flowers may be more decorative or personally pleasing (and you can use them in the exercises in the next section), but this thorny rose Sentry will help you to maintain a better separation.

Your Sentry works in many ways and on many levels. In its simplest form, this rose is a symbol of your spirituality. It will transmit a peaceful, nonthreatening greeting to everyone you encounter. Additionally, because it is grounded, your Sentry has more complex functions and abilities. This symbolic rose can stand guard outside your aura and intercept other people, much like a hostess or a bouncer, by accepting and grounding the energy sent to you.

Your Sentry can help create an atmosphere of peace and privacy, because its very presence tends to make people feel they have been communicated with on some level. More often than not, people attempt communication simply to be noticed, and nothing more. Even very aggressive, bothersome people usually want only a simple, heartfelt "Hello in there," which of course they won't get if they throw aggression around. Your symbolic rose communicates that greeting very effectively. Often, people will be able to interact with your rose and not need to disturb you! Though you have created your Sentry for protection, the message this lively symbol gives is one of love and acceptance, both of which tend to make protection unnecessary.

People *think* they want to talk to you for a specific reason, but all they really need is some love and communication. When they come in contact with the love and beauty of your Sentry, and it accepts and grounds their communication feelers, that is very often all the communication they need.

Keep your Sentry out in front of you and check it and its grounding cord periodically. If it's wilted or worn out, thank it for a job well done. If it has changed, it has been intercepting the energy and communication of others—great job! Let your tired or wilted rose go, then create a new, sturdier rose with a brightly colored grounding cord. Make sure your new Sentry isn't too delicate for the job. If you like tiny pastel baby flowers, put them all over your room and all throughout your aura, but use a meaty, thorny, deep-colored rose for your Sentry. Clearly, this flower needs to have a bit of an attitude! I envision mine as a broad-shouldered, nimble, highly aware, and energetic being with a goofy sense of humor. Nothing really fazes it, so I'm not constantly replacing or repairing it.

During your daily meditation check, feel free to repair your Sentry if necessary. You can try other types of flowers or plants to see how they work. Mix and match their colors to blend or clash with your aura boundary, your grounding cord, the walls in the room in your head, your attitude, or your shoes.

Take the time during the day to check your Sentry's grounding. Peek at it after you encounter people you love, as well as people you'd like to pinch. Note its appearance after each of your encounters in the days ahead and make a note of the people who tend to damage it. These people probably need a dozen free, ungrounded gifts from you in order to make their separation from you easier. Make sure that the free gifts you send have no grounding cords attached to them. If your gifts are grounded, your recipient will get the message that grounding, safety, and psychic ability reside in you and your symbols, and not in their own lives. This will undermine their abilities and turn them into evermore energetic, badgering pests, which will erase all the benefits of giving them a present in the first place. Your free gifts should be just that, with no calling card or ulterior motive attached.

If your symbols are grounded, they are less ephemeral. They're harder to throw away. They also come at the recipient with a gift card, as it were, and the recipient now has the uncomfortable choice of accepting something unwanted or insulting *you*. That's not responsible spiritual communication; that's garbage. This work isn't about controlling or intimidating others and forcing them to behave in ways that make you feel more comfortable! It's about taking control of your own life and learning to create safety for yourself. You can't do that if you require other people to do your bidding, on any level. They can't move onward if they get the psychic message that beauty and peace reside in and come from you! Enough said.

A note about destructive people: There are people who have received so much bad attention in their lives that all they can manage is behavior that draws more bad attention. You are free to be furious with people like this, but it will usually make you their new best enemy. Your bad attitude will attract them. You will feel like home. Using Sentry roses with people like this can be frustrating, because they tend to destroy beautiful things. It's very hard not to take the destruction of your rose personally. Don't. If these people can wilt or melt or destroy your Sentry, *they are doing you a favor!* They are showing you which energies your current Sentry can't handle.

Your job, in this instance, is to make a fresh, vibrant, resilient Sentry that loves a challenge. See your Sentry accepting destructive energy with relish, and growing stronger as it eats and then grounds out that person's energy. Remember, it's only energy.

Real plants and flowers grow more beautiful with fertilizer. Consider a destructive person's energy as fertilizer for your Sentry. Know that anything thrown at you is just that—energy. You can work with energy. Your Sentry was created to work with energy, and intense energy doesn't need to scare it off or damage it. Use the challenge of energy-damaging people to help you create a lean, mean, Sentry machine.

Don't forget to send your Sentry-trashers a bunch of free, ungrounded gifts. I know this is counter-intuitive. If people are treating you badly, why should you do anything nice for them? Why not ignore them, or glare at them? Why give them something beautiful? Because it will surprise them. If people come at me with volatile energy and destroy my Sentry, I immediately send them a dozen ungrounded gift flowers—not to reward them, but to divert their attention for a minute. I need that minute to recreate and revitalize my Sentry. I need the destructive person neutralized for a moment while I work.

When I am ready with a new, stronger Sentry, I see what these space invaders are up to. They may have destroyed all the gifts I sent and gotten their destructive energy out, or they may be in a state of shock that anyone would send them anything nice. They are almost never in the same place they started, and I am now ready to get out of their way or start again. The next round is usually much less intense, and may even evolve into reasonable communication.

Remember, everyone is intuitive and everyone longs for spiritual communication. Our culture denies this. Any spiritual communication from you will be a breath of fresh air, even for crotchety, unloving souls. Your responsible spiritual communication will create a loving atmosphere around you. People will begin to respond positively to you, even if they're unpleasant and unaccommodating to everyone else. For more help on dealing with unsettling, unsafe people, the next section on Destroying Images (see page 56) will be very useful.

Your daily meditation at this point should be to get grounded and call your name down your grounding cord, to get into the room in your head, to light up your aura and ground and heal it if necessary, and to put up your Sentry. Check in with your Sentry every morning. If it's healthy, just call your name down its grounding cord and go on with your day. If your Sentry has taken a beating, thank it, let it go, and create a stronger, scrappier symbol. Remember to ground your Sentry and to call your name down its grounding cord each morning, or each time you create a new one.

With only two more beginning skills to master, you're almost done with the basics. If you are feeling overwhelmed or stuck on any technique, skip forward to the Troubleshooting Guide (see page 259). It will give you alternative techniques for creating your tools if you can't manage these more elementary forms.

Don't consider yourself a failure if you cannot master these techniques all at once. I couldn't. I suffered from a serious spirit/body split throughout most of my life. Now I'm back together, but it took work. As I said, it's good work, if you can get it.

DESTROYING IMAGES

As you proceed with this work, you may notice that people are contacting you more frequently. Your parents and family members may call to check in, old relationships may pop up, and old animosities may flare up. People may intrude on your daily meditations by calling or coming over when you sit and ground, or by constantly appearing in your thoughts. This is all quite normal.

Spiritual communication and growth are generally invalidated in our culture, so any hint of them creates excitement, fascination, fear, and confusion. When you take on a journey of spiritual growth, you send ripples out through the psychic fabric of your life. Many people are intuitive enough to know where the ripples have originated, even if their knowledge is completely unconscious. They may not know why they're calling you or what they want to say, but they need to check in. They need to find out what's happening. They need to maintain the status quo and their sense of stasis.

Some people who show up will just want to say hello and study what you're doing. These are the people who will soon help you maintain your newfound skills, in all probability. My suggestion, however, is that you keep your energy work to yourself at this time. Nothing will gum up the works of an inner growth process more than having to get permission from others: permission to move on in life, permission to use spiritual healing techniques, permission to grow beyond your social milieu.

If people around you have noticed that the status quo is changing—that you're moving beyond their established comfort-levels, you'll need a responsible, peaceable, and confident way to diffuse their stasis-seeking attentions. You'll need to remove them, their needs, their hopes, and their wishes from your psyche. Once again, your symbolic gift symbols will come to the rescue.

We've worked already with free gifts, which we give to people who like to be destructive. Our next type of separation and healing is called *destroying images*. Its function is more specific than the act of offering a free gift of a loving symbol. Destroying images actually allows us to move people out of our auras. Although this technique may seem startling at first, it often has wonderful results.

HOW TO DESTROY IMAGES

To destroy an image, get grounded and into the room in your head, inside a clean and colorful aura, and behind a strong and vibrant Sentry. Get yourself into a comfortable, seated position, because you'll be here for a few minutes. Now think of someone in your family—whoever comes up—and imagine an ungrounded gift plant or flower in their favorite color. Place this symbolic gift inside your aura, on your left or right side, whichever feels best.

Quickly place your image of this family member into the gift you made for them. Superimpose their image onto the plant or flower. Move their gift to the outside of your aura and away from you, and destroy it as swiftly as you can. I explode my gift images with dynamite, but you may burn yours, make them vanish with a POP, or see them disintegrate into a million tiny bits of nothing.

Check in with your meditative state. Are you still grounded and in your head? How are your aura and Sentry doing? Were you able to maintain your energy tools and abilities around your awareness of this person, or during the act of destroying his or her image? If you notice any disturbances in your energy tools, take a moment to fix them. These changes are either the normal effect this person has on your life (for instance, if you just lost your grounding, your aura definition, or your Sentry, you probably do that in a face-to-face meeting with this person as well), or the punishments you impose on yourself when you try to move on to new levels of awareness and break your ties with old relationships or behaviors. If you experienced any weakening of your energy or tools, reground and redefine yourself with stronger, more vibrant tools. Thank your energy tools for showing you, in this safe place, some of the ways this relationship helps to keep you from moving forward.

If you noticed positive changes, such as a brightening of the colors in your aura or grounding cord, or a reduction of mental chatter, you have experienced the healing effect of removing people from your inner life. It usually feels quite wonderful, and it brings you to a very important point in this healing path: the point at which you begin to realize that other people and their needs should have no place inside your aura or your inner self.

This is individuation. This is finding your authentic self, regardless of the messages of the people around you. Grounding out and re-examining messages was your first step in making room for yourself inside your own life. Defining your aura and the room in your head gave you a finite area to care for and inhabit. Your Sentry delineated the edge of that personal area. Now you have a way to remove other people's images from your inner life.

Inside your aura, there should be only one person: you! Your aura should not be a family-reunion area filled with chatter, expectations, admonishments, and societal rules. Your aura will be at its healthy best when you live inside it and it can talk to you without having to look over the heads of your parents or around the shoulders of your siblings and friends. No matter how much people love you, their energy does not belong in your aura or in your mind. Their energy belongs in their own auras. The act of destroying images makes that fact startlingly clear.

If you had a hard time destroying your gift image, you're not alone. The idea of using violent techniques seemed to go against every idea of spirituality I had ever encountered. You must learn, however, that when you create a gift in the favorite color of your intended person, you offer this person a symbol of acceptance and beauty. When you place that person's image inside the gift, you envelope the person in that beauty. You surround that person with love.

When you move someone swiftly out of your personal territory and destroy that person's image, you make a certain, clean, and lightning-quick break. Then, it's over. You are through with that image, without having to call, plead, bargain, or inflict pain. You simply let go, with absolute clarity. You let go from your side of the relationship, which is the only place you can ever effect any change. You let the image go in a split second, and nobody gets hurt.

How does it feel to have your image destroyed like this? Actually, it feels wonderful, especially if you are in conflict with the person who is placing dynamite under your image. After the release, you may feel free to get back in touch, to relate differently, and to do it right this time. You may feel free of your old attitudes, or free of your image-destroyer's pictures of you. This is one of the most beautiful things about destroying images. It can move relationships forward.

Since all people are intuitive, all of us use intuitive communication. Whether we know who's on the phone or where a parking place will show up, whether we can sense another person's covered-up bad mood or know that certain people are trustworthy, we all use intuitive reading and communication skills. We also know how people see us and we react to that knowledge. The destroying of images takes advantage of this fact.

For example, my best friend and I generally have a good relationship, but it has lately become one-sided. She has unconsciously taken on the role of protector, and I have become the person-in-need. When we talk, it's all about my difficulties and my struggle, and she spends most of her time advising me. I love and value her, but I am starting to feel like a helpless little sister. She is uncomfortable too, because she has pain in her life that she would like to share, but she doesn't want to intrude on my *poor me* soliloquies. We are stuck.

One morning, my friend decided to put her image of me inside a bouquet of my favorite flowers. She created a number of tiger lilies in my favorite color, and put inside them a picture of how she saw me at the moment (helpless, clueless, and time-consuming). She swiftly moved the flowers out of her aura and blew my image away with extra dynamite, because she was frustrated with our relationship.

Suddenly, on my side of the relationship, I felt free. That weak, snivelling picture I knew she carried of me was gone. I didn't know that she had blown me up, and I didn't feel sharp bits of flower shrapnel hitting me. I just felt free of the weakness in myself and in our relationship. I called her that morning and for the first time in weeks, asked her about her marriage and her family issues before barreling into my own troubles. We were once again back on more equal footing, because she was willing to release me. Now, we are both able to try something new.

※

People usually know how you feel about them. It's as if you carry around a picture of them and they can almost see it. If your picture is flattering, you have a friend. If it is unflattering, you have either an enemy or a pest who can't leave you alone until your picture matches what they want you to see. In either case, people do know—even if it's in a completely submerged area of their psyche—how you view them. Your relationships are controlled, to a certain extent, by the images you hold of others. The act of responsibly destroying these images helps relationships evolve. By clearing out old, limiting images, you can be in the moment, not only in your grounding, but in your response to the people and relationships in your life. This makes your relationship to the outer world as clean as your relationship to the inner world.

Destroying images doesn't just clear you out, it also helps the evolution of the people around you, because it sets them free. Whenever you destroy your image of another person, they get a healing of inestimable value. They get to move forward in consciousness, because you were willing to release your tired, past-time views of them. They get to come into the present and make new decisions about how they want to behave in relationship to you.

Your willingness to heal and change your relationships with others will give them a safe practice arena for making the same changes in other areas of their personal lives. When you release your images of others, they will be able to move forward with you, if they so desire. They will also be able to move on.

Of course, people can also decide to be stubborn, to maintain the status quo and the old images—but you can just destroy their image again. It takes almost no energy for you to release your limiting concepts of others, but it takes a ton of energy for others to resist change. They'll tire out eons before you will. Even if they don't, you'll have more freedom in the relationship. You will have changed it from your side.

The destruction of old images is the best way to deal with people who sense your psychic ripples and check in on your spiritual growth. It is a loving, responsible, and easy way to show them what you're doing on a spiritual level, without having to stop and explain everything in a logical, linear way.

When you destroy their images, the people in your life can get a small intuitive taste of what it feels like to clean out and move forward in consciousness. In addition, you can have the spiritual peace and privacy you need for your healing, without having to halt your process. Destroying images will calm down the people in your life, clear out the noise in your mind, heart, and aura, and give you the chance to heal and give without giving yourself away.

Your symbolic gifts and flowers, all of them, come from your inexhaustible spirit. As such, their use will never affect your day-to-day energy levels. You can bring forward and destroy images all day long and never run out or need to rest, because your gifts come from the constantly replenished nursery of your inner self.

※

Try destroying a few more images, but this time, revel in their destruction, if that was hard for you before. Remember that your resolve in getting rid of old, limiting images of others relates directly to the quality of healing they will receive, and of the separation you will achieve. If your gifts flutter away gently or make a dainty little pop, you won't really be allowing the people inside them to get on with things.

When your destruction of your image-carrying gifts is not certain and swift, the people inside them will feel a small, somewhat confusing communication that won't give them much direction. They won't feel the release that the real, serious destruction of your images would give them, and they won't really be able to move on. If you can become comfortable enough to blast all the energy away from your old pictures and really mean it, you'll be doing your relationship-mates and yourself an irreplaceable service. Let go and allow yourself the freedom to get rid of old images, relationships, and expectations. Create beautiful, loving gifts, nestle your images of other people inside them, and obliterate them!

⁂

At this point, your daily meditation should look like this: ground yourself, get into the room in your head, light up your aura boundary and clean it out if necessary, check in with your Sentry and its grounding, and create and destroy ungrounded gift symbols for anyone who shows up in your consciousness. You can blow people up one by one, or you can destroy them in pairs, trios, or groups of whatever size you like. Remember to superimpose your image of people onto your ungrounded gift symbols *inside* your aura, and then to move the gifts outside of your aura to destroy them. These are important steps, because they help to remind you that the pictures you have of people belong to you.

The images you have of people are ones you create out of your experiences with them, but they are only imperfect and incomplete images that come from your current level of understanding and compassion. These images are not the whole story about this person's spirit; they're just the parts you can identify.

For example, your mom's spirited attention may drop in during your meditations, but your reaction to her presence and the images you create inside your mind will belong to you. The images are *your* creations. They are made up of your responses to your mother. Your mother is as many things and has as many different facets as you do. She is not just those aspects you perceive. She is a million things, and she is a spirit unlike any other. Your pictures limit her spirit and, depending on how important your views are to her, they can limit her growth as well, when she tries to measure up to (or resist) those views.

When you create a gift for your mother's image inside your aura, you are taking responsibility for your view of her. You are owning up to how you see her by projecting her symbolically and enveloping that projection in a symbol of your love and spirituality. When you move your mother's image outside of your personal territory, you are bringing that image into the light, where it can be released into the psychic fabric once again. As you destroy your mother's ungrounded gift and the image of her that it contains, you are examining your response to your mother, returning energy to her, and setting both of you free.

You can begin again in that moment and choose to see your mother in her completeness, instead of viewing her in relation to your needs, your reactions, and your past limitations. Creating her image inside your aura, and then destroying it with resolve, not some pseudo-spiritual gentility, helps both of you move on in the real world.

You can destroy images at any time and in any place. If people become obtrusive during the day and hello gifts don't calm them down, blow them up right then and there. It's fun to talk to someone and keep nodding and saying, "Yes, I see," while you watch your image of them turn into shrapnel! It's even funnier to see them lose their train of thought and begin to relate to you more peaceably, for no apparent reason.

❋

You are almost done with your beginning skills. The next skill, the Gold Sun Healing, will give you a way to retrieve and rededicate all the energy you've been grounding and vacuuming and releasing and destroying. If you want to stay with destroying images for a few days, however, by all means, do so!

We have very little support from our culture to move on in healthy ways and to grow away from the group consciousness. For many people, this exercise will represent the first time they have ever had the permission to clear the decks and get into their own lives. Many students stay with this process for a few weeks, or even longer. That's perfectly appropriate.

Have fun blowing the stuffing out of people, *especially* if you love them. Blow those old entrapping images away. You'll be surprised at how much freedom it will afford you, and how much more love you'll feel when you can relate to people as your own authentic self.

THE GOLD SUN
HEALING

Your task, up to this point, has been to create a peaceful reading space by clearing out your energy and finding your authentic self. Now you need to find a way to help cement the changes you are making, so that old expectations and behaviors don't throw you backward into old ways of relating.

Getting yourself into the room in your head and behind your protected aura has helped define your territory, while grounding and releasing images has helped you to separate yourself from the foreign messages and energy surrounding you. The next step is to retrieve the grounded energy and exploded picture fragments that belong to you and to call energy back into your life, on your terms.

The Gold Sun Healing is a way to feed yourself with your own cleaned out, rededicated energy on a daily basis. This healing is a constant reminder that energy just *is*; it's not good or bad, healing or damaging, right or wrong. Energy just is. It is the currency with which you can purchase anything—love, happiness, grief, hatred, worry, laughter, insanity—anything. Energy can be redirected, renewed, rededicated, and reused. Energy itself cannot be created or destroyed, but the attachments you have to energy can.

You already know how to redirect and rededicate energy. You've collected it and turned it into grounding cords, gift images, and a room in your head. You've altered the edge of your aura; you've released energy from your images of other people; you've drained out the energy of old messages. You already know how malleable energy is, and how much it loves to move, flow, and transform.

The fluid properties of energy have formed the basis of your work. If you remain connected to your own energy source and maintain its fluidity at all times, all movement, all transformation, and all healing becomes possible. Nothing can hold you back, in life or in consciousness, if you have access to your own constantly rededicated energy.

The Gold Sun is a symbol used to represent the endless supply of energy you have, with which you can create any kind of life you desire. The reason your life often *doesn't* flow is that family and society usually need you to be understandable and controllable. Most of us get stuck in some kind of stereotypical, societally-induced, energy-wasting pattern, essentially from birth. If you belong to a certain gender, you've got one set of responsibilities; if you belong to a certain race, you've got another. Usually, by the time you're two years old, you've got huge slices of your Gold Sun dedicated to fitting in, making other people happy, living up to stereotypes, and not being any trouble. Our confused, fearful, and control-obsessed society tries to contain us—to stop us from stirring up our families, our neighborhoods, and society in general.

The Gold Sun Healing, and all of the work of this book, seeks to heal that containment and diminishment of spirit in you. The Gold Sun Healing also works through you to heal society. Whatever releasing work you do has repercussions in the energy fabric, not only of your inner world, but of the outer world as well. We'll focus on you and your own psychic fabric for now, however.

Your own personal energy is limitless. The symbol of the Gold Sun reminds you that your energy is alive, renewable, and constantly available. You can't ever run out of energy, no matter what you do. You can give too much energy away and forget to refill yourself, but the vast sum of your energy remains available to you at all times. The Gold Sun Healing gives you a way to gather and utilize your own energy, which contains your own information, your own healing abilities, and your own answers.

ENVISIONING YOUR GOLD SUN

To perform a Gold Sun Healing, sit comfortably and ground yourself. Get into the room in your head, within your clean aura and behind your Sentry. Destroy a few images if you need to. Now, envision a large, golden sun right above your aura, directly over your head (see figure 6, page 68). Feel the warmth of your Gold Sun, which symbolizes the limitless amount of energy you have available to you in this lifetime. Your Gold Sun contains your highest information, your healing powers, and your humor. It is also your eighth chakra. Your sun chakra contains an endless supply of energy that you can use at any time.

If the word *energy* confuses you, replace it with the word *attention*. They mean the same thing. If you have your attention on something, part of your energy will be there as well. Your attention requires mental and emotional energy; the first part of the Gold Sun Healing helps to remind you of that. When you are not paying complete attention to the present, you won't have the energy available to function at top efficiency.

During the first part of this healing, your Gold Sun will act as a beacon for the energy you've lost or given away to relationships or situations in your life. When you ask it to, your Gold Sun will call back that energy and clean it out so you can re-use it. Ask your Sun to call back your energy, and stay inside your room as you watch it come back.

Don't be surprised if your attention is everywhere except inside your aura, and a virtual traffic jam of your lost energy gathers in a holding pattern around your Gold Sun. Maintain your grounding and centering and allow your energy to come careening back to your Sun. You might see the energy of disagreements or conflicts with other people, the energy of desperately wanting some material possession, or the energy of ignoring important tasks. You may also receive disjointed snippets of relationships, conversations, or emotional states. Stay centered and open, and just watch yourself.

As your energies come back, allow the attachments you created to burn up and fall off as the energies hit the edge of your

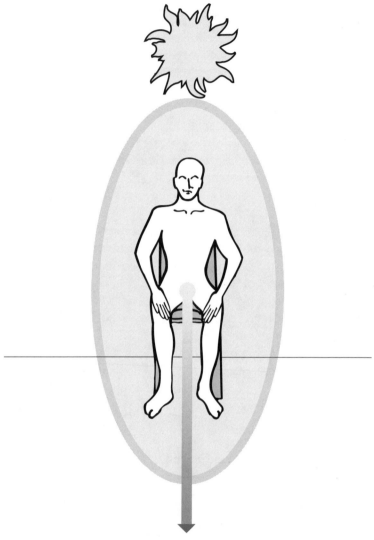

Figure 6. Envisioning your Gold Sun.

Sun. Watch each bundle become clean energy again as it re-enters your Sun. For example, your energy may come back in the form of a remembered fight with a lover. You may either see or feel the quality of the conflict as the energy nears your Sun.

Once the energy touches your Sun, however, the images of conflict will burn up and fall away. The newly clean energy then becomes one with your Sun. You now have that much more energy available to you. You can choose to revisit the old conflict with your lover in any way you like, now that your energy has returned to you, or you can move on completely.

The purpose of the Gold Sun Healing is to help you center and call back all your energy and attention from wherever it may be hiding. What you decide to do with your newly cleansed energy is your own business.

If you can't see or feel anything coming back at this point, don't worry. Your Gold Sun will collect and cleanse your energy, whether you can sense it or not. The Gold Sun chakra is a powerful energy beacon, as are your grounded, centered state, your ability to release old images, and your ability to separate from others through maintaining a healthy boundary. Everything about you right now is already calling energy back. The Gold Sun is simply helping you to focus and get into conscious control of this process by acting as an energy placeholder of sorts. Your energy and attention are coming back anyway. This Gold Sun Healing is a tool with which to collect, cleanse, and rededicate the energy that is already available and waiting to be acknowledged, accepted, healed, and reused.

Each time you put up your Gold Sun, different energies and qualities of energy will return to you. You can observe the ways your attention is diverted from your present-time awareness, or you can trust your Sun to do its collecting work and relax into the healing.

When you don't know why you're feeling uncertain or scattered or deeply emotional, you can put up your Sun and closely monitor your incoming energy. When you can see where your energy has been, you can ground out the attitudes that have kept you trapped. You can also destroy images or strengthen your Sentry in order to keep your energy in one place. Or, you can let your Sun do its work on its own and know that your energy is now cleansed and available to you, no matter where it has been.

PERFORMING THE GOLD SUN HEALING

To proceed with the second part of the Gold Sun Healing, check in with your grounding and your general meditative state, and release a few images if your Sun work has brought other people into your consciousness. If you need to, dump attitudes down your grounding cord, change the color of your aura or your Sentry, or move to a more comfortable place in the room in your head. Whatever changes you experience in the first part of this healing need to be addressed. Thank your Gold Sun for providing this self-healing practice arena. If you experienced no changes in your meditative state, thank your Gold Sun as well. It is doing its work without needing to contact you or disturb you in any way.

When your meditative state is as you want it to be, make a small opening at the very top of your aura, and let the energy of your Sun shine in (see figure 7, page 71). See or feel this warm, soothing, tingling energy fill your entire aura and cover your skin. Feel the warmth on your face, on your hands and feet, behind your back, under your legs and arms, and all the way out to the edge of your aura. Let your aura and its boundary become completely gold.

Breathe in the energy of your Sun, and feel its warmth as it enters your lungs. As you breathe, see and feel your Gold Sun energy travel through your bloodstream along with the oxygen you have just inhaled. Feel your clean, present-time healing energy as it lights up your bloodstream, your muscles, your organs, and your bones. Feel your gold energy throughout your abdomen, in your hips and legs, in your arms and hands, throughout the inner layers of your skin, and in your chest, neck, face, and skull. Breathe.

Now turn your grounding cord gold and feel the energy inside your body flow down your cord, cleansing the cord and your body and rededicating your grounding cord with present-time healing energy. Stay in your head and turn everything in your room gold—the walls, the furniture, the scene outside your window—everything. Stay in this newly golden room in your head and shine your Gold Sun onto your Sentry symbol. Turn your

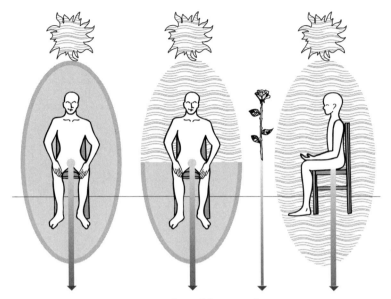

Figure 7. The Gold Sun Healing.

Sentry gold and change its grounding cord to match. This gives your Sentry a present-time healing as well.

Sit for a few minutes and experience your own energy. This warm, calming, tingly, wonderful energy is your own. It is constantly available at your discretion, absolutely free, and completely within your control. Feel it as it travels throughout your body, moving gently, lighting up each cell. Watch it as it moves through your aura and your energy tools, cleansing and rededicating your energy, and making each tool more real to you. Get in touch with what it feels like to be safe in the present moment, surrounded by your own energy.

Check in with your grounding and make sure your cord is still gold. Running your Gold Sun energy through your body and out your grounding cord is a wonderful healing. As each portion of your body is lit up from within, old messages, pains, and stored emotions will be dislodged and fall away. When you turn your grounding cord to gold, you'll be able to drain off a lot of old, clogged energy, so that your body can begin to flow into the present. Healing your grounding cord with Gold Sun energy also makes grounding much more effective.

When you are ready, close the opening in the top of your aura, and allow the golden energy to settle in your body and your aura. Stay grounded, bend over and touch the floor with your hands, and let your head hang downward. Allow the golden energy inside your body to drain out of your hands and feet, or out the top of your head, if that feels right to you. Stay in this position until you feel cleansed, then sit up again, slowly. Check your grounding and make sure you're still inside your head. You're done. Excellent work!

＊

You must always give your body a chance to drain out after you add energy to it. Your body works very well on its own and can be seriously disturbed when you add light and colors and energy to it willy-nilly. Because it exists in the physical world, your body is very different from your aura and grounding cord and images that live in the ethereal world. It holds a stupendous amount of responsibility, survival information, and information in general. Your ethereal information may not coincide with that right away. In addition, your body exists in real time, which means that its work proceeds at its own pace—which may be quite different from the pace your spirit can keep. Though you nearly always mean well by it, adding healing energy to your body can be done in the wrong way at the wrong time, according to its individual time schedule. Your body needs to have control over what it accepts.

Your Gold Sun energy shouldn't have any negative effects on your body, but you need to let your body decide how much of the golden energy it wants to release, how much it wants to retain, and where it wants to store it. Bodies work with a different set of challenges than spirits do, but they know exactly what they're doing and when everything needs to be done. If your body needs the spiritual energy you give it, it will keep it. If not, you must give it a chance to release it.

Don't *throw* energy work at your body; it may have been living without your attention for a very long time. If so, it will have its own way of doing things. Let it have the power to choose what it wants and needs. If you don't, your body may not trust you. Work with it, not at it. Your body knows what it's doing.

✳

After each Gold Sun Healing, you will have brought all of your tools into your conscious awareness. Now your grounding cord and aura will know that you've called back your energy from this person or that situation, and they'll become stronger for it. Your Sentry will know where you are and can now transmit a clearer, stronger energy. The room in your head will have received a major spring cleaning. Each part of you will be newly aware of and tuned into your current level of spiritual awareness.

The Gold Sun Healing connects your spiritual self to your body in a safe, warm, and real way. With this connection, you will suddenly have access to a number of safe and sane responses to the experiences around you. You won't need to rely on runaway healing, emotional benders, dissociation, or fearful boundary-making. You will have not only the tools taught in this book, but the whole of your knowledge as an unlimited spirit.

Use your Gold Sun Healing every day, at the end of your regular check-in meditation, or any time you lose your boundaries. As with each of the other skills we've learned, this healing can take as little or as much time as you like. In essence, as soon as you've got the gold flowing through you, this healing is done, However, you can keep your Gold Sun energy lighting and warming you for as long as you like, just as you can turn on your grounding vacuum, cleanse your aura, or destroy your images for an extended period. It's up to you.

✳

You have now learned all your beginning skills and are ready for deeper work. Your daily meditation at this point should go like this: sit and ground yourself, get into the room in your head, define your aura and cleanse it if necessary, check and renew your grounded Sentry if necessary, and release any number of relationship images. When you're done, call up your Gold Sun and feed yourself with your own energy. Finish by bending over and letting your body release energy if necessary. You're done!

If you feel a bit hazy during the day, you can quickly fill your aura with Gold Sun energy, without going on to fill your body as well. This is a very swift way to redefine your aura. It can be done at work, in the car, or anywhere else. This simplified aura-fill is easy to do in the presence of others, because it's less involved than a complete Gold Sun Healing. Since you don't bring the Gold Sun energy into your body during this quick mini-healing, you won't need to bend over and release, which can be hard to explain at a PTA meeting or in the ticket line at the airport. Actually, with a little discretion, you can do most of your meditation in public if you have to. None of these skills requires privacy, quiet, or even external peace, which makes them very useful for busy people like us.

Congratulate yourself for getting this far. Don't undermine yourself if you haven't been able to work with some of these tools. Some skills will be easy, while others will take a lot of practice, depending on where your energy is stuck. Skip ahead to the Troubleshooting Guide (see page 259) and look up your specific area of difficulty or your symptoms. You should find the answers you need. Give yourself time to revisit skills you haven't mastered, because the work undertaken in the next section depends on the skills you learned in this one.

PART II

FURTHER INWARD

BURNING CONTRACTS

You've learned to ground and center yourself in a safe, meditative sanctuary within your body. You've become proficient at cleansing and defining your aura. You've learned to create and destroy images to release other people's messages from your inner life. You've created a Gold Sun Healing to channel your cleansed energy into your aura and body. With these foundations in place, you're ready to delve a bit deeper.

You may already have discovered a few relationships, attitudes, or ideas that you cannot ground out or destroy completely. Some energies or relationships may show up in your meditations every day, regardless of how much releasing work you do with them. In these cases, it is very likely that you have entered into a psychic *contract* with this relationship—a contract that needs to be examined, renegotiated, or destroyed.

When unaware or incompatible people interact with one another, they often set up a series of expectations, behaviors, reaction patterns, and comfort zones in an attempt to create intimacy and connection. These postures and expectations often define the quality and scope of the relationship and act as contractual maps or unifying placeholders for both participants. Through conscious and unconscious agreement, many relationships evolve (or decay) in precisely delineated, contractual patterns.

When people are truly compatible and live in the present moment, their relationships will not require such contracts. Compatible relationships tend to grow, fluctuate, move, and change in response to the growth and awareness of each partner. If you have a friend to whom you can say absolutely anything, even if your paths diverge for months or years at a time, you will understand the ease, freedom, and security that compatible relationships provide. When people can communicate freely, contracts that specify rigid behaviors or expectations are unnecessary. They can even be damaging to the relationship.

When people are not compatible, however, they often rely on relationship contracts to create an illusion of closeness, or a least a reliable sense of continuity with other people. In these instances, a relationship contract can remind people of how to behave when their own truths and needs are unimportant (or unwelcome) in a relationship.

Work relationships or casual social acquaintanceships are perfect examples of instances where contracts may provide support when the true relationship does not. Relationship contracts are also helpful for people who would rather not be awake and aware in every moment. Contracts can help to remind you to be serious with this person, social but not too close to that one, funny but guarded with this one, and so on. The problems arise when the contracts erase your true relating skills and force you to comply with their tenets and bylaws.

In these contract-governed situations, authentic communication and connection is swept aside as the contracts grow larger and more rigid. In many relationships, people actually spend more time attending to their contractual obligations than they do relating to their contract partner. For example, we all know married couples who stay together for reasons we can't understand. Each person is miserable, they can't communicate, they are lonely and have affairs, or require endless support from their friends. But they don't split up and move on. Their relationship usually revolves around money, obligations, or the kids, but their love for one another has no life or healing in it anymore.

In these instances, two people are bent under the weight of an unyielding, 20-foot monster contract. Neither can reach (or even see) their partner through this behemoth called Their Relationship, and both are incapable of communicating around it. Still, they continue to feed and honor the contract, even though it may destroy both of them. These people have been taught that it is honorable to obey contracts and to live up to the expectations and demands of others, no matter what it does to them or to their relationship.

Their unwieldy marriage contract is usually made up of societal and familial rules about how marriage should be. Often, both partners will unconsciously imitate their own parent's marriage contracts in a sad game of playing house, missing out on the excitement (and the work) of creating their own love and relating styles. Their contract may also be filled with trivial and often outdated information on each partner's likes, dislikes, and opinions—so much so that most of their conversations will center around reminders of how the other person is *supposed* to feel and behave, based on old information ("You *hate* Mexican food. . . . We agreed to have children *after* graduation. . . . This never bothered you *before*. . . .").

What these and all other relationship contracts do not contain is room for freshness, surprise, change, acceptance, or flow. Relationship contracts require conventional, reliable, and stereotypical responses. Relationship contracts exist to guarantee *stasis*.

Stasis is a natural and wonderful thing, just as change is a natural and wonderful thing. Contracts, however, do not leave room for the natural wonder of change. They only support stasis. They are one-sided and unhealthy, and should be avoided in an active, whole, and healing life. Imagine how unbalanced and exhausted you would become if some agreement in your life required you to change constantly, no matter what. Your life would soon be unworkable. The same unworkability ensues when relationship contracts, which require a complete avoidance of change, are allowed to prevail over natural human communication.

Contracts may seem, at first, to provide a useful support system in the difficult realm of human relationships. As with many supports that exist to make courage and honesty unnecessary, however, contracts soon become incapacitating. Relationship contracts are often set up to make honesty in incompatible relationships nonessential, so that people who really don't belong together can manage their relationship on a superficial level. This may seem logical. In fact, contract-building would be acceptable if human relationships were logical and dependable. But they're not and, because of that, contracts in human relationships fail miserably.

When a contract is set up to help people *avoid* intimacy within a relationship, the people involved become *incapable* of intimacy or honesty. The seemingly logical contract becomes illogical in the real world, as the people within it become trapped in webs of misunderstanding, frustration, and isolation. Release and freedom can only come when someone is willing to take responsibility for their part in the agreement and *burn the relationship contract.*

HOW TO BURN CONTRACTS

Let's use our unhappily married couple as examples. When the husband grounds himself and goes through his meditation process, his wife may show up in his thoughts, even after he has released her with a loving image. This will signal to him that he is holding on to more than an old *image* of his wife; he's got a *contract* with her as well.

From inside the room in his head, the husband checks his grounding, his aura, and his Sentry, and fixes any problems he finds. Then, he imagines a long piece of paper or parchment inside his aura, upon which he places the qualities of his marriage contract. He may write his wife's name on the parchment, or a description of the emotional content of their marriage, or he may project a movie of their interactions onto the parchment. Whatever comes up for him with regard to his wife will go onto the paper, in plain view.

As he places his marriage agreements onto the parchment, he also places *his* stances, reactions, and requirements, alongside those of his wife. As he does so, his first parchment may soon become crammed with images and emotions. If so, he moves it aside a little, and creates a second, clean parchment in order to continue with his releasing work.

When he feels a sense of peace and relaxation in his body, he rolls up his many parchments so that the information on them is no longer visible, and he imagines tying up each roll of paper with a healing golden cord. He then moves or tosses the sealed-up parchments away from him, to the outside of his aura, where he sets them on fire. As he watches his relationship contracts transform into neutral, unreadable, unattached energy, he rechecks his grounding and meditative state, and performs a Gold Sun Healing to feed this clean, newly available energy back into his life.

When he burns the contracts of his unworkable marriage, the husband examines, takes responsibility for, and releases vast amounts of enmeshed, entangled energy. This step alone will help to heal his marriage, because it requires him to take responsibility for his part in the character and condition of that marriage. In addition, because his work involves releasing a contractual agreement with his wife (which she agreed to on some level), his contract burning helps to release her as well.

If his wife is ready to move forward with him, this work will free both of them. She will no longer be ensnared in his controlling, stereotypical expectations and reactions. She may be able to respond authentically to him for the first time in years. If his wife is unwilling to move forward, and still wants to keep the old, "You ruined my life!" pot brewing, his work will still have a freeing effect on both of them. It does not matter if the wife refuses to burn her side of the contract. If the husband burns his portion, the contract will get smaller. It has to. When it does, the wife's position will be less supportable, less charged, and less fun. It is not possible for this man's wife to maintain conflict with him if he won't fight back. Nor is it possible for them to have a damaging relationship contract if he won't sign it.

Regardless of the wife's wishes, the husband has moved forward. Because he is an individual, he has that right. The marriage contract he agreed to revoked his right to move forward, but he revoked the contract. Now he can make decisions based on his present-day needs, wishes, and realities. The marriage may heal and renew itself, or it may end, allowing both husband and wife to live again. The outcome, and the next steps, are as individual as the parties involved. Burning their old contract allows both to be freed as individuals, instead of remaining slaves to a psychic document.

Contracts are everywhere. It is not unusual to have separate contracts with every person in your life, as well as contracts with emotional states like despair and fury, contracts with gender identification and social standing, contracts with finances and security, and even contracts for how you live up to contracts!

Do not punish yourself for relying on contracts to pilot you through the tempests of human interaction. Contract-building can be an important connection tool in instances where connections might not otherwise be possible. If most of your relationships require you to amend your personality, and if your aura is littered with contracts, congratulate yourself for trying to connect, before you despair over how much contract burning you will have to do.

BURNING YOUR OWN CONTRACTS

To burn a relationship contract, get into your grounded body, seat yourself in the room in your head, light up and cleanse your aura, and check in on your Sentry. Destroy a few of the confining images you have of others, and be aware of which images come careening back into your consciousness. These are almost certainly your contract partners. If you question the existence of a contract with anyone, create yet another gift in their favorite color, place them inside it, move their image outside of your aura, and release them again. If their image reappears after this second release, there's no doubt—you've got yourselves a contract.

Now, create a large piece of sturdy parchment paper in front of you and inside your aura. This parchment originates *inside* your aura to remind you that your views of people and your side of any contract belong to *you*, not them. Choose a warm and soothing color for this parchment. Bright or strong colors can be too reflective, and you'll want this paper to accept all your energy and projections, without reflecting anything back onto you.

With the paper in front of you, allow yourself to think of your contract partner. Let your thoughts be transmitted to the parchment. You can write your partner's name on the parchment, or you can write the name of the relationship. You can project your contract partner's image onto the paper, or transmit a video of their movements, actions, and behaviors. If your first parchment becomes crowded with images, move it gently aside, and create a fresh parchment, so you can continue to release the relationship. Some relationship contracts will require many parchment pages before you are through with them.

As you continue to work, your own image will begin to emerge alongside the image of your contract partner. You will be able to see your conflicts, your body postures, your own attitudes, and your responses to your partner. Place those images and attitudes on the parchment as well. They signify your involvement in the contract, your payoffs, and your reasons for agreeing to the contract in the first place.

Don't waste time abusing yourself if your reasons and justifications for agreeing with or reacting to the contract are less than wonderful. Stay in your head, observe yourself, and keep working. Allow the energy of this relationship contract to flow out of you. Use as many parchment sheets as you need. Your body and aura will signal the end of this session by making a shift of some kind. You may feel a sudden sense of relaxation, or the impatient need to get up and move around. When you feel this shift, roll up each of your contracts so that all you can see are the blank, exterior portions of each parchment.

As you roll up each contract, tie it closed with a piece of golden rope. Binding your contracts with golden energy will remind the contract that this is the present, where its laws and by-laws no longer apply. When all your parchments are rolled and tied, move or toss them three to five feet outside of your aura. Gather or stack your contracts together and burn them up. Depending on your feelings at the moment, you may light one match under your contract or pile of contracts; you may set them ablaze with a flare or a stream of intense energy; or you may torch them with a militaristic flame-thrower.

When your contracts are blazing, stay in your head and watch their energy feed the fire as they lose their attachments and become neutral energy once again. As the once-important contracts turn to ash, know that they are no longer readable, viable, or binding.

Check in with your meditative state, and attend to any disruptions in any of your tools. When you are centered, perform a full Gold Sun Healing. The burning of relationship contracts frees up and cleanses much energy. Your Gold Sun will help you to gather, rededicate, and feed this energy back into your system. When you have your energy back, you can use it to heal yourself, to forgive yourself, and to communicate authentically with your once-contractual partner. Remember to bend over and touch the floor at the end of your Gold Sun Healing so your body can release any energy it doesn't want. You're done!

※

Don't be surprised if your burnt-up relationship contracts attempt to reanimate themselves. Like all bad habits, contracts tend to hang around in the shadows of your being, waiting for the day when you become tired or unaware, and BANG!, they're back.

If you can treat contracts like the untrained, immature animals they are, and gently but firmly remind them to go on the paper (or parchment), they will eventually get the message. If you accord the contracts some respect as you create and release them, and realize what a valuable service they provided when you *wanted* to be unconscious, they will leave you with more dignity and finality.

When you are less reliant on contracts, you will find that your relationships, even if they are purely social or work-related, will usually allow you the freedom to be yourself. Of course, this freedom in relationships only comes *after* you become centered and grounded enough to give yourself freedom in your own life. The process of burning contracts simply supports this liberation.

When you are free of contracts, relationship difficulties will become less prevalent. You will soon find it odd to be stuck and unable to relate, or in need of guidance and support in your relationships. Instead of identifying yourself as someone unable to relate (or denouncing the human race as untrustworthy), and using contracts to protect yourself from intimacy, you will begin to flow in and out of relationships that feed, instruct, or challenge you. Your conscious awareness will support you in saying what you feel, asking for what you want, and trusting the human experience.

Burning contracts won't suddenly turn the world into a safe or logical place. What it will do is free up your energy so that your inner world becomes safe and logical for you. When this happens, your needs and requirements in relationships will change from being unworkably self-centered, give-me-everything-you-have-or-I'll-know-you-don't-love-me expectations into a realistic, love-centered willingness to experience the fullness of another person, without having to control, amend, objectify, or destroy them.

When you have the energy to meet your own needs, you won't require every relationship to be perfect and unwavering in its devotion to your specifications. When you burn your relationship contracts, you'll free up the energy to meet your own needs. You'll also free up the people in your life so they can begin to meet their own needs, which will make them less dependent on you, and more able to relate authentically, *sans* contract.

As you burn your contracts with people, take a few moments in each session to burn your contracts with ideas, emotional states, and attitudes that hold you back as well. For instance, you can create and burn the contract you have with your gender identification by placing all the pictures and ideas of how your gender should behave, dress, eat, parent, or make money onto a parchment. You can also burn contracts with your work ethic, your attitude about money, your fears of success or failure, or your reactions to certain religions, ideologies, or health regimes. You can free yourself from trapping, stereotypical relationships with anyone or anything.

You've already worked with grounding out various ideas and attitudes. It is very likely, however, that some of these grounded items have come careening back to you. You may have tried to ground and release gender issues or emotions, but with very little lasting success. This lack of release signals a contractual relationship with the idea or attitude—a contract that has been set up to keep you a controlled member of *the group*, whatever group that may be. Burn your membership card, please.

When you release your attachments and burn your contracts with ideas and attitudes, you certainly free yourself, but you also begin to dismantle the ideas and attitudes in your culture as well. Investigations of human history have shown that many hallowed beliefs and practices simply disappeared when enough people examined and rejected them.

Some beliefs, like the flat Earth theory and the practice of medicinal blood-letting, were rejected through scientific investigation, but some prevalent beliefs just lost their energy as people turned away from them. Many ideas, inventions, and requirements that were concrete realities for our grandparents have no meaning for us today, because energy and attention were withdrawn from them. We can withdraw our attention and energy from any of today's concrete realities, and live in our own reality.

✳

Emotional states can also bind you contractually. You may become addicted to a certain emotion, but ignore the issues and circumstances that caused the addiction in the first place. Rage, despair, and suicidal urges are three favorite contractually addictive emotions that take up an enormous amount of energy.

When you burn contracts with recurring emotions, you free up your entire emotional body so that it can heal itself. When you burn contracts with ideas and attitudes, you remove energy from them, so that they do not have such a fiery presence in your awareness or your milieu. When you burn your contracts with gender, career, or financial identifications, you release energy from the fabric of those belief systems, so that their intensity is lessened and they become less binding for others. When you release yourself from contracts, you also heal and release the people and energy around you.

When you burn your contracts, strangely enough, you become more connected to your world. You become more able to connect to the humans who share it with you, because you move away from limiting rules and expectations, and into the flow of life.

Inside your aura, you are in charge, not only of your internal issues, but of your relating skills and responsibilities as well. From inside the room in your head, you regain control of your reactions to anything that comes at you from the internal or external world. You may not be in control of what comes at you (you're not all-powerful), but you are in control of how you *deal* with what comes at you.

In your centered life, you can choose to leave or stay in abusive environments. You can choose to leave or stay in unhappy relationships. You can't always control the money coming in, but you can choose where you spend it. You can't control your friends and family, but you can manage your reactions to them, and choose to see them in different ways.

Your spiritual healing work will not make everything in your external life magically smooth and wonderful. This planetary experience is not about peace and plenty right now, nor should it be. You're here to grow, learn, experience life, and become stronger in your individual expression. When you have a clean, available, and lively inner life, your individual expression will occur naturally. When that happens, your outer life will not have to be perfect. Instead of placing unrealistic burdens on other people and the state of the world *before* you deign to blossom, you will be able to cultivate yourself. By doing so, you will become a real asset to the world, instead of a burdensome pile of want and need.

Burning your relationship and mind-set contracts releases others from the impossible task of providing for all of your needs. It releases the external world from the burden of having to be perfect before you feel safe, comfortable, or happy. It releases you from the fetters and blinders that keep your individuality imprisoned. Burn your contracts and let them go. You will set your heart and your spirit free.

※

The way to support yourself in this releasing process is to ground, ground, ground, and ground. Grounding will keep your spirit and your body in communication with one another, which will make the room in your head more comfortable. From inside your room, you can heal and redefine your aura, check on your Sentry, ground out pain and difficulty, destroy images, and burn your contracts. Grounding makes it all possible.

It is also vital to perform as many Gold Sun Healings as you can during this time. Your Gold Sun energy contains specific, individual healing energy for you, as well as health information, behavioral guidelines, personal support, and information on your direction and your most healing spiritual path right now.

As the old energy leaves you, make certain that you replace it with the cleansed, healing, and supportive information and energy of your Gold Sun chakra.

When you add contract burning to your set of spiritual tools, you will become, for all intents and purposes, a miracle worker in your own life. When you can remove old ideas, attitudes, expectations, and other unwanted energies from your life, and can cleanse, retrieve, and repossess their neutral, healing energy, you will be a gifted psychic self-healer.

Know, however, that ridding yourself of old, unworkable relationship patterns or belief systems can and does bring emotions forward. Sometimes the emotions will be understandable, sometimes not. In our culture, this important, emotionally volatile process is almost totally misunderstood, as are emotions themselves. This is a shame.

The next section, and the rest of this book, attempts to bring emotions out of the shadows, and into your hands. I know you thought this book was about the exciting world of psychic knowledge. Actually, it is about the real excitement of knowing yourself. Your emotions hold much knowledge and more healing power than any external mystic or healer ever will. You'll see.

CHANNELING YOUR EMOTIONS

I don't know what happened to emotions in this society. They are the least understood, most maligned, and most ridiculously over-analyzed aspects of human life. Emotions are categorized, celebrated, vilified, repressed, manipulated, humiliated, adored, and ignored. Rarely, if ever, are they *honored*.

Many psycho-rational therapies, religions, and New Age teachings split emotions into categories like good and bad and then spend enormous amounts of time and energy teaching their respective disciples to agree with them. In order to truly fit in, followers must court, invoke, and experience the teaching's accepted emotions while they ignore, pray away, and run from the forbidden ones. The only problem is that the therapies and teachings can't seem to agree on which emotions are right, and which are wrong. Some religions and teachings shun all emotions, while others shun only anger and fear. Most New Age teachings make do with one emotion (joy), and strive to sublimate the rest. As in any perfection-instead-of-wholeness regime, the damage caused by the denying of true human emotions creates truly inhuman problems.

In our society, the "bad" emotion is grief. After a few hundred years of repression, we have become a cold-hearted people, mesmerized by, but incapable of accepting, death. Disallowed, repressed anger turns to inner rage, torment, and suicidal urges, while denied fear turns into panic attacks, spirit/body splits, and an underlying distrust of people and life in general. These are the rewards of repressing the emotions.

Expressing the emotions is better than repressing them, because it allows a flow of truthfulness in the body and spirit. If emotions are very strong, however, expressing them can create both exterior and interior turmoil. The exterior turmoil occurs when we pour our strong emotions all over some unfortunate soul and try to make him or her responsible for our mood. The interior turmoil occurs when we realize we have startled or hurt someone with our outpouring, which makes us feel dismayed and ashamed of ourselves. Then we either repress the emotions again, or express them even more loudly, neither of which will help anyone.

Often, our strong emotions make us lash out and blame others for our feelings, which traps us into believing that someone else is in control of our emotions ("You *made* me angry, you *made* me cry!"). Expressing strong emotions can be damaging to our egos. So, what's left? If we can't *repress* emotions without getting into trouble, and we can't *express* them either, what can we do, live in a cave? No. *We can channel our emotions.*

When we express our emotions, we hand them over to the outside world, where we hope they will be noticed, honored, healed, and transformed into something bright and beautiful. Emotional expression relies on the exterior world and on other people to decipher and transmute emotional messages into action. When we repress emotions, we hand them over to the interior world, where we hope they will be taken care of, healed, and transformed into something more acceptable to us. Emotional repression relies on the unconscious, interior world to accept and *do something* with the emotion.

Neither hand-off works for very long. Emotional expression makes us unworkably dependent on therapists, books, friends, family members, clergy, and external action for emotional relief and release. Since all of these exterior people or supports can leave or be taken away, we emotion-expressers can become stuck with a life full of feelings, but no emotional skills of our own, and nowhere to go with the feelings and energies we have.

Emotional repression, on the other hand, makes us unworkably dependent on a body or an unconscious that can only hold so much repressed material before it has to get rid of something. When you hand off your emotional responsibilities to your body, it stores them somewhere until they eventually show up as pain or illness. If you hand off to your unconscious and tell it, "No anger or grief, okay?" your unconscious works very hard to obey you, but it has to create something else with all your angry, grieving energy. Suicidal urges usually do the trick.

Both the expression and repression of emotion have serious drawbacks. The hand-off never works. On the other hand, when you listen to, honor, and channel your emotions, you don't need to hand them off to anyone or anything. Emotional channeling lets you handle your emotions yourself. When you are able to take care of your own emotions, they will take care of you in ways you may not be able to believe right now.

All emotions are messages from our unconscious aspects to our conscious ones. Emotions may spring from our bodies, from our deep memories, or from unused and unnoticed aspects of our psyches. They carry with them the absolute truth of the sending aspect. Strong or uncontrollable emotions carry, not just truth, but enormous amounts of energy, which is the essence of this work. Strong energy makes this work stronger. Therefore, strong emotions carry absolutely all the healing energy we need to deal with whatever brought about the strong emotion in the first place. Strong emotions contribute the energy we need to heal ourselves and evolve. Strong emotions are the energetic warehouse of the soul.

Expressing and repressing emotions are subtle ways to leave your body and your experience, and to squander your energy. Though you may remain grounded and in the room in your head while you pour your emotions all over someone (or ignore an unacceptable feeling), these are not centered or aware actions. You can get away with them for a while in a grounded and centered body, but eventually, your refusal to accept and honor your emotions will activate the old spirit/body split again. To circumvent any further dissociation, let's learn to honor and channel our emotions.

CHANNELING THE FLEETING OR IMMEDIATE EMOTIONS

There are two kinds of emotional channeling: one that can be used in any normal healing and meditation session, which channels fleeting emotions, and another that deals with very powerful or repeated emotional states and requires a special meditation of its own. The simpler method of emotional channeling is actually a lot of fun. All that is required is your willingness to be aware of and available to any emotions that come up during your regular healing and separation sessions.

As you release your images and burn your contracts, emotions often spring forward. If you have been taught that emotions are bad or unspiritual, their presence may interrupt your process (and end your healing session) while you use up your energy reacting to or suppressing them. If you learn to see them as good, healing, and integral to you, they will enrich and support your process. Emotions will not be in the way of your spiritual work; they will show you the way to spiritual health.

Releasing and destroying images with emotional energy is very simple. As you create the images you will release, be aware of the emotions that come up in response to the people you imagine. As you move these people outside of your aura, use the energy of the emotions they bring forward to help you destroy the image you hold of them. For example, if someone's presence in my awareness makes me feel angry, I will destroy their gift and image with fiery red-orange, angry energy. If another person's presence causes a fearful reaction in me, I will release them with a spiky green, frightened energy. If someone else's presence fills me with grief and sadness, I will let them go more slowly, with a fluid, dark, and grieving energy.

When I release people with the emotion I have in reaction to their presence, I honor the fact that I *do* react. I honor the fact of the emotion, the fact of my status as a human artwork-in-progress, and the fact of my lack of strong boundaries with regard to this person or that event. By honoring my emotions, I learn about myself. I become a clearer and more centered intuitive healer.

I learn to strengthen my aura and my Sentry. I learn to stay grounded. I learn to create a better room in my head. And I learn to feed myself Gold Sun energy if my reaction to people or ideas drains me. If I pretend that I feel powerful and complete at all times, and try to use my spiritual separation skills to tell myself lies about my power in the world, or my power over other people and the supposedly lower emotions, I'll soon have a whopping spirit/body split. I won't have learned my lesson.

Spirits are powerful and fearless, because they never die. Bodies, on the other hand, must expend enormous amounts of energy ensuring their own survival. Bodies die and are injured and made ill every day. Bodies are not all-powerful. Neither are they fearless or emotionless.

Emotions exist to help the body protect itself. They also serve as a connecting link between the reality-centered body and the light-and-energy-centered spirit. Emotions are fluid, ever-changing, and extremely versatile energies. Emotions *move*.

Emotions, if properly honored and channeled, create a flowing, healing, and communicative link between the needs of the body and the knowledge of the spirit. If we can listen to, validate, and use our emotions in our spiritual healing sessions, our bodies and our spirits will come into closer accord. There will be a fluid medium between them.

Though the body is not lower than or inferior to the spirit, its grounding in real time, real food, real money, and real life can make its communications with the other-worldly spirit confusing at best. Conversely, the spirit's timeless, formless, and limitless information can sound like gibberish to a body in immediate distress.

The intellect does its part to translate and direct information between the body and spirit, but without the fluid medium of the emotions to carry the information, very little real work is accomplished. When the body and spirit are at odds, and the communicative abilities of the emotions are ignored, the intellect will often go into high gear. Such situations create people who think too much, often to the point of tormenting themselves with all their misused and overburdened mental energy. Nothing gets accomplished, but lots and lots of energy is used up in planning, scheming, what-iffing, and obsessing.

The intellect was never meant to do the work we moderns have forced upon it. Its translating and explanatory abilities are absolutely vital in a working quaternity of body, spirit, mind, and emotion, but the mind can't magically run the quaternity alone. Without the support of the fluid conveyance of the emotions, which carries the mind's translated information between spirit and body, the mind can only escalate its process. It can't transfer workable physical information to the spirit all by itself; nor can it help the body understand formless spiritual realities without an emotional assist.

What the mind can do by itself is think, think, and think, create fantasies and battle plans, go over the same issues hundreds of times, and torment both body and spirit, as well as itself. However, when the emotions are utilized properly in the healthy quaternity, when the emotions are used to carry information from one reality to another, the body/spirit split simply disappears, as does the mental torment. In a healthy, emotion-supported-and-supporting quaternity, the body's information reaches the soul in a spiritually tangible, "So *that's* how life feels!" form. Conversely, when the emotions are allowed to transmit spiritual information to the body, the information arrives in a physically understandable form. The body receiving this information can say, "Oh, so acceptance feels like *this*, anger has *this* energy*, and my reactions mean *that*. I get it."

When the emotions are honored and channeled, the intellect can take its rightful place as the overseer of the spirit/body translation process, instead of being expected to actually carry the information from body to spirit and back again. Since, within the quaternity, the mind is being asked to do what it was meant to do, it need not torment itself or its owner. It can rest, lie back and concentrate on its studies, and let the emotions do the walking.

When you include your emotions in your healing work and your life, you will be able to almost fly through issues that once kept your mind, body, and spirit in turmoil. You will have reserves of energy available—energy you used to throw away when you handed off your emotions in one way or another. The emotions make the body more aware, the mind more able to process in calm and centered ways, and the spirit more grounded and comprehensible. Channeled emotions also make separation work very swift and sure. If you can release an image with real energy, or if you can burn a contract from within your actual feelings, your separation process will be far more certain and valid than release work done with some supposedly spiritual gentility shtick.

As you release your images and move turmoil away from your center, let your emotions give you a hand. The function of emotions is to transport energy from one place to another. They can make your separation work easier if you let them usher and transport unwanted or confusing energy out of your life.

As you burn your contracts, remember that the emotions you have in response to your contract partners are the specific emotions needed to transport information about the contract between your body, mind, and spirit. Your emotions also contain the specific amount of energy required to help you release yourself from contracts.

Anger can help you burn contracts hot and bright. Fear and anxiety can help you incinerate them in a split-second flash, and sadness can help you create a funeral pyre, so you can mourn your losses properly as your contracts are cremated. Each of your emotions will help you to release yourself and the people in your life from limiting images, contracts, and expectations. Your honored and validated emotions will help you to flow more smoothly through your life. Use them.

CHANNELING THE DEEPER
MOODS AND EMOTIONS

Channeling deeper, repetitive, or intense and unrelenting emotions is not difficult. In this process, we dedicate ourselves and our spiritual territory to the emotion at hand. During a deep channeling session, we choose a color, quality, and movement for the energy of our emotional state, but, instead of releasing images and contracts with the energy, we channel it into our body, our aura, our grounding cord, and all of our energy tools.

Emotional channeling is very like the channeling you have done with Gold Sun energy. The only difference is that your emotional energy is not neutral like Gold Sun energy; it has something very specific to say! If you'd like to hear the messages your emotions have for you, wait until they pull you into a deep mood, then listen and learn.

When a mood or an intense emotion comes up, your being is signaling the need for serious release work. When you can, please sit and ground yourself. Get into the room in your head, define your aura, ground it with its own grounding tube, and check in with your Sentry. If you have to stop and fix any of your energy tools, go ahead. Your emotion will wait for you. When you are centered, allow your mind and body to bring your emotion to its fullness. Let your body feel its intensity, and let your mind describe the emotion in words and images.

From within your head, choose a leading color and movement for the energy of your emotion. Anger might be a hot and swiftly-moving orange energy; fear may be an electrically-charged green swirl; sadness may be a drippy blue energy; and grief may be a solid and unmoving brown cloud. Your mind and body will help you choose your own colors and movements. If you have trouble visualizing, get a feel for the shape, movement, or sound pattern of the emotion, and use that instead.

When you have envisioned the energetic quality of your emotional state, allow it to fill your body completely, and then breathe it out into your aura. Fill your aura with this energy, and change its colored boundary to the color and quality of your emotion. From inside your head, watch and feel the movement of this emotion's energy in your body and your aura. When your body and aura are full of the energy of your emotion, fill up your Sentry until it, too, is made up of the energy of your emotion. Allow the emotion to come into the room in your head, and fill the floors, walls, ceiling, furniture, and plants with its energy. For a few moments, sit in your head and study this energy. Listen to it.

You may experience sudden changes in temperature or energy flow in your body or your aura. This can happen when your emotion alerts you to problems in your physical or spiritual circumstance. Your emotion may require you to speak, yell, scream, cry, or move around the room. Do it. Be available and keep listening. If the emotional energy tends to gather around one specific part of your aura or your body, ask it why.

Another emotion may emerge from within the energy of your chosen one. Choose a color or quality for the new emotion, and channel that emotion into your body and aura as well. If you have relied on repression in your life (and who hasn't?), your emotions may run in protective pairs or packs in response to your censure of them. Forgive yourself, welcome the new emotion, and keep channeling. This second emotion will also have instructive and healing messages for you.

After a period of one to five minutes, or however long you like, turn your first-chakra grounding cord into a vacuum. Create a large grounding tube for your aura, and turn it and your Sentry's grounding cord into vacuums. Use these vacuums to suck the energy of the emotion out of you. Let the energy leave the room in your head and watch it as it leaves your body. Let the energy of the emotion move down and out of your aura, and let it flow out of your Sentry as you watch it from inside your room. As the emotion grounds out of you, remember that its attachments will dissipate until it exits your grounding cord as clean and reusable energy once again.

Right now, note any places in your body where the emotional energy is stuck and resists grounding. Ask the emotion why. Know that you can release and ground these areas separately in a moment, but take this moment to look at where your body holds this emotion. Ask it why, thank the emotion, and let it go. You may need to attach a special grounding cord to the resistant area. Do that now.

When you are done and the emotional energy is drained away, turn off the vacuums in all of your grounding cords, and relax for a moment. Breathe.

All that's left is a Gold Sun Healing to replenish you with clean and neutral energy. Before you put up your Gold Sun, however, *please drop the grounding tube out of your aura.* You don't need this tube unless you are performing a special healing that pulls energy out of the aura. The aura grounds itself very well by grabbing onto your body's grounding cord just below the floor. Your aura doesn't need any more grounding than that in most cases, and right now, you don't want all the golden energy you're about to receive to drain out immediately.

When you put up your Gold Sun, it will be surrounded by a large amount of cleaned-up, ready-to-use emotional energy. Welcome this refreshed energy back and know, as you channel it through your body and your energy tools, that you can use it in any way you choose. Bend over and touch the floor to let your body pour off any Gold Sun energy it can't use immediately. Get up, and you're done!

All emotions are tools for our use, if we accept them, channel them responsibly, and take the time to listen to their healing messages. Not surprisingly, the "bad" emotions can bring us amazing insights, because they carry so much energy with them. Anger and fury can signal a lack of boundaries, and then contribute the energy to rebuild those boundaries into strong protectors. Sadness and despair can signal an arid harshness in the self or the environment, and then contribute the healing fluidity that was missing. Anxiety, fear, and terror can signal the presence of dangerously wrong people, ideas, or environments, and then contribute protection, or the energy to move out of harm's way. Grief signals loss, and then contributes the energy to cherish, honor, and release the lost entity. Suicidal urges demand liberty or death, and, when channeled, contribute the energy to kill off unworkable aspects of life and to liberate the spirit from unendurable pain (*without* killing the body; see the Troubleshooting Guide, page 280).

Although it may seem as if emotional channeling lets moods take our lives over, nothing could be further from the truth. Inside our heads, we decide on the colors and qualities of the emotion. We direct its flow, and we ask it questions. When we are done, we vacuum the emotion out of our body and our aura. We *give over* our body and aura to an emotion, but this is entirely different from being *taken over* by one.

People who dishonor, repress, or irresponsibly express their emotions are taken over by them. Emotional channelers take over the emotions instead, and use their energy in healing. Emotional channeling reminds us that a healthy psyche is a complete one. Completeness includes light and dark, good and bad, love and hate, perfection and flaws, solemnity and silliness, wisdom and idiocy, and everything else.

If you attend only to the nice-nice parts of yourself, you become dissociated, no matter how grounded you may appear. If you ignore your own shadowy emotions and try to hide them, or throw them out with the trash, they may loom up and attack you with a sword created out of all your own repressed energy. Ouch. When you accept and channel your "bad" emotions, the sword retreats; it becomes, instead, a ceremonial dagger with which you may cut away the lies, contracts, unworkable attachments, and shackles in yourself. When you accept and honor the power and wisdom of your shadow, you become a multi-dimensional, whole human being (see bibliographical references to the *Shadow* books by Robert Bly, Robert Johnson, and Connie Zweig).

Emotional channeling does not interfere with the expression of our needs, feelings, and moods to the aware and supportive people in our lives. Rather, it offers a stronger (and more personally empowering) support. When we work with the energetic material of our own emotions, we no longer need to rely on others to help us deal with or validate them.

If you have been to a competent therapist, you will recall that, in the office, all emotions, reactions, dreams, and ideas were acceptable. When you channel your emotions, you can create this exact atmosphere for yourself at any time. In the safety of your own meditative sanctuary, you can bring your Earth-wise body, your energy-and-information-filled emotions, your intellectual brilliance, and your spiritual awareness to bear on any difficulty, question, mood, or opportunity that arises—and save thousands of dollars in therapy fees.

When you can bring your emotions to bear on your life's issues, you will move through them with a fluid ease and grace. Your fluidity may require periodic yelling, crying, reacting, and stomping, but these momentary reactions won't bother you. You will have matured enough to accept your emotions as they are. When you accept, honor, channel, and refuse to punish your emotions, your life will flow more easily.

In order to remain whole and alive from this moment forward, you'll need an environment that lets you cry when you're sad, squeal and jump when you're exhilarated, move quickly when you're anxious, protect yourself when you're fearful, stomp and snap when you're angry, dance when you're happy, and grieve when you lose someone or something. Whole people accept and honor all human emotions. Whole lives require them.

Your life right now may not be whole, but when you commit to channeling your emotions, you will move toward completeness. Your inner life, at least, will be the environment where you will be free to feel. Your inner life will be the place where you can work with your feelings. What are you waiting for? Go and destroy a few images and contracts with your emotional energy right now, or channel any mood that keeps you stuck. The rest of the book will wait. Your emotions have waited long enough.

You may notice that I haven't gone into detail about what your emotions may tell you. I feel very strongly that your emotions can do this for you far better than I. The Troubleshooting Guide at the end of this book (page 259), however, contains definitions of more than a dozen different emotions. You can skim through these definitions before you get started on your own emotions. You don't *need* to, but you can peek anyway.

As a support for your emotional body, I cannot recommend the Bach Flower Remedies highly enough. These English flower essences were created to bring emotional balance to the body and spirit, and their healing abilities are nothing short of remarkable. One of the best books on the subject is *Bach Flower Therapy*, by Mechthild Scheffer (see bibliography, page 285). Forget psychotropic drugs; these remedies actually work!

ADVANCED TECHNIQUES

Your grounding and image-making abilities may change and evolve as you do. Fluctuations in your skills and abilities are normal and healthy. If your grounding does not feel real to you at this point in the game, however, I would suggest that you look into your entire chakra system, instead of concentrating on your first chakra alone.

In many cases, difficulty in grounding can be a sign of disturbances in the communicative fourth and fifth chakras, the protective third chakra, and the Earth-centered foot chakras. When the chakra system is blocked or disturbed, the flow of energy between body and spirit can become blocked as well. Please take the time to study this section, but know that more help is available in sections to come if you still can't get or keep yourself grounded.

When your body is grounded, it's easier to live there. Simple. The same is true for your home, your workspace, your car, the room in your head, your aura, or anyplace else you may be. Grounding creates a connection between your spirit, the grounded object, and the center of the planet. It also provides a spiritual dumping ground for energy, and a constant source of energetic safety, renewal, and awareness. Awareness, however, requires responsibility. Therefore, you must learn the rules of grounding.

ADVANCED GROUNDING RULES

The grounding rules for areas and objects are similar to the grounding rules for people. Just as you should not ground someone else, you should not ground someone else's house, office, car, or computer. Objects, buildings, and machines have their own energy, their own karma, and their own destinies which involve the people who own them. The energy of your grounding cord would interfere with those destinies.

If you ground other people's possessions, you will interfere in their lives. This is not good. Pay attention to your own energy and don't try to live other people's lives. Grounding machines and possessions transmits your attention, ownership, and responsibility to the grounded object. If you own the object, machine, place, or any portion thereof, you have every right to ground it. Otherwise, you should leave it alone.

Before you learn how to ground the places and objects you own, let me give you a few specific exceptions to these grounding rules.

Grounding your area: If you live in a room in someone else's house, or inhabit a space, cubicle, or office in someone else's work building, you have every right to ground your area. Your sleep and work areas should always be grounded, but don't worry about transitional places in someone else's area. For instance, you shouldn't ground the communal kitchen in a rooming house or office building, because it's not your private space. Your own personal grounding cord will be enough to keep you centered while you're making meals.

If you have no private area of your own in any place you live or work, make sure that your aura is always grounded. Adding aura grounding to your regular grounding will provide some privacy and distancing for you. Do what you can to move on to a situation that is more respectful of your separateness and your humanity. Privacy is an absolute necessity.

Grounding your responsibilities: When I borrow objects from people, use their car or their computer, or take care of their house, I become responsible for these things. If I'm responsible, I want my own energy in charge of what goes on during that time, so I ground these objects. I consider that, if anything happens to something in my care, I'm going to have to deal with it, financially or otherwise. I'd like the things that happen to have something to do with my energy, my path, my lessons, and my karma. I don't want to have to deal with another person's theft or damage fears when I have to rely on their possessions. I ground the objects or machines for which I am responsible as soon as I get them, and renew my grounding each time I use them.

When I return the borrowed item, I remove my grounding cord (by dropping it out of the object). This is a vital step, because, just as I shouldn't have to deal with another person's energy in any item or machine I use, other people shouldn't have to deal with my energy once their possession is returned to them. As far as alerting people to my spiritual safety techniques, I tell people about what I am doing with their item if they understand grounding, and I keep it to myself if they don't.

Grounding your tools: This is a combination of the first two exceptions. When you are working with tools, machinery, and other skill-requiring objects, you are expected to be responsible for them. Therefore, it is best to ground them, even if you don't own them. The drill press or computer you use already have an energy connection with you. That connection will be stronger, safer, and more real if you ground the tool during use. Grounding the tools of your home or workspace helps protect those tools from breakdown, misplacement, and inadvertent borrowing.

Within the category of tools, I include any vehicle you use for work, including commuter planes, fleet cars, rented construction equipment, and even elevators, if they make you queasy. Work machines and vehicles are in a hazy category for these grounding rules, because no one person really owns or relates to them individually. I personally think that aware users do these metallic beings a great service by grounding them and giving them our focused attention. I know we do ourselves a great service when we allow our centered awareness to connect and protect us in all the places we go.

Grounding your healing area: I always ground any place where my body is being treated, including massage rooms, my acupuncturist's treatment room, and operating rooms. I ground these places because, when I pay for a professional healing service, I want real healing to occur, with no foreign energy getting in the way. I also want my body to feel completely safe, so I can let go and receive the healing I've asked and paid for.

If you have a special place where you read this book and meditate, make sure it's grounded (see below), and it will be easier to keep yourself centered. I always ground rooms where I give classes, because I have to be very open and receptive in those situations. Once again, I want to protect myself and my body as much as possible when any healing work occurs. When my healing is done, I let the room-grounding cord go until the next session.

HOW TO GROUND ROOMS OR AREAS

This skill isn't hard to master, but it is hard to explain (see figure 8, page 105). The grounding cord you provide for an area will help to define its territory, whether the area is a normal room, a whole house, a partitioned cubicle, or an oblong lean-to. Your grounding will define your space as a separate, protected area. When grounding rooms or areas, you will identify the energetic boundaries of the area you wish to ground, and attach cords to the uppermost and bottom-most corners of your chosen location.

Starting at the ceiling, visualize four cords of golden, present-time energy, and attach them to the uppermost corners of your room or area. When these cords are attached, allow them to reach down diagonally to meet one another at the very center of the space. This center should be at about eye-level.

Attach similar cords to each bottom-most corner of your area and visualize these cords traveling upward to the center of the room, where they meet and connect with the cords you brought down from the ceiling. Each of these eight cords should meet at the very center of the area you wish to ground.

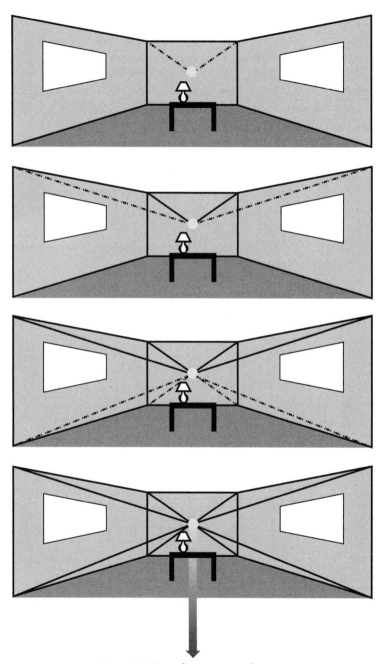

Figure 8. Grounding rooms and areas.

Now, attach a grounding cord of any color you desire to the conjunction of these cords (pretend that this energetic conjunction is the first chakra of your room), and send it down to the center of the planet. Anchor this cord, and your area is now grounded.

You will need to check on this area-grounding cord a few times to assure that it stays put. If it disappears regularly, there may be an ungrounded person using the area and grabbing your cord unconsciously. It is a good idea, in this instance, to use gold cords only, because gold is a neutral, depersonalized healing energy. If people inadvertently pick up your gold area-grounding cord, they won't become trapped in your energy. They'll just get a nice healing. If you use gold grounding cords, they won't be able to identify you as the source of that healing, unless they are very intuitive.

It is a good rule, when grounding your portion of a public area, to surround that portion with a blanket of ungrounded gift images or roses. This symbolic blanket will help to define your area and stop people from snatching your grounding cords and undoing your work. This blanket usually stops cord-snatchers, who will instead walk off with an armful of your free gifts or flowers. Since the gifts are there for the taking, this presents no problem. Ungrounded gifts are easy to replenish.

Usually, I ground my healing area or office space each time I arrive. I don't even check to see if my previous area grounding still exists. I want my portions of other people's space to be freshly grounded each time I use them. In my home, I check my grounding much less often. I find that my customary body- and aura-grounding cords tend to freshen my home's grounding, and vice versa. Maintaining a grounded home, office, or area around me also helps me to stay in the room in my head, and to remember my Sentry. Once again, the use of each of these spiritual tools tends to support the health of the others.

In addition to surrounding your home, workspace, or general area with an aura of ungrounded roses, it is always a good idea to place a grounded Sentry symbol at the door or entryway to your grounded area. The act of grounding is very noticeable in your local psychic fabric, and people may be inexplicably drawn to you. Your free gift blanket will give these people the communication and healing they seek, and your grounded Sentry will help them to remember that you are a protected individual in a protected area. Without the help of these psychic tools, you may find that your grounded area is the new "hang-out," and that you have to replace its grounding cord every few hours or so.

Do yourself and the people around you a favor. Use your grounding, your gift blankets, and your Sentry to gently tutor people about where you start and where they end. Don't let unaware intuitives waste their time paying attention to your new skills. Be a responsible spiritual citizen, not a show-off. If you notice a few people who can't seem to stay away from your grounded area, and you feel they really need a healing, don't stop your forward progress or slow yourself down to heal them! Let them borrow this book, or draw them a picture of grounding, and continue with your own healing and separating skills.

HOW TO GROUND CARS
AND OTHER MACHINES

Some people have an uncanny way with cars and machinery. Machines don't break down for them and although they're not usually mechanics *per se,* they always seem to be able to remedy mechanical problems. These people are usually very grounded, and their grounding generally extends to anything they touch or use. This grounding of machines works just like the grounding of energy in an electrical current; it tends to make machinery run more efficiently and, therefore, more safely.

Ungrounded people, on the other hand, have a different experience. If a machine is going to have difficulty at some point in its life span, it generally waits until these people are in control. A lack of grounding seems to create or exacerbate mechanical and electrical difficulties in machines, while strong grounding seems to drain the quirks and difficulties right out of them.

It is wonderful to learn to ground your machines, and to become a person who doesn't create chaos in the mechanical world around you. Grounding machines and objects is very like grounding areas. Attach four cords to the upper corners of the machine or object, and four cords to its lower corners, then bring all eight together in a conjunction at a central point. Attach a large grounding cord to that central conjunction, and you're done! (See figures 8 and 9, pp. 105 and 108, for a clearer view.)

We can take advantage of the fact that machines like to be grounded. We can ground our cars, computers, tools, and appliances. By grounding, we not only create a safer arena for the electrical and mechanical beings in our lives, we increase our own present-time awareness as well. When we are able to ground and connect with all the mundane and useful items in our everyday lives, our meditation and healing will not have to stop when we're driving, working, cooking, or performing all those real-world activities. The real world will become a part of

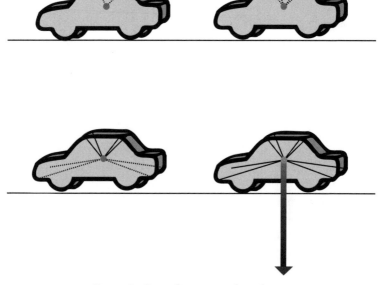

Figure 9. Grounding cars and machines.

our spiritual world, so we can continue to ground, heal, grow, and process, no matter where we are or what we are doing.

Though these auxiliary grounding skills are very useful, grounding your own body is still by far the most important skill taught in this book. If you forget everything else and simply ground from your first chakra or through your foot chakras (see the sections on those chakras), your life will travel along more smoothly. All the other skills have their importance, but the ability to ground is the centerpoint of everything we have done and will continue to do.

When you are grounded, you live in the present moment. You live in your body. When you live in your body, you are aware of and available to your surroundings. You notice your needs, your thoughts, your reactions, and your emotions. You begin to care for yourself. When you care for yourself, you protect yourself and create separations. It all starts with grounding, so feel free to go on an all-out grounding binge, especially when you get a little out of sorts. You can always get back to center when you ground yourself. When you are centered, your ability to ground, not just yourself, but all your "stuff" will make staying present in your body and your life easier. When your world and the "stuff" around you is cleansed of past-time, excess, or foreign energy and expectations, peaceful awareness is far more likely.

As you move through your day, feel free to ground as much or as little of your surroundings as you see fit. If your body- and aura-grounding cords are strong and secure, you may naturally and unconsciously transmit your grounding to everything you use. It's very comfortable to be on this planet when you get to that level of groundedness.

If your area or object grounding cords disappear, be aware that someone in your life needs grounding, and that your areas or objects are giving them that grounding. If you react emotionally to the theft of your grounding cords, use your emotional energy to recreate the missing cords in more vibrant and energetic colors. Be sure to place an ungrounded gift blanket and a grounded Sentry just outside your grounded area or possession. This should correct the problem.

It is okay for people to take your area- or possession-grounding cords a few times, but it is not at all good for them to make a habit of it. If you allow that, you will be teaching them that grounding resides in your life, and not in their own. You will also be allowing a totally unnecessary victim-perpetrator game to flourish. You are strong enough now to prevent people from acting against you on an energetic level, or to get yourself out of their way. You're not a victim. Allow your natural emotional reactions to come up during energy-tool thefts, but channel your emotions appropriately, so that they can lend their strong and decisive energy to the recreation of your external tools.

Protect and honor your life by making it safe from unaware people. If you think it will help, you can talk to grounding-cord thieves about learning to ground for themselves. You can also place a copy of this book where they will be sure to see it. In any case, protect and separate yourself, and go on with your own healing.

ADVANCED IMAGING TECHNIQUES

You've already used gift images in a number of spiritual communications. There are also ways to use gifts to heal and cleanse specific areas of your body. Try this next gift healing when you are overstimulated and headed toward a frontal-lobe headache.

THE GIFT FACIAL

When you meet or interact with people, the bulk of their attention is usually focused upon your face and eyes. If their attention is there, their energy will most likely be there too. Sometimes, your face can have so much of other people's energy on it that you will feel old and wizened before your time. Too much external energy and attention on your face can even feel like a sinus headache. Try this gift facial at the end of a public-relations filled week, or anytime you feel yourself squinting or clenching your teeth with stress and fatigue.

Sit in a grounded, aura-defined body, and look out from inside the room in your head at a large, soft-leaved plant or flower.

Place this image directly in front of your face. This gift symbol should be a little bit larger than your head, and close enough to you so that you can see the veins and dew on its leaves or petals. This gift symbol should be large enough so that all you can see before you is the gift itself.

Ground the center of the symbol with a gold grounding cord. See this cord moving down through the plant's stem and roots, and downward to the center of the planet. Don't follow your grounding cord. Direct your cord from inside your head, and know that it will do what you ask.

Turn this gift symbol's grounding cord into a vacuum, and let it pull blocked and foreign energy off your face. You may feel the pull in your eyes, your jaw, your teeth, your cheekbones—even in the back of your head or your neck. Let the energy go. See your gift symbol becoming stronger and healthier as it grounds the old energy out of your face. See this clogged, foreign energy as fertilizer for your plant. Know that all departing energy will be cleansed and returned to its owner (or to you, the next time you perform a Gold Sun Healing). Let it go.

Continue with this gift facial for as long as you like, and be aware of how much energy comes off you. If you feel noticeably lighter afterward, you need to take a look at your Sentry. Does your Sentry normally stay in front of your face, or do you move it aside when you interact with people, almost as if it's an over-sized centerpiece? *Don't!* Keep the entire flower part of your Sentry directly in front of your face. If you shed a lot of energy in this healing, your Sentry needs to be stronger, because too much of other people's energy is being deposited on your face.

If you are in a people-intensive job, or a life situation where intense energy is directed at you, you'll need to adjust your tools accordingly. I suggest a Sentry blanket, instead of just one Sentry, a phone, door, or window gift (see page 112), and a steady supply of ungrounded free gifts at your disposal. If you are prepared to deal with a barrage of people, you won't be affected by all their energy. If you're not prepared, your healing and meditation work will be more involved, because you'll be full of trivial bits of other people's attention, needs, demands, and energy.

You can be more effective as a receptionist, retail clerk, or seminar leader when you are in charge of your aura. It doesn't make you colder, less aware, or less humane to separate from people. It helps you to live as an individual within your own life, your own lessons, and your own karmic pattern. What could be more effective?

DOOR, PHONE, OR WINDOW GIFTS

Door, phone, or window gifts are very like ungrounded hello gifts, which you send to greet people before they reach you. The only difference is that these specific gift symbols are placed in areas where you can't always see who is coming.

When you work with the public face-to-face or over the phone, you really can't prepare for all the differing attitudes, relationships, or difficulties that might occur. Placing a large number of ungrounded door, phone, or window gifts at the area of initial contact can help calm people down as they come into your sphere of influence. The use of these public relations gifts will make your personal Sentry's task much easier. Your Sentry won't have quite so much work to do to protect you, because people will have received a bit of free love and beauty before they actually get to you and your aura.

Door, phone, and window gifts are placed liberally and freely at the entrance to your sphere, whatever that is. If people enter your workspace through a door or an opening in a cubicle, place at least a hundred ungrounded gift symbols at the door or opening every morning. If people contact you through the phone, intercom, or computer modem, place another hundred ungrounded gifts inside each machine. Envision one or more of your gift symbols traveling across the transmission cables, directly in front of your standard typed or vocal greeting (of course gift symbols can travel through cables; they're made of energy!).

If you work behind a sliding window, as in a doctor's office, place another hundred or so ungrounded gift symbols just outside the window, in addition to those you have placed at the doorway. I've never seen an office with a sliding window that wasn't filled with stress (which came first?), so it's a good idea to plan ahead for that stress and provide as many door and window gifts as you can.

Using these specifically-placed gifts can help to make your workplace as safe as your home. They will also provide excellent spiritual communication to anyone who is fortunate enough to come into contact with you.

THE NEGATIVITY-EATING GIFT

The negativity-eating gift symbol is a fun little friend to have! It grows and thrives on other people's intense and disruptive energy. This symbol especially loves it when other people try to project their shadow material (which is signaled with any phrase that sounds like, "Do you know what your problem is?") in order to control you through fear or shame. In situations where negative attention is being focused (at a job interview, in court, when the police pull you over, when someone says, "You know what your problem is?"), you can create a gift symbol that absolutely thrives on projection and disruption!

While your regular Sentry and your aura boundary deal with keeping you separate, your negativity-eating gift will bop around your aura eating up the human fertilizer that makes you so uncomfortable and it so happy. When this gift gets big and full, you simply give it to the person whose energy helped create it, and you'll both experience release and healing.

Here's how: Create a medium-sized, *ungrounded* gift plant or flower somewhere inside the front of your lit-up, protected aura, and dedicate it to any negative or threatening person you encounter. This gift is ungrounded because it will be given away. Give the plant or flower a face, with teeth that like to gobble up energy, and the ability to move so that it can zip around eating any energy that gets past your Sentry. I usually place my ungrounded negativity-eating plant somewhere between my eyes and my heart. Sometimes I place this gift on my lapel, and sometimes directly in front of me, but it is always able to move around like a little Pac Man, searching for delicious bits of projected energy. I make it into a thorny, fist-sized flower with a silly, hungry face and pointed teeth, like the man-eating plant, Audrey, in *Little Shop of Horrors*.

As my negativity-eating plant seeks out and eats energy, it grows bigger and healthier, grinning all the while. When it eats enough energy to make it grow to the size of a cabbage, I send it to the person whose energy it has been eating. Sometimes, my plant grows that big right away, before the disruptive encounter has even begun! No big deal. I send the gift symbol to the person who helped it grow so big, make another negativity-eating plant, and start again. I've got a million plants and flowers in my garden.

When the negativity-eating symbol has eaten its fill, and you give it away, you have the chance to sit back and see that you are separate from other people's relating styles. In addition, the person who fed the plant or flower gets an intuitive look at how much energy they use in being threatening, unkind, or controlling.

Many times, the receipt of this gift symbol will shock such people terribly, because they rarely see themselves as negative forces in the universe. They think they're dominating, unwaveringly honest and direct, or trying to take care of their own or their company's interests in the face of a world filled with crooks and liars. When their silly gift comes at them—fat, happy, grinning, and absolutely stuffed with their own gruffness—they suddenly have to take a look at what they're doing in the world. Sometimes the results are as funny as the negativity-eating plant itself.

A student of mine used a negativity-eating bird-of-paradise on a motorcycle cop who pulled her over by mistake (he thought her license plate had expired—it hadn't), and then hung around looking for reasons to have done so. He started checking her lights, her turn signals, her insurance certificate, and anything else he could think of. Halfway through the inspection, my friend remembered her skills and created a negativity-eating flower for him.

This flower got so big, so fast, that my friend had to give it to him almost immediately. Apparently, the policeman stopped talking in mid-sentence, turned on his heel, got on his bike, and left her standing by her car, stunned! Because of this immediate and startling result, my friend worried that she had somehow manipulated the police officer into action. In truth, the simple return of his energy snapped him back into shape. He couldn't speak to her rationally and apologize, because what affected him did not come from the rational world. He was aware enough to realize he was making a pompous fool of himself, but not aware enough to talk about it. Leaving was all he could manage at that moment.

※

Don't criticize yourself if your Sentry and aura boundary can't keep certain types of disruptive energy out of your aura, and don't be worried if all of your negativity-eating gifts grow very large, very quickly. Take the hint and recreate your protective boundary symbols in stronger, more vibrant colors, and make sure your Sentry rose has a good number of large, pointy thorns. On the other hand, don't be afraid to support your normal boundary tools with the use of your negativity-eating plants and flowers. They are very good gifts for all occasions.

If, during a stressful encounter, your negativity-eating gift doesn't grow, and there's still a lot of projected energy in the room, congratulate yourself. It means that your regular Sentry and aura boundary are keeping you separate on their own. When it's time to go, give the grumpy person their little gift anyway. It couldn't hurt.

THE SENTRY BLANKET
We've already talked about Sentry blankets, but they are so useful that it is good to go over them again. Sentry blankets can be used in their *grounded* form as a very strong Sentry system around the entire aura. With a grounded Sentry blanket on guard, there is no place at all where people can get through to your aura or your body.

People coming at you with the intention to disturb, harm, drain, or control you will be met at every possible entrance with hundreds of thorn-filled, grounded roses (you can also throw in other favorite flowers, plants, or trees if you like). The pest's energy will be accepted, honored, and grounded; your aura will be protected; and the pest will be calmed and neutralized simply by having their energy accepted by *something*. By honoring spiritual communication, you will make other people's lives as spirits on this planet more real, which is a healing in and of itself.

With Sentries and Sentry blankets, you decide where that healing spiritual acknowledgement will occur (*outside* your personal auric field), and how you will protect your own reality while the spiritual contact is happening. By placing a rose-and-gift-filled, protective facsimile of yourself outside of your aura, with the express job of greeting others and keeping your personal territory sacred, you are not retreating from the world. On the contrary, you're right out there, offering an intuitive ear, a lesson in grounding and separation, and a whole lot of free beauty, love, and consideration for all the other beings on this planet.

In their *ungrounded* form, hello gift blankets are excellent placeholders for any grounded areas you create in other people's spheres. When your office, room, or cubicle is grounded, it may attract people who either need grounding, or want you to stop grounding. You won't have any privacy. Placing a blanket of free, ungrounded gift symbols at the edges of your defined area will give people a chance to see your life and energy needs as separate from theirs. They'll come toward your area to find out what you're doing, or to stop you from taking control of your life, but they'll go away with the love and attention your free gifts provide. Through the use of gift blankets, you'll be able to more easily maintain your privacy, while the people around you receive healing spiritual contact.

Remember to refresh your grounded and ungrounded blankets daily. If you sensed that they were necessary for your safety, you are probably in a situation that is fatiguing for you and your normal Sentry. Give your blankets lots of attention and support, and replenish them frequently. Feel free to create new and novel uses for your gift symbols. They are, after all, symbols of your ability to love and heal and protect your reality. Your life's challenges will be as individual as you are. Whatever you feel you should do with your gift symbols is what you need to do.

Remember to ground the symbols you use in your aura and your body, but not to ground the gift symbols you provide for others. You must be able to hold on to your personal healing symbols (which is why you ground and anchor them), and you must be certain that your spiritual communications are neutral and responsible (which is why you don't ground or anchor the symbols you send to others). You must never imply that spiritual healing and communication come directly from you, which is what would happen if you grounded the symbols you sent to others.

Beyond that, have fun creating and destroying gifts and images and learning how easy it is to communicate spiritually when you communicate responsibly and with love. People really do want to live in peace and happiness. If you can apply the lessons and the love your gift symbols offer, both you and they will tend to remember that.

PART III

THE OWNER'S MANUAL

READING YOUR AURA

Most of my education about, or experience with, aura readings has been confusing at best. I think I could take my aura to a dozen otherwise competent intuitives in one day, and get a dozen or more conflicting diagnoses—because auras are very much alive and constantly changing. It's really hard to nail down what each color, nuance, or fluctuation means.

I believe a competent study of the aura might require an exhaustive, encyclopedic series of books, because each aura contains a wealth of information. But then, the study of the body requires encyclopedic knowledge, and most of us get along quite well without a conscious awareness of each of the untold thousands of functions therein.

When we live in and care for our bodies, we tend to require less external healing or expert advice. Our health becomes a simple issue when we listen carefully enough to what our bodies tell us about which food, exercise, environment, emotional state, or relationship we should choose. This same simple knowledge is available with regard to the care and understanding of our aura. If we live in and listen to our aura, it will tell us very clearly what healing or attention it needs. We will become excellent aura readers, not by studying all auras at all times, but by becoming aware of the specific needs of our own energy boundary.

Auras, like bodies, are individuals. While there are auric similarities that can be relied upon, blanket statements like "Purple auras mean spiritual advancement" can send an aura reader down a very precarious path. Though I will include a list of the possible meanings of color in the aura, I don't want you to take it too seriously. Besides, auras change color on an hourly, or even a minute-by-minute basis. Color interpretations are extremely subjective. If I tell you that green in the aura means change and evolution, but the green in your aura reminds you of frustration, then your green *is* frustration. It's *your* aura, which means it understands your inferences and experiences. The colors and images it displays will have personal, specific meaning to you.

When I read or heal other people, I don't usually read the colors of their aura. In a sense, I put on blinders. Instead of reading specific colors and trying to guess what they might mean to each new person, I feel around (with my open hand chakras) and get a sense of where each aura is in relation to each person's body.

During aura readings, I check for hot or cold spots, holes, completeness, size, bulges and so on, and I talk about what I'm sensing as I work. Usually, the person's aura will begin to mend and reshape itself before I can lift a finger.

Each aura I see is completely different, both from other auras, and from itself from reading to reading. Auras are, as I said, malleable, changeable, and completely individual. The only thing all auras have in common is that they always exist in some form or another. If they do not appear right away, the normal energy hovering around the body can be fashioned into an aura (through the aura definition technique, on page 31). With this help, auras soon right and reform themselves. I've seen some tremendously drug-and-psychosis-damaged auras, but they always hold on in some way, shape, or form.

I also see energy or deviations in auras that have no meaning to me whatsoever. In such instances, I check in with my own aura, which sends me a feeling or a picture in *our* individual language to describe what that other aura is doing.

This is an important point. Psychics always read from their own understanding, though they may get help from spirit guides or other sources. The main trick to becoming a good psychic is to live fully and collect as many bits of knowledge and experience as possible, so you will have a wide base of knowledge and experience to use in unusual reading or healing situations. A good psychic simply trusts that the information received is correct. This is as true in self-readings as it is in the reading of others.

As you go through these aura-reading guidelines, I want you to feel free to replace any reading technique that doesn't work for you. I have very sensitive hands and do my readings through a form of empathic ability. You may have very sensitive eyes or ears and be able to do your readings clairvoyantly or clairaudiently. If I ask you to feel the aura, but you can see, hear, or sense it in other ways, use your own psychic abilities. Don't rely on my reading techniques if they don't work for you. Your abilities and your aura will differ from mine.

GENERAL AURA-READING GUIDELINES

To read your aura, sit in your usual, grounded meditative state. Cleanse your body and your aura of old energy by using your grounding vacuums, then light up and define the oblong boundary of your aura with golden light. Gold energy is present-time healing energy; it will be a signal to your aura that you want to see what it is doing at this very moment.

After you have established your correctly-shaped, complete, and golden aura boundary, stay inside your head and allow the gold energy to fade into whatever colors your aura wants to show you. Be aware, too, of any shape changes, or other deviations that come about when the color changes. If you can't see anything at this point, close your eyes and use your hands to feel the edge of your aura. Hand chakras can pick up color vibrations. Don't worry that your closed eyes will give you a monochrome aura. Your brain can very easily receive and interpret color vibrations through your hands. It's the way a lot of psychics work.

AURA COLORS
These are general ideas. Your own interpretations, of course, are the correct ones.

PINK: Healing humor, protection from abuse, indecision.

RED: The first chakra, the foot chakras, the physical body, power, anger, sexuality.

ORANGE: The second chakra, the emotions, the muscles, fury, sensuality, healing.

YELLOW: The third chakra, the intellect, immunity and protection, impatience, fear.

GREEN: The fourth chakra, the hand chakras, love, transformation, healing, frustration, loss.

BLUE: The fifth chakra, communication, spiritual knowledge, mourning, separation.

PURPLE/INDIGO: The sixth chakra, spiritual power, telepathy, victimization.

VIOLET: The seventh chakra, spiritual certainty, release, religious confusion.

BROWN: The foot chakras, Earth energy, groundedness, past-time issues.

BLACK: Finality, death, rebirth, delay.

WHITE: Spirit guide presence, purity, shock, erasure.

SILVER: Spirit world information, ungroundedness, uncertainty.

GOLD: The eighth chakra, healing, neutrality, Christ energy, transformative illness.

As a rule, any pastel color can indicate a less intense reading of its base color, and darker colors can indicate a much more intense reading. Mixed colors indicate a mixed message. For example, a pale yellow in my aura may mean that I'm slightly trapped in intellectual process, slightly impatient, or using a light level of fear energy in a somewhat unsafe environment. A very bright yellow may mean that I'm thinking all the time, I'm very impatient, or I'm using a lot of protective fear because I'm in a terribly dangerous environment.

On the other hand, an orange-ish yellow in my aura may mean that I'm trying to bring sensual realities into my thought process, that I'm using the energy of fear to protect my sensuality, or that I'm impatient with my emotions. In your aura, these same colors may mean something entirely different. My suggestion is that you rely on the certainty you have when you channel your emotions, and reverse the process.

When you channel your emotions, you choose a color scheme and an energetic quality for the emotional state you want to heal. Then, you let that chosen color represent your emotional state as you work with your energy. When you read your aura, you can reverse the process by asking its colors or qualities to tell you what emotions or situations they represent. To do this, stay in your head and sense your aura's color or quality of color. Wait for your body to bring up an emotional state or memory in response to the color or energy you sense.

Your mind may also help you interpret the energy by offering a series of images or explanations about the energy. In either case, thank the translating aspect of yourself, and move forward in your reading with the information provided.

Don't get married to the colors you see in your aura right now, or judge yourself on their level of evolution up the vibrational scale. Your aura may be a scuzzy green and black right now, but it will be purple and gold later, and bright pink or electric blue in between. During this reading, your aura essentially freezes itself in place so you can see it. In normal situations, your aura moves and fluctuates so quickly that you'd never be able to keep up with it. The colors you see now are only momentarily valid.

What your aura is showing you right now are the issues that require your immediate attention. Your grounding and centering *are* that attention. The Gold Sun Healing at the end of this aura reading will cleanse and process any issues your aura has right now.

Far more important than color, in my practical experience, is the shape and condition of the aura. Our aura work up to this point has dealt with redefining the aura into what I consider to be its ideal shape and size. The bright colors we have chosen for its boundary are not directives on color management, but placeholders, for us and for them, signifying where we would like our auras to be in relation to our bodies.

My bright magenta-bounded aura can be any color it likes inside its boundary, even if I create a pastel wash of that magenta inside my aura. My use of the magenta energy helps me to maintain a constant awareness of the completeness and integrity of my personal territory. My magenta boundary lights up and defines the area I wish my aura to inhabit, which helps remind my aura of where it should be. The pastel wash of magenta is used to connect my bodily awareness with my auric awareness, not to replace my aura's natural colors with ones I might like better.

When your aura shows you its real color and energy patterns, it may also show you any deviations it has in its size and shape. These will be healed during the Gold Sun Healing at the end of this section, but first, let's take a look at what each deviation might indicate.

Be Aware: These explanations and exercises are included to give your aura a little help when it is out of sorts. If your aura is constantly "whacked out" and wavering, *and you are not currently using drugs or alcohol,* your chakras are very likely out of alignment. This is not a big issue, but you can't fix your chakra problems by manipulating your aura.

If your aura boundary is still incomplete or full of unsettling energy, even after you have done your Gold Sun Healing and the healings described below, please skip ahead to the section on Reading Your Chakras (page 245). When your chakras are healed and aligned, your aura will usually be able to take care of itself.

If you are currently using drugs or alcohol, your energy will be chaotic. You most likely won't be able to maintain a healthy aura, a constant grounding cord, or a healthy set of chakras. If you want to stop using these substances, all of the tools in this book will make moving out of abuse easier, but the work we're doing (and in truth, any work) won't help much if you're actively abusing your body and your energy with drugs.

AURA SIZE
The following size categories relate to the arm's length, oblong-shaped aura we've been defining all along.

TOO SMALL: A tiny overall aura boundary (anything less than twenty inches from your body) indicates a reaction to an unsupportive, even life-threatening, environment. If your invisible aura cannot take up its required space in your life or relationships, it's certain that you don't have the personal freedom you require for your highest growth and evolution.

In many cases, we will unconsciously choose engulfing environments—for two very ingenious reasons: they take away our ability to move forward, so we don't have to face the terrors of growth and change, and they force our awareness into a smaller-than-normal area, which may keep us in or near our bodies most of the time. Since we now know how to stay in our bodies, however, there isn't any need to squash or hinder our auras any longer.

It makes no difference where you are in consciousness, your aura needs to be at its healthy size, and you need to be in an environment that allows your aura to take up its requisite space. If your aura has been confined, your attempts to expand it may have already created difficulties in your presently engulfing environment.

If you have a smaller-than-usual aura, take care of yourself, and burn your contracts regularly. Move on to a situation that gives you and your aura the room to live in freedom. I know it's not easy. It's just absolutely necessary.

TOO LARGE: An aura boundary that is all over the room is a sign of a bored and under-used spirit, or a drug user. Don't make me recite the drug speech again. Just get your energy back together, okay? A huge aura (anything larger than thirty-six inches from the body) denotes a tremendous amount of spiritual and physical energy that is essentially being ignored. People with huge auras are usually out of their bodies, mostly because their lives have almost nothing to do with their true path as questing, intelligent, immortal beings.

Pulling this type of aura into the requisite area can be very uncomfortable, if you want to continue to ignore your life path and fool around. When your aura and your energy take up their correct dimensions again, you may feel hemmed-in and forced to make decisions that ask you to travel down a narrower path than you think you want right now. Those are fears talking. Choose a color for those fears and channel their emotional energy to see why they are protecting you, and what they have to tell you.

AURA SHAPE

Auras can deviate from the oblong in any number of ways. These deviations can include bulges, tears, holes, indents, and other flaws. We will talk about the specific deviations in the next section. Here, I'd like to give an overview of what each segment of the aura indicates.

THE FRONT: Any deviations in the front of the aura are related to the future and to the conscious mind. A person with a very large front section (and a small, close-to-the body back section, see figure 10, page 129) is throwing a lot of energy into his future, into plans, schemes, or dreams. This person is most likely out of his body, ignoring the past and any unconscious messages, and living in a frenetic, jumping-out-of-the-skin state. Plumping out the back of his aura, and making room for the lessons and unfinished business of the past, may help to calm him down.

Injuries to the front of your aura can signify an upcoming trauma to which your aura is clairvoyantly alerting you. You can bring this trauma under your conscious control by making, and then burning, your contract with it. When you see a future event clairvoyantly, you can usually change it.

THE BACK: The back of your aura is the past, the unconscious, and the foundations upon which you base your current life view. A very skewed, too-much-back and not-enough-front aura signifies a person unable to move forward. She is focusing all her energy and attention on past issues. Because she doesn't have the support of the front, or forward-facing, portion of her aura, she may not be able to bring these past issues into consciousness. The past may haunt her.

Injuries and tears in the back of your aura indicate unremembered or past-time injuries that have not been addressed. Gold Sun Healings will help to bring the issues into present-time, where you can heal and confront them with your present-day awareness and abilities. Plumping out the front of your aura, which can make more room for you in the present and future, will help as well.

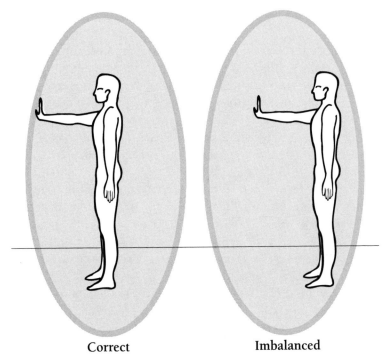

Correct   Imbalanced

Figure 10. An example of aura-skew.

THE LEFT SIDE: The left side of your aura signifies your feminine energy, whether you are a man or a woman. Your feminine energy contains your diffuse, intuitive, receptive nature, and the functions of the right side of your brain. When there are indents or injuries on the left side of the aura, look for a denial of the receptive feminine aspect of the self, or an interference caused by a person who uses a lot of feminine energy.

The left side of your aura also shows how able you are to receive, from the spirit world of information and guidance, and from the physical world of contact, support, and love. A huge left side in an aura implies a serious dependency on receptivity, while a squashed left side implies an unwillingness to listen and receive.

THE RIGHT SIDE: The right side of your aura signifies your masculine energy, which is present in both men and women. Your masculine energy contains your focused, discerning, expressive nature, and the functions of the left side of your brain. Injuries or deviations in the right side of your aura denote a denial of your expressive masculine aspects, or difficulties with a person who uses a lot of masculine energy.

The condition of the right side of your aura illuminates your ability (or permission) to give, to teach, to speak, and to express your inner self in the outer world. A huge right side in an aura implies a serious dependency on expression, while a cramped right side implies an unwillingness to act, to speak out, or to express yourself.

THE TOP (from chest-level to the upper edge of your aura): The top of your aura relates to your connection to spirit and your comfort with the guidance or information you receive from spirit. Spirit can include God, your spirit guides and angels, or anyone you know who is not currently in a body. If the top of your aura is squashed flat around your head, it can mean that you don't believe in or trust spiritual information. On the other hand, a huge and elongated top portion of the aura can mean that you focus so much energy on the cosmic aspects of life that you ignore your body and your physical life almost completely.

Injuries and deviations in the top of your aura can signify a punishing religion, a rift in your belief system, or a separation from spirituality and the support it provides. Plumping out the upper portion of your aura can make your spirituality more useful and comprehensible.

THE CENTER (from your chest to your knees, all the way around your body): The condition of the center of your aura relates to your daily physical life. Deviations in this portion generally refer to physical problems and challenges that your aura is either signaling to you, or is trying to heal on its own.

Sometimes, your aura will show you a blob of color or a pulse of energy right around a body part that is having, or is about to have, difficulties. Channel your Gold Sun energy into that area of your aura and body, and go see your acupuncturist. Chinese medicine has worked with energy for over five thousand years, and it is invaluable in maintaining a clear, grounded, healthy spirit/body connection. Chinese medicines are also very energy-respectful; they won't kick you out of your body and create side-effects, as Western medicines usually do.

The center of your aura also points to the fit or communication between you as a regular human and you as an immortal spirit. Central aura sections that are wobbly and indistinct usually denote a less than ideal body/spirit relationship. Keep grounding. You'll get it.

THE BOTTOM (from the knees down): The bottom of your aura relates to your ability to ground. Incompleteness and deviations in the bottom portion of your aura point to an unwillingness to stay grounded, or an inability to ground. Hazy lower auras can even denote a lack of exercise (which is naturally grounding), and a lack of care for your body.

Be aware of your top-to-bottom aura skew. Are you grounding very hard and pulling in the top of your aura so you don't have to listen to spirit? Or are you pulling up your grounding so that the top of your aura can go flying off in search of magical answers? A little tip: the magic is right here. You'll find it faster if you're grounded, in your body, and connected to your spiritual information at the same time. It's fun to go off on a body-only or a spirit-world-only afternoon every now and then, but being healed means being whole. We are spirits *in* bodies, not just spirits and not just bodies. Being whole means working to keep all of our aspects in balance most of the time.

Any skews, tears, bulges, or insufficiencies in any part of your aura can be healed by re-forming your aura boundary with present-time gold energy, and then performing a full Gold Sun Healing. In fact, you can consider any aura boundary definition and any Gold Sun Healing a quick reading and healing of your aura.

The more advanced reading techniques that follow are only called for when an aura deviation does not respond to simpler healings, and keeps showing up, unchanged, in your meditations. At that point, a full aura reading is in order.

DEVIATIONS IN THE AURA

Now that you have an idea of what each area of the aura depicts, let's look at what specific deviations and injuries can mean. Remember that, in almost every case, healing of these injuries will be accomplished during the Gold Sun Healing you have already mastered.

BLOBS: Defined blobs of color in an aura can signal stuck energy, in the energy body or the physical body. See **COLD SPOTS, HOT SPOTS** and **PULSATIONS**, below, if your blobs have specific attributes. If not, ask the blobs why they are there. They will usually show you a stuck relationship or thought pattern, if they come from the emotional, intellectual, or spiritual bodies. You can clear such blobs away by burning contracts or destroying images.

If the blobs are connected to your physical body, they will usually hover around an area where a disease or difficulty exists. Sometimes the blobs will show you a picture of the way that you hold your body, or a food that you eat which is causing difficulty. Pay attention to any blobs of stuck energy. For support, see your acupuncturist. Acupuncturists see the body as a system of energy meridians; they are usually able to find and release energy that is stuck and gumming up the works.

If your energy blobs show you pictures of other people, it usually means that you are in an uncomfortable contractual relationship that allows your contract partners direct access to your aura or your body. The blobs in these instances are actually bits of your contract partner's personal energy, which can't work in your aura. Burn your contracts and images, and steer clear of your contract partner for a day or so, until you've made a real separation. Sometimes, it will take a few image-burning sessions before you can truly break the connection and move on. As you work, remember to channel your Gold Sun energy into the area the blob once inhabited, and to cover your aura with a grounded

Sentry blanket. This will make an unconscious contractual re-connection less likely.

BULGES: Bulging areas usually denote an aura skew, meaning that the opposite side or portion of your aura has an indent, which is either the reaction to, or the cause of, the bulge. Bulges usually signify that a part of you is feeling trapped and indented by limitations (your own or society's). Your opposing side will then try to bulge out and take up more space in the world. For instance, if you have an indent in the right side of your aura, which means you don't have permission to express yourself or your masculinity, you may swing over and depend on too much feminine, receptive energy in response. However, your one-sided use of feminine energy won't be very healing in the long run, because it will not be balanced with your masculine energy. Such bulge-dent difficulties can be healed in regular aura-boundary redefinitions, or in a Gold Sun Healing, during which you use your hands to pull in the bulge while you plump out its opposite dent. Add lots of bright, healing, golden energy to both sides of the skew.

BRIGHT SPOTS: Areas of bright light or color denote a portion of your being which is being examined, highlighted, and healed right now. The awareness of the difficulty and the application of this light may have come from you directly, from your aura's own healing ability, or (if the bright spot is white or silver) from your spirit guides. I generally leave bright spots alone, unless they are very hot (see **HOT SPOTS**, page 139). These bright areas are already in the midst of a healing, so I don't often interfere.

COLD SPOTS: Auras should maintain an even temperature, but sometimes, brighter or cooler colors will slightly change the temperature in their area. This is nothing to worry over. If you feel a spot in your aura that is noticeably colder (by more than five or ten degrees) than the rest of your aura, however, it may need attention. Cold spots generally denote a part of you that you have allowed to die off through lack of use. They can also denote an area in your life where specific people can enter into your awareness and abuse you. Refer to the section on aura segments and their meanings to gain an understanding of what this cold spot may signify for you. Cold spots need to be filled with a great deal of warm and healing Gold Sun energy, and then surrounded with a grounded Sentry blanket.

Burn your contracts with the cold, unused, and denied aspects of yourself, or with the people who have had permission to siphon off your energy. Burn these contracts in a very bright and hot flame. Keep an eye on this area through successive Gold Sun Healings. Be sure to define your aura boundary with very warm and vibrant colors as you take this area back into your life and into your conscious awareness.

COLOR SPLOTCHES: Skittery and indistinct color splotches (as opposed to more distinct and slow-moving or motionless **BLOBS**, page 132) denote a great deal of activity in the aura, usually related to spiritual growth and transformation. Splotches are usually a transitory deviation. If they show up more than once, or are all the same color, they may signify energy damage related to drug or alcohol use.

Drugs and alcohol scatter physical energy, each in their own specific way, but they also do a lot of damage to the auric and chakric fields. If drugs are in your current or recent life, the work in this book will be very difficult, and splotches of color will probably be all your aura can manage right now. Nurture your aura with golden healing energy, and try to pull yourself together by cleaning drug energy out of your body and your life. See an acupuncturist, a holistic nutritionist, a Bach Flower practitioner, or a rehab counselor for support.

DARK SPOTS: Dark spots in your aura signify areas of punishing, judgmental harshness, from yourself or others. Entirely dark quadrants can signify a complete deadness in the darkened area, or an unwillingness to accept that aspect of your being. See the section on aura segments for an idea of what the deadened aspect might be.

I see dark energy as a place where the lights have been shut off, through punishment or fear. Channeling Gold Sun energy into darkened spots and lighting up the aura boundary can help make the transition to acceptance of the area or areas a much easier task. Remember to burn contracts with your old pictures of the darkened aspects of yourself, and to light up and reoccupy the area as you create a grounded Sentry blanket for your entire aura.

DENSE ENERGY: Areas of dense energy, where you can actually feel edges and shapes, often signify the presence of other people or beings in your personal territory. This presence is always contractually allowed; no one can be in your aura without your permission.

Auras work best when their colors and energy patterns have fluidity and freedom to pulsate, move, twist, and flow. Dense energy places a blockage in the aura that cannot flow and is not conducive to healing. Dense energy can feel hot, warm, or cold, depending on the intensity of the contract. This contract needs to be brought out, examined, and burnt up. In addition to contract burning, areas of denseness need to be grounded out and released.

To remove areas of dense energy, place a brightly-colored grounding vacuum right in the middle of the energy, and vacuum the dense spot out of your aura. As the denseness drains away, immediately fill your aura with your Gold Sun energy, and see the golden energy pressing the denseness down and out of your grounding vacuum. Use your hands to smooth your golden energy into the once-dense area, then surround the area with a protective blanket of grounded Sentries.

If you know who helped you create this denseness, burn your contracts with them again, after the denseness has been removed. If not, place a picture of the size and quality of the dense area onto a contract, and burn your relationship with it. This will work just as well.

It's not always necessary to identify the contributors to your psychic discomfort. The only real necessity is to clear out old, unworkable patterns, and to replace them with better skills and a higher level of awareness. Blame is good for a while, because it helps you to pinpoint your wounds, but concrete actions that remove you from victimizing relationships are better for every-one in the long run.

DENTS: Dents indicate areas where you don't have the freedom you need to express yourself safely. Dents usually indicate that this lack of safety originates in your environment, and not in yourself. Sometimes, dents are a part of an aura skew you have created through the belief that you can be one thing *or* the other, but never both.

I see a lot of people who dent off the grounded bottom por-tion of their auras so they can bulge out the portion at the top and become more *spiritual*. I remind them (and you) that we are striving to become whole, centered beings, not split, one-sided reactions to our environment. Whole beings have Earth and cos-mos, male and female, dark and light, peace and chaos, past and future. Whole beings are one thing *and* the other.

Smooth out your dents and bulges by redefining your aura boundary as a continuous and well-balanced oval. Remind your-self that, even if you are having issues with a certain portion of your being, your aura will be happier and healthier if it has a workable, wholly defined space in which to process your issues, and to function as your protector.

ELONGATIONS: Elongations (which appear as long tentacles or ropes of energy extending from your aura) are areas where you are reaching out to grasp a concept that you judge to be beyond your current range of ability or understanding. This judgment is a residue of a belief that safety, peace, and information are any-where but in your own life and experience.

Elongations need to be called back into center as you remind yourself that all information, all healing, and all safety reside with you: in your grounded, protected body, and in the present moment. It is also helpful to smooth out the edge of your aura manually at the site of the elongation, and to keep an eye on that portion of your aura in subsequent readings and healings.

FLIMSY, WAVERY EDGES: Through your regular aura-bound-ary definitions, your aura should be able to maintain a fairly clear delineation between itself and the outside world. If your aura shows you a flimsy, indistinct boundary, it can be signaling a lack of health, in itself or in your body.

Examine your sleep, diet, and exercise routine, but also check in with your interpersonal or work relationships. If your life is unsafe or unsupportive, your aura won't be as healthy as it could be. A beautiful aspect (or a scary one, depending on your point of view) of this inner work is that your suddenly healthy body, aura, and inner self won't put up with abusive energies anymore. You and they will begin to react strongly to abuse as you evolve into a more conscious life. Though you are truly becoming stronger and more alive, you may feel weaker and less free as your body says "no" to this lover and that food, "no" to this job and that neighborhood, and as your aura says "no" to this relationship and that health regime.

When your aura shows you flimsy boundaries, it's saying that your health, both physical and spiritual, are at risk in your current milieu. You can certainly beef up your aura boundary and load on the grounded Sentries, but I'd also like you to realize that safety and support is available, right now. You don't have to stay in a boundary- and health-compromising situation at this point in your life. You can move on to other lessons. Or you can stay where you are and discover all sorts of new energy tools for protecting yourself in unsafe environments. The choice is yours.

HAZY AREAS: Haziness in your aura relates to confusion in or between aspects of your whole self. The haziness may come from other people's refusal to let you explore the aspect, or your own refusal to support yourself in regard to it.

If you have no idea of how to express your feminine side and your aura's left side is hazy, or you just don't *get* spirituality and the top of your aura is wavering, put up your Gold Sun and place in it a picture of yourself as a feminine being, a spiritual being, a grounded, earthy being, or any other aspect of your wholeness that is hazy for you right now. See yourself, inside your Gold Sun, fully becoming and realizing this aspect of yourself. As you bring the Gold Sun energy into your aura and your body, pull this whole being into you. Let this being's legs fill your legs, let it sit in your pelvis, let its arms reach into yours, and let it look out from behind your eyes.

Allow this previously unrealized aspect of yourself to place gold energy in and around your aura. Give this aspect a strong gold grounding cord so that it can stay with you. Sit and feel what it's like to be this feminine, or masculine, or spiritual, or earthy being. Let yourself experience the wisdom and beauty of this previously ignored or invalidated part of your whole self. Let this aspect of you speak and feel and live. Let it share all the information, healing ideas, and life energy it has been forced to hide.

When you've gotten this lost part of yourself firmly installed in your body, let your Gold Sun vanish, and close off the opening in the top of your aura. Bend over and dump any excess energy out the top of your head. Watch to see how much of this aspect your body wants to keep. Don't be surprised if it wants all of it, and you feel completely comfortable right now. You've lived without this portion of yourself for long enough.

Let this aspect of you have its head for now, and try to listen to the stories, warnings and feelings it has about your life. You may find its information counter to what you believe right now (or its area wouldn't have been hazy), but listen anyway. Invite this aspect of yourself to help you heal your aura in subsequent reading and healing sessions. You may find your life and attitudes changing in surprising ways once you revitalize a hazy and unrealized portion of your being.

HOLES: Holes in the boundary of your aura are places where your energy can leak out, and other people's energy can sneak in. Holes can be a sign that your Sentry is not the right one for the situations you encounter, because the edge of your aura is becoming involved in the energy intrusions of others. A hole-filled aura needs a grounded Sentry blanket right now, and don't skimp on the thorns.

Holes also ask you to be more aware of the quality of interactions you have with the people or situations in your life. Step up your image destroying and contract burning until you pinpoint any specific boundary-injuring people or events. If you ask them, the holes in your aura will often show you the shape of the person or situation that created them. Once you identify the cause of such holes, you'll need to burn specific contracts, send dozens of hello gifts, and remember to be grounded when in contact with hole-making people or situations in your life.

Holes will also appear in your aura through your use of drugs, especially depressants, alcohol, hallucinogens, and marijuana. All Western drugs and mood- or consciousness-alterers scatter energy. Sometimes that's called for in certain situations, but not nearly so often as we moderns tend to think.

If you use drugs, your aura will show it, and your energy will have a less evolved, less able, and less aware reaction to the many challenges of living in a body. You can continue your drug use and fix your incomplete and unhealthy aura more often, or you can give your body a break and clean out!

HOT SPOTS: Areas with a temperature increase of more than five or ten degrees denote intensely concentrated energy, from your conscious attention, from your aura's own healing ability, or from the attention of another person.

Heat is usually a sign of intense healing energy, but its presence can disrupt the delicate balance in your aura and take healing energy away from other equally deserving areas. A healthy aura needs healing energy in all areas at all times, and hot spots denote an overall lack of clean, readily available healing energy. More frequent Gold Sun Healings are called for in this instance, so that the aura can experience a constant flow of healing energy, instead of having to take energy away from one area to heal another.

Ground out any hot spots to cool them before running your Gold Sun energy throughout your entire aura. Keep an eye on the area and on your body to see what was going on. A visit to your acupuncturist or other holistic practitioner would be wise. Remember not to compartmentalize yourself or your aura by obsessing on one spot or aspect to the exclusion of all others. Keep your healing energy flowing everywhere.

JAGGED EDGES: Jagged, spiky edges on aura boundaries, or in holes or tears, denote a serious need to pull in and redefine all boundaries. I usually see jagged spikes on what I would call "all-encompassing" people, or people who try to love, accept, and experience everything they encounter.

When you do not use your discerning abilities to make separations between what does and doesn't work for you, your aura may have too much input to process. If you try to accept all beings, all external experiences, all contact, and all information, without filters, you depersonalize yourself in the process. Though a sense of universal love and acceptance of all experience is considered paramount spiritual behavior, it can really get in the way of healthy individuation, unless it is arrived at truthfully.

Real individuation requires real emotions like anger, jealousy, prejudice, fear, and exhilaration. Emotions and reactions help us to separate input into chaff and wheat; that difficult and messy process helps us to evolve. Opening up after reading a book on how to be evolved, or doing a weekend seminar on advanced *beingness* doesn't usually work well in the real world of specific life purpose, karmic patterns, and unsafe experiences. The process of opening up requires actual work, not just the denial of your supposedly unspiritual emotions, your reactions, your discerning abilities, and your aura.

Jagged edges in any part of your aura are a call for help. When your aura gets spiky, it means you are not giving it enough definition or conscious support. When an aura is undefined, it is unsafe, nonfunctioning, and endangered. Spikiness is evidence of the aura's inability to separate from the experiences and people around it. Without your conscious help in such instances, your aura will create edges, points, and straight lines to try to protect itself and make up for the delineations you are not providing.

Don't get me wrong. I am not asking you to cut yourself off from humanity and hide behind your aura. Instead, I want you to engulf yourself in a protective blanket of your own individuality. Within your individuality is your true path, your true healing, your own answers and karmic pattern, and your own ability to love and honor the world as it is. It is much easier to love and accept people from within a healthy aura than it is to drop all your boundaries and your individual responses and pretend to be something you read about in a book or heard about at a seminar. It is also much more evolved and true.

When you live within your own reality, you will be of more use to the world. *You* are the individual, unique person God sent here to live your life, to think your thoughts, to feel your feelings, and to find your answers. When you move onward into the spirit world, you'll have endless opportunities to be neutral and faceless. While you live in your body, it's best to be your flawed, silly, stupid, majestic, reactive, wonderful, human self.

When you find jaggedness or spikiness in your aura, it can also mean that you are trying too hard to go beyond specific "bad" emotions, and that your aura is having to do all your emotional protection and reaction duties for you. Please reread the section on Channeling Your Emotions (page 89). Remind yourself that, in a healthy quaternity, we have body, mind, spirit, *and* emotions. Emotions are not simply reactions to thought, or signs of bodily imbalance. Emotions have a life and an experience and a wisdom that is absolutely integral to balance and wholeness. If you ignore or try to transcend them, you'll induce a body/spirit split, and you'll soon be in a dissociated position. Trust your emotions, channel them, and they will move on peacefully, after giving you their indispensable messages. Ignore and denigrate them, and you'll be stuck inside an unhealthy, overly intellectual life, without the tools you need to process, grow, change, or love.

If your aura is filled with jaggedness and spikes, your Gold Sun Healing will need to include a rehearsal of your earlier skills, such as grounding, getting in your head, and creating a strongly grounded blanket of Sentries. Take some time alone to dance around with your own moods, feelings, and reactions to life. Use your hands to smooth out the edges of your aura boundary and to close any jagged holes or tears. Massage your healing gold energy into your aura. Also, pay special attention to the sections on the second and third chakras.

PULSATIONS: Pulsations in the aura that skitter around (as opposed to the normal pulsations of an aura, which look like the movements inside a lava lamp) signify a great deal of scattered, excitable energy. When you begin to work with your energy, your aura will go through periods of excitability. This is not anything to be concerned about. This is proof that you are doing your work and moving energy out of your inner life. Most skittery pulsations will be calmed during a normal Gold Sun Healing.

Pulsations that center around or within a specific area can be a sign of physical distress or an upcoming injury. Thank these pulsations as you ground them out and perform your Gold Sun Healing. Cover the pulsating area with a grounded Sentry blanket, and go see your acupuncturist or holistic practitioner.

Pulsations and lightning bolts of energy can also be a sign of drug damage, especially from stimulants, hallucinogens, and cocaine. Once again, drug energy rears its ugly head and shows how completely unhelpful it is in the evolved, conscious care of the self.

RIPS: Rips in the aura, as opposed to holes, are signs of injury to our view of ourselves. These injuries can be self-inflicted, or they can come from the views other people have of us.

As with any opening in the aura boundary, rips are places where your energy can leak out, or other people's energy can sneak in. Rips need to be mended during a Gold Sun Healing, and covered with a blanket of *strongly* grounded Sentries. Burn your contracts with the injury, and with your position as a victim of your or anyone else's thought forms. Remember that all thoughts and ideas are bits of energy and attention trapped in an attachment. When you release the attachment, your clean and cleared-out energy is available for you to use in any way you like.

As you mend the rips in your aura, sit inside the room in your head and watch the energy inside the rips fly up to your Gold Sun. See the once-trapped conflict, or anger, or self-hatred burn off as its energy enters your Sun. Welcome that lost energy back into your total energy bank. Then, do something different with it.

※

Almost all auric deviations will be healed in a regular Gold Sun Healing, which you should do now if you are currently reading your aura as you are reading this section. It is only when deviations show up repeatedly that they need to be singled out for a special healing.

Remember that your aura has come to an almost complete stop to enable you to see it. While you're sitting and reading its momentary snapshot, it may already be going on to heal all the deviations you've noticed. Perform your Gold Sun Healing and trust your aura to do its work—just as you're doing yours. Don't obsess about it. If you pick at it, it will never heal!

AN INTRODUCTION TO YOUR CHAKRAS

Chakra is a Sanskrit word for a series of circular energy centers in and around the body. There are chakras, or energy centers, in the palms of your hands and on the soles of your feet, and there are seven central chakras in a line up the center of your body. There is also a chakra just above your aura, called the Gold Sun chakra. Your grounding cord originates in your lowermost central chakra, or your first chakra.

The chakra system is intimately connected with the endocrine system. The second through the seventh chakras are each associated with a specific gland or glands, while the first and eighth chakras act as physical and spiritual regulators of the endocrine system. Imbalances in either the glandular or the chakric system, or in any specific gland or chakra, can disrupt the other system. Conversely, healings on either system can benefit the other system. Keep the endocrine system in mind as you heal your chakras. For excellent and comprehensive information on the glands and hormones of the endocrine system, see the book *Healthy Healing,* by Linda Rector-Page (see bibliography).

Many Eastern religions offer a great deal of information about the chakras. Their seven central chakras have seven different names, each with its own musical note, color, shape, animal, and other attributes. All these classifications are interesting, but, just as with the aura and the body, you could spend years studying all the possible functions, meanings, and histories of the chakras without ever learning to work with them in useful ways. I will not spend much time with these classifications, because they

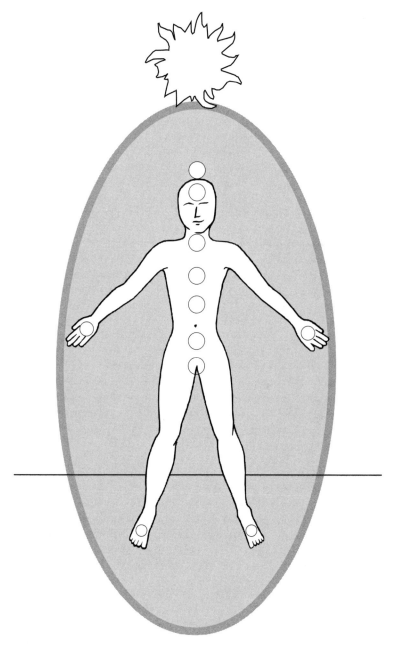

Figure 11. Your chakra system.

take our attention off healing. Besides, once you become aware of your chakras, they'll show you all their auxiliary information themselves.

In the most rudimentary definition, each chakra is a kind of placeholder for a specific set of abilities. In a sense, the chakras are gauges or meters that can tell you about the relative health of the ability in question. If you want to know about your ability to work with spiritual information, you can look at the chakra right above your head (the seventh chakra) and check its condition. If you want to look at your ability to balance spirit, body, and self-healing, you can zero in on your heart chakra (the fourth chakra). If you want to see how well your immune system is working, both physically and spiritually, then look at your solar plexus (the third chakra).

Energy troubles in your aura are a reflection of what is going on in your life, but the root cause of the troubles can usually be found inside your chakras. You can puff out the upper portion of your aura and heal an overly grounded aura skew a number of times, but if you don't look at what is going on in the energy centers of your chakras, you may just be applying Band-Aids to significant, ongoing energy problems. If you constantly have to place protective images in front of your first chakra area, or grounding is impossible, you really need to look at and heal your first chakra to get to the root of your difficulty. Or, if your aura boundary is constantly hazy and your Sentry doesn't function, those are clear signs that your protective third chakra needs a healing.

When injuries or difficulties are cleared from within your chakras, the clarity achieved can be startling. Through reading your aura, you can get an overview of your energy strengths and weaknesses; you can learn how you function. When you read your chakras, you can zero in on the foundational energies that determine *why* you function in the ways you do.

And now, another warning: Students in any discipline often develop a group narcissism that helps them to feel special and separate from the unwashed, untutored masses. Don't be surprised if you get a little cocky about healing your chakras when everyone around you is unaware (in your opinion) and spiritually undeveloped. Don't celebrate your superiority, however. You'll be stupid again, don't worry.

If you study your chakras in a healthy way, your knowledge will bring forth more questions—often very difficult, foundational questions. Sometimes, the things you see in your chakras will make you want to collapse and leave all your training behind. You won't feel superior; you'll feel like a dope. This is good. This is what real learning feels like, at times.

When your learning takes you off in too many directions, go back to the beginning. Keep grounding. Reread the early parts of this book. Go over the Troubleshooting Guide again, and keep things simple. When you are regrounded, go back to the place where you were overwhelmed, and you will find that you can come at the issue differently. By keeping your feet on the ground, you will be able to learn to fly. When you can fly through your own issues, you won't have time to look down on other people. Remember, everyone has an aura and chakras. Many people can maintain their spiritual health without ever learning a thing about them. Don't assume that other people's chakras are not healthy just because they have never heard of chakras. Other people have other paths, that's all.

If you've read other books about the chakras, this information may contradict what you have already learned. My only defense is this: I've never read a book on the chakras! Whatever I know about chakras was learned on the job, from the chakras themselves. This is not a treatise about the chakras; it is a tale translated directly from the world of the chakras. Hopefully, it will lead you into the world of your own chakras, where you will be able to discern any discrepancies for yourself.

THE CHAKRA CHECK

Before you start to read or study your chakras, it's always a good idea to give them a mini-healing. The chakras, like the aura, have a certain basic form. If this form can be established before a reading, the ensuing reading will flow more smoothly.

I envision each chakra as a forward-facing disk of swirling energy. Healthy central chakras are usually anywhere from three to five inches in diameter, and the hand and feet chakras are generally somewhat smaller (two to three inches) in diameter. The Gold Sun chakra usually takes whatever size it likes, depending on how much energy it has to feed back to you. In depth, chakras can range from a cylindrical length of two to three inches to as much as a foot, depending on the energy output of their owner. Longer, thicker chakras mean more energy output; shorter, thinner chakras mean less.

In healthy chakras, I look for a clearly delineated, circular border; a clean and healthy color that is specific to the chakra; and a constant, gentle flow of energy within the chakra. Deviations from this norm are to be expected, and even celebrated, in early chakra healings and readings. Deviations mean that you are becoming a good reader, and that your chakras are aware enough to send you messages about their difficulties.

Chakras, like auras, are extremely active and busy. If you don't clear them out and get them calmed down before you start to read, you could easily spend an hour on each chakra as it tells you stories of past, present, and future. The stories are fascinating, but not always valid for you in the present moment, and not always indicative of what you can do to alleviate any difficulties.

The healing I call the Chakra Check is a simple way to remind the chakras about their ideal shape, size, and color. During a reading or healing, your Chakra-Checked chakras can show you any deviations they are experiencing right now, as opposed to deviations they have experienced in the past, or will experience in the future. The Chakra Check cleanses your chakras and pulls them into the present; it calls them to attention.

During the Chakra Check, it is important to remember that you are, at this point, *telling* your chakras what to do, not listening to their stories. If you stop and listen to them at this point, your Chakra Check will not be a quick healing, but a time-consuming reading. You should be in a directive attitude here, instead of a receptive one. Receptivity will be called for in the actual chakra studies and readings to follow.

HOW TO PERFORM THE CHAKRA CHECK

Envision your Gold Sun chakra touching the edge of the top of your aura. See it as clear and open, with bright golden energy moving freely within it. Envision a strong delineation between its edges, the edge of your aura, and the energy outside of your aura.

Starting with your seventh chakra, right above the crown of your head, envision this energy center as healthy, open, circular and defined, and filled with a clear, flowing, lively purple-violet energy. Now direct your attention to your forehead and see your sixth chakra (or third eye) as healthy, open, circular and defined, and filled with a clear, moving, vibrant indigo energy. As you shift your attention down to your fifth, or throat, chakra (just above that depression at the base of your throat) see this chakra filled with a clear, moving, sapphire-blue energy. Stay in the room in your head. Do not fly out of your head to visit each of your chakras. You can see them just fine from inside your room.

Center your attention on your fourth, or heart, chakra (which is centered over your sternum), and see this chakra open to the same diameter as the chakras above it. See your heart chakra as circular and defined, and filled with a clear, moving, emerald-green energy. Your third chakra, or solar plexus, should be healthy and open, circular and strongly defined, and filled with a clear, flowing, sunny yellow energy. Now see your second chakra (just below your navel) as healthy and open, circular and defined, and filled with a clear, moving, persimmon-orange color.

Stay in your head and envision your first chakra (just above the testicles in men, or at the low-center of the vagina in women) as an open, healthy, and defined energy center filled with a clear, moving, sparkling ruby-red energy. Make sure to include a picture of your healthy grounding cord in your vision of your first chakra. See your hand chakras (in the center of your palms) open to two or three inches in diameter, and see your foot chakras (in the center of your arches) open to those dimensions as well. Do not assign colors to your hands and feet, but be aware of any colors already present.

✳

Now your chakras are awake and aware of what they're *supposed* to be doing. Though you can go on to study or heal them now, this Chakra Check is an excellent mini-healing that you can do at any time, whether you are intending to go on to a full chakra reading or not.

If you do go on to read your chakras, your reading will be much more valid, because your active and busy chakras will be calmed and centered. If you don't go on to a full reading, your chakras will be happy anyway. This mini-healing gets them back into alignment and connection, with you and with each other. Like you, your chakras love to be noticed and talked to, even in seemingly inconsequential ways.

As you read through these following chakra descriptions and try a reading or a healing, remember that any deviation or damage you see in your chakras is a sign that you are becoming a competent, aware chakra owner. The problems you can identify are the problems you can fix. Remind yourself that you are now an intuitive healer. You can deal with any problems your chakras share with you.

The First (or Kundalini) Chakra

This bright red, expressive chakra (all odd-numbered chakras are primarily expressive, all even-numbered chakras are primarily receptive) is located at the very base of the spine, just inside the vagina in women, and just above the testicles in men. The first chakra (some people call it the root chakra) is the chakra of basic survival, the primal sex drive, and bodily life energy.

The first chakra is not associated with any particular gland. Instead, it acts, in cooperation with the eighth chakra, as the physical energy regulator for the endocrine system. If there are problems in the first chakra, the functioning of the chakra system, and the endocrine-hormonal system, may be adversely affected. See the Troubleshooting Guide for information on endocrine imbalance (page 259).

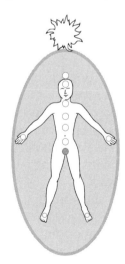

The first chakra is (or should be) connected to the chakras in the soles of the feet. If this connection is not healthy, grounding may be very difficult. In any study of the first chakra, the foot chakras must be included. Please refer to the section on the foot chakras for an in-depth look at the connection between these energy centers.

The energy of this chakra is very powerful. When first-chakra, or *kundalini* energy, runs upward and through the body (the first is the only chakra that does this), its powerful life force can help to ensure physical survival in the face of danger. First-chakra energy is responsible for sudden bursts of strength. It can help people run from or competently face violent encounters, or lift trucks off small children.

Kundalini energy will also flow upward in some instances of spiritual awakening. Because of this, many spiritual groups have developed techniques to get the kundalini to run upward, even when there has been no awakening, and there is no danger. When the kundalini runs upward, it blasts through each of the other six central chakras and out of the head, like a column of fire, or a cobra ready to strike.

The physical sensations resulting from this upward flow are very like a cocaine rush. One feels invincible, extremely awake and alert, psychically aware, and totally uninterested in food, sleep, or any other mundane life process. This is a good feeling, but running the kundalini to get it has its consequences. I can't begin to count the number of jumpy, ungrounded, exhausted people who have come to me to have their kundalini rerouted. A little bit of first-chakra energy goes a very long way. Even during a short kundalini rush, the body can't handle the excess energy, not to mention the lack of food and sleep.

Kundalini meditations used by advanced and centered yogis can bring about healing evolution. However, many kundalini teachings in the West are not taught by or to advanced yogis. Here, kundalini work is often used as a recreational drug. Using the kundalini energy starts out to be a really exciting idea, then turns into a catastrophe. If people are not completely sure of how they managed to raise their kundalini (usually, one chants, fasts, and sits in deep meditation until the first chakra wakes up and starts blasting), they won't be able to lower it with any certainty. Coming out of meditation and eating again do not always work.

Interestingly, cults use chanting, fasting, and sleep deprivation to bring recruits into the fold, all of which will send the kundalini up and out (the kundalini can turn itself on, as a protection, in times of starvation and insomnia). For Westerners who have no experience of spiritual or psychic energy, this kundalini rush can be overwhelming. Instead of acknowledging their own first chakra's power, many spiritual seekers give their power to cults and the cult experience. This helps create and sustain the entrapping culture. If people are not allowed to explore or experience their own energy, they are perfect prey for cults, gurus, and anything else that offers the illusion of power and spiritual knowledge.

Even though the kundalini energy can cause many problems, the first chakra is very responsive. It's very easy to reroute, even if it's been running up and out of the top of the head for a very long time.

❋

One of the worst kundalini cases I ever saw was in a female cult member. She had kept her first chakra blasting upward for so long that she had broken out in an all-over rash that looked as if her skin had been burnt. The fire of the kundalini was actually beginning to affect her skin. She came to me for a healing, so I grounded her and created a blue moon (see the Kundalini Healing, page 275 in the Troubleshooting Guide) above her head. Almost immediately, she went into a series of seizures as she re-entered her body and her first-chakra energy drained out of each of her upper chakras. I kept working, and the seizures stopped when her first-chakra energy got back into its correct place. Then, she began crying in big, racking sobs. I kept working. Soon she was grounding from her first chakra again, and her energy had evened out. Her upper chakras were damaged and distorted because they had been forced to run first-chakra vibrations instead of their own, but we soon got them back to normal.

This woman told me it was like waking up from a dream that had turned into an endless, hallucinatory nightmare. She felt that she had been seduced and then trapped in another world. Her cult was one that fell apart in a big, ugly way a few years later, leaving many wounded people in its wake. She was relieved to have gotten out when she did, even though she was vilified for doing so by the people she thought were her new family. Her rash went away the day after our first healing, and she was able to resume her life as a wiser and more centered (if somewhat less idealistic) person.

※

If left to its own devices, the blasting capability of the first chakra will turn itself on and off, triggered by danger or emergency, illness and depression, or an opening of psychic awareness. During times like these, the energy of the first chakra will channel itself up and through the other chakras as a kind of wake-up call. When the first chakra turns itself on in response to real-need situations, it will turn itself off in its own time, without any help. The kundalini energy is self-governing. It knows more than we do about its own functioning and responsibilities.

I would not suggest playing with the kundalini as if it were a toy or a drug, or using it to take a shortcut to spiritual awareness. It might be fun to play with the power of the kundalini for a while, but it wreaks havoc with the other chakras, which cannot function very long at the vibrational level of the first chakra. The blasting can also damage the aura, which will not remain healthy if it is allowed only one color (red) and one frequency of vibrational energy. Added to those two serious drawbacks is the fact that it is almost impossible to ground when the first-chakra energy is running upward.

OPEN OR CLOSED FIRST CHAKRA

In any first-chakra problem, difficulties may also occur in (or originate from) the foot chakras. Since these chakras should be connected to the first, please include the foot chakras in your study or healing of the first chakra. Healthy foot chakras will support any first-chakra work you do. The foot chakras are covered in a later section.

A very large and open first chakra is usually a sign that you are in complete survival mode—financial, emotional, and physical survival. If you are right in the middle of a catastrophe, let your first chakra remain large so that it can assist you, but be aware that it may start running upward in a kundalini rush. Your first chakra will generally turn this rush off by itself when the danger has passed. If not, and your kundalini runs upward into your other chakras for more than a day or so, see the Kundalini Healing in the Troubleshooting Guide. If you are not in immediate trouble, your large first chakra may simply be opening to new levels of awareness. This is very good, but I will ask you to keep an eye on your large first chakra for now.

The first-chakra energy is very brave—even foolhardy at times—which is why it is so good at helping you survive. Your newly-healed first chakra needs your guidance and leadership, however, as it awakens. It may get a little better and suddenly think it can run a marathon, spiritually speaking. It may think it can heal your every issue and stay open and unguarded, because life is suddenly safe. Be aware that your current lifestyle and surroundings may not be healthy enough yet. Protect your powerful first chakra from the harm that may be implicit in your environment (get your protective third chakra up and working, please). Bring the edges of your too-open first chakra into the normal three-to-five-inch diameter. Your chakra may be open to a larger size out of habit only, especially if you are always poised for danger. Chakras open and close like camera shutters, if it helps you to use that visual support in your attempts to change their shape.

A closed first chakra is a sign of a shutting down of life energy, or an attempt to ignore it. Closed first chakras appear on people in great physical or emotional pain, not from being in survival *per se* (which would create a too-open first chakra), but from being in deep denial of their own life path or lessons. The closing of this chakra can also signal an individual's denial of the necessity of straightforward, unemotional, rocks-off sexuality. Closing the first chakra may seem like a good way to escape all of its issues (especially the sexual ones), but it doesn't work. Closing off and ignoring the first chakra only disrupts the grounding and the rest of the chakra system.

I always tell people with any closed chakras that it is perfectly normal to have painful issues, but that closing the chakra associated with those issues will increase the issues, problems, and difficulties a hundredfold. It is very possible to have difficulties with sex, survival, and grounding while maintaining a healthy first chakra. Punishing our chakra system because we don't want to deal with certain aspects of our wholeness is silly. It is our responsibility to make sure that we aren't penalizing ourselves or our chakras just because our lives aren't perfect. Regardless of the issues at hand, it is always correct to keep all of the chakras in working order.

If you have a closed first chakra right now, but are not in any dangerous or survival-based situation, it is possible that your chakra is closed for repairs. In a healthy and balanced chakra system, chakras may close down for a little while in order to heal and divest themselves of bad habits or damaging energy contracts. During these times, the other chakras look out for the closed one. They let it take a little vacation. You will recognize a first-chakra vacation by the health and color of all the other chakras, by the absence of immediate survival issues, and by the fact that you can stay grounded even though your first chakra is closed.

If your first chakra is on vacation, congratulate yourself and all of your other chakras, and give them each a hello gift. When one of your chakras can take a safe rest like this, it means you have achieved health and communication in your chakra system as a whole! Support your chakra system further by placing two Sentries directly in front and in back of your first chakra. These Sentries will guard and heal your first chakra, which will open back up as soon as it is ready—usually in less than a week.

If your first chakra does not open by the end of a week's time, ask it what is needed. Usually, your first chakra will require a better Sentry and aura boundary system, or perhaps a new grounding cord. It may even need its neighboring chakras to be healed first. Trust this basic chakra to tell you what it needs in order to open up again.

TRAITS OF A HEALTHY FIRST CHAKRA

When the first chakra is open to the right size, defined, and flowing with a freely moving, ruby-red energy, the grounding cord will be healthy and defined as well.

Beyond all the positive effects of being grounded, people with healthy first chakras will be in touch with their body and their sexuality on a purely physical, unemotional level. They will know what is right for them in terms of food, shelter, and sex partners without needing to emote or ruminate on the rightness of each decision. They will have a solid stance, a strong, balanced gait, and an awareness of where they are, where they left their car, their car keys, and their energy.

Such healthy first-chakra people will feel centered, powerful, and able to handle any health concern that comes up, even if that means being sick for a while until their body clears out old, unwanted energy.

If a person lives from their first chakra only, they can be earthy and basic beyond belief. They won't have the tempering influence of their other chakras to balance their physicality with their spirituality, their intellect, and their emotive nature. We won't spend too much time discussing unbalanced people, though. We're working toward wholeness.

THE SECOND
(OR HARA) CHAKRA

This warm orange, receptive chakra sits just below the navel in the center of the body. The second chakra is the center of the emotions, the musculature, gender identity, and sexuality beyond the first chakra's primal need to procreate. The second chakra is associated with the gonads: the testes or the ovaries.

The sexuality of the second chakra is about connection, specific gender roles and identities, and the ability to bond and become one with a lover. The second chakra energy also allows us to bond in nonsexual situations and experience true body-level empathy. This is not always good, especially in interpersonal situations where clear boundaries are crucial.

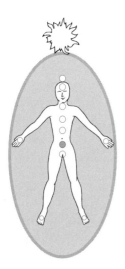

In many cases, people who are not connected to their first chakra because of its earthiness will over-identify with the energy of the second chakra and try to ground and center themselves there. This is a problem, because the second chakra exists to bond things together through emotion. In a healthy chakra system, this bonding can be used safely as but one of a number of relating skills. In an unhealthy system, a second-chakra focus can create a person with very few emotional boundaries.

The sexual energy of the second chakra is unhealthy if used all by itself. Second-chakra-centered people will be deeply emotional lovers who require profound, to-the-dying-breath commitments from their partners. They will spend vast amounts of time seeking a transcendent, in-love feeling, as opposed to taking people as they are and loving them without so many superhuman requirements. Trying to manage an adult sexual life from the second chakra alone can be emotionally exhausting for everyone concerned. It is best to get the first chakra up and running to create a balance between its "hunka-hunka-burnin'-love" sexuality, and the second chakra's romantic ideals.

The second chakra is also the center of gender identity. All humans are supposed to maintain a psychological, emotional, physical, and spiritual balance between male and female, but most of us do not manage to do so. Gender and sexuality become confused. Signs of imbalance are expressed in the functioning of the second chakra. The second chakra reveals how much focused, expressive, masculine energy we allow in ourselves, in contrast to our diffuse, receptive, feminine energy. As in any other case of balance between two poles, a lack of balance in regard to gender is not an ideal state.

A good way to check in on your gender balance is to place two small reading roses just in front of your second chakra. On your left, place your feminine energy rose. On your right, place your masculine energy rose. Let each rose become a symbol of its gender, and watch them both to see how they change, specifically in relation to one another. If one rose gets big and bright while the other goes dark and wilted, you've got yourself a strong gender skew.

Study these roses, and go back to the chapter on rose readings if you need to refresh your memory on stem length, colors and other attributes. Remember that these roses are an illustration of where your gender balance is right now. If it is very unhealthy and skewed, remind yourself that this is not a guarantee of a life-long gender imbalance. This gender imbalance can be examined, worked with, rehabilitated, and healed.

After you have read your primary gender-skew information, thank and destroy your reading roses and place new, extremely healthy, grounded Sentries in their place. Dedicate these new

Sentries to the healing of your gender skew. Endow them with protective abilities, groundedness, and radiant colors, and these Sentries will stand guard in front of your very receptive second chakra. They will not only serve as healing placeholders for your masculine and feminine energy, they will also confront and ground out all the crazy societal messages about gender that infect our society. For help in recognizing and honoring the differences between masculine and feminine energy, I recommend the books *He* and *She* by Robert A. Johnson (see bibliography). They're tiny books, but they are powerful!

Each chakra has a specific psychic ability attached to it, and this chakra's ability can be rather tricky in a time as chaotic and unconscious as ours. The second chakra heals and communicates through complete body-level empathy, or *clairsentience*. Through its clairsentience, your second chakra can actually bring someone else's pain, emotions, or conflict inside your body. A good, everyday example of this kind of body-level empathy occurs when you double over in sympathy when you see someone else's testicles get kicked. You can actually feel the kick, even if you haven't got any testicles.

Being able to feel another's pain and to deeply understand their emotions and reactions is an important skill. The problem with this depth of understanding is that other people's energy cannot work in your body. You do not have the ability to truly heal their pain, because you do not have their tools. Each person's pain is specific to them, and all pain comes with its own specific tool set, as it were.

While I cannot heal your gender skew for you, I can help you find the tools to heal it yourself. If I tried to pull your pain and confusion into my body, you would feel lighter for a while, but you wouldn't have learned your lesson. The problem, or something very much like it, would come back soon enough. In addition, I would have your pain stuck in my second chakra, unless I were conscientious enough to ground it out.

Clairsentient healers who work from the second chakra are called *sponge healers* and, though they can perform miracles, they usually die of cancers and organ-wasting diseases. This is because their bodies cannot process that which is not theirs to heal. Their systems are simply overwhelmed by all the foreign energy they ingest. Though they may perform a fair number of healing miracles in their careers, the long-term costs are very high.

For example, my own suicidal depression was created by my energy and my cells for a specific reason, and healing my depression brought me to a new level of personal awareness. Though I required guidance, nutritional support, and information, the tools I needed to heal my own illness came with the illness. My ability to access those tools came from using my second chakra energy on myself. By coming into direct empathic contact with my suicidal urges, I was able to understand why they were manifesting in my body. When I saw the importance of the depression in protecting me from seeing or knowing the truth about my childhood, I was able to thank it and let it go. Instead of fighting and hating and drugging my disease, I was able, with the help of my own empathic abilities, to use its energy as an ally in my healing.

My second chakra taught me that each imbalance exists for a specific, often protective, reason. The body in turmoil is not giving up, but trying its best to continue on in the face of trauma and hardship. When my depression showed me that it was a reaction to my assault, I was able to heal the split of my assault, which released the need for any further insanity.

My deep depression served a deep purpose for me, not the least of which was the imperative to no longer pretend everything was okay in my world. If I had given the responsibility of healing my psychiatric disturbances over to a healer of any kind, I could easily have ignored the message within my turmoil. If I had been healed miraculously by someone else, I would have experienced none of my own healing power. I might also have thought that the power to heal existed only in the miracle worker, and not in myself.

If you, as a healer, miraculously sponge someone else's illness off them, you not only take away their opportunity to learn and move to new levels of personal power and awareness, you place yourself in unnecessary danger. Because you don't have their illness, you don't have the tools to deal with their illness. You have no business bringing their pain into your body. If you love people and want to help them, allow them to have their own pain. Try to guide them out of their misery, but don't suck their misery into your body. If you love yourself, don't damage yourself to prove that you are a good healer. Use the healing abilities of your other chakras, or, better yet, heal from all of them at the same time. If you do, you will be able to understand other people's pain without having to become one with it.

※

Be aware of how open and receptive your second chakra is, because you can unconsciously sponge energy in any number of seemingly mundane situations. People who are very good at cleaning, organizing, or mucking out usually sponge up old energy with their second chakras as they scrape off grime or create a new filing system. People who are very good personnel managers or counselors normally sponge off the stress of others without realizing it. Nurses are notorious sponge healers, as are massage therapists, court reporters, office managers, bookkeepers, parents, and humane society workers. The list goes on and on, and, though women are more famous for sponging, men do it just as well and just as often.

The best way to find out if you are a sponge healer is to examine your fatigue levels and the condition of your third chakra. If you are knocked out and exhausted at the end of a work week, if your stomach is constantly hurting, if you pack protective fat over your solar plexus or below your navel, and if you require long vacations far away from your home, you are probably sponging on a daily basis. The exhaustion and the urge to get away from everything can be a sign of normal fatigue, but the stomach-ache or padding in this instance signals that your protective third chakra needs your help. It's trying to get you to protect both it and your second chakra. The constant need for far-off vacations is also a dead sponging giveaway. People with functioning spiritual and emotional boundaries do not have to leave town to relax.

Place many grounded Sentries in front of your second and third chakras as an anti-sponging defense mechanism and check in on each chakra's size and general health as often as you can. Remind yourself, over and over, that you can exist and be important, even when you don't fix everything and everyone around you. Your sponging abilities are important, but only in a healthy, balanced, and aware energy body. If you've got sponging abilities that are far greater than your other intuitive abilities, you'll create tremendous spiritual and physical imbalances.

Clairsentience is an important healing ability within the self. It is also vital as a part of a whole and healthy spiritual healing arsenal. By itself, though, sponging is safest between members of the same family, especially in the case of parent-to-child sponging. A mommy-or-daddy kiss on a cut or bruise has absolutely magical healing properties. The pain drains right out of injuries when parents kiss them. While children are under the age of thirteen, they are psychically connected to their parent's energy anyway, so this kind of parent-to-child sponging will have no ill effects on the parent.

Sponging between siblings or between older children and parents or grandparents can also be done safely, because the genetic and emotional material is similar enough for the body to process without too much damage or difficulty. This is really the only time I recommend sponge healing on its own. Other situations are simply unsafe and unnecessary. People cannot learn their lessons if their difficulties are removed as if by magic.

※

Sponge healers are often disconnected from their interior emotional reality. Because their second chakras, which are the centers of emotions and emotional protection, are always busy with anything but their owner's needs, sponge healers really don't know how they feel. Their emotional confusion is such that one could abuse a sponge healer for years before they become aware of the abuse. Most of the people in a sponge healer's life depend on this fact.

Out-of-balance clairsentients are so filled with other people's energy that they can't even find their own feelings anymore. Their emotional energy is used up on other people's problems. This is the reason many sponge healers stay with their healing work, even though it starts to kill them. Sure, it hurts, but it also has a big payoff: they don't have to feel their own feelings! The pain *seems* to come from the present, and they can deal with that. The pain that sits inside them in the dark seems too big to handle. For these people, the dangers of sponging seem preferable to the terrors of their inner trauma.

Clairsentients are very much at risk in relationships with manipulative and off-center people, because they have a lack of boundaries that makes abusers feel so welcome. A sponge healer's aura and chakra system say, in effect, "Come on in, the water's fine!" No protection there!

This abuse is unfortunate, but it can be halted. Remember, sponging is a contractual agreement, and contracts can be rolled up and burnt as easily as they are written and entered into. Just because spongers have spent a long time sponging doesn't mean they have to keep doing it. It is a pattern that can be changed. Sponge healers can become aware of their own second chakra and its ability to channel emotional states that instruct and heal. In a surprisingly short amount of time, spongers who reconnect to the healing strength of their second chakras can become uninterested in sponging for others.

Healthy, balanced clairsentients have so much fascinating information and healing energy available for themselves that they don't have to stick their second chakra into other people's healing processes. They can find the healing information their own emotions hold for them, and they can learn to connect and empathize with others in healthy, nonclinging ways.

＊

Working with the second chakra is simple. You don't have to spend weeks worrying over it or begging it to close. All that is required is awareness, and the willingness to change. When you get to the sections on readings and healings that follow these chakra descriptions, pay close attention to your wounded second chakra, but spend most of your time getting it back into alignment and contact with the rest of your chakra system. This balance, more than anything else, will heal your second chakra.

The overuse of the second chakra creates problems in grounding (the first chakra), psychic protection (the third chakra), self-love and body/spirit communication (the fourth chakra), and on up the line. Healing the second chakra alone will help, but it is imperative to rebalance the entire chakra system and to pull each chakra into present time. Otherwise, the associated problems in the other chakras can throw the second chakra back into a sponging position once again.

The healthiest chakra is one that is a working member of a functioning system. A second-chakra problem requires, not only your help, but the help of all your other healed chakras as well. Once you heal it and place it back into alignment and communication with your chakra system as a whole, your second chakra will receive help, support, and healing from all your other chakras.

OPEN OR CLOSED SECOND CHAKRA

A very wide-open second chakra in an unbalanced chakra system must be brought back to size (three to five inches in diameter) immediately. Since this chakra is so receptive and generally unprotected, it can draw foreign energy into your body before you are even aware that any energy was lurking around. Resize this chakra by imagining the closing mechanism of a camera shutter, or use your hands to re-form it. When you are new at closing off a life-long sponging tendency, it is very good to keep this chakra at least an inch smaller than the others. Cover it with strongly protective, grounded second-chakra Sentries, front and back. After any period of nonfamily sponge healing, your second chakra may need a long rest.

When closing a too-open second chakra, it is advisable to take a vacation from needy or manipulative people for a while. Seek out only those friends and family members who honor, understand, and value you. You may have difficulty finding such people if you have spent a long time as an unbalanced clairsentient, but there will usually be one or two caring individuals hidden away somewhere. If anyone in your sphere has urged you to rest or take care of yourself, or offered you help and healing, even though you always refuse, seek them out. Your second chakra (and your overused clairsentient ability) will require the support of another human being who knows how to give without giving everything away.

A wide-open second chakra in a healed and balanced chakra system is the sign of an emotional or sexual opening that is necessary to growth and wellness. You can tell if your very-open second chakra is healthy by its color, which should be a very clear and warm orange, without any other colors mixed in. If your other chakras, specifically the first and third, are also healthy, you can let your second chakra remain large for as long as a week.

Place two strongly grounded Sentries in front and in back of your open second chakra to protect it from moving backward into sponge healing, and keep an eye on it. It should get itself back to normal before a week is out. If it hasn't, resize it yourself.

A closed second chakra is a sign that either the emotions, or the connective and emotive aspects of sexuality are turned off. A closed second chakra, along with a very open first chakra (a skew that creates an earthy, nonempathic, unemotional personality and sexuality), is a societally condoned position for men to take. If you're a man, or a woman who runs a heavily masculine gender skew, don't be surprised by this imbalance. It's not a tough skew to fix in the quiet solitude of your meditative moments, but the resulting level of emotional openness and empathy can be difficult to support out in the world.

If the people in your life have known you as a cold and unemotional person, they may see you as someone who just doesn't care. They may not confide in you, or include you in social events, which has probably been fine with you. As you re-open your second chakra, however, you won't think its fine to be isolated anymore. It will feel awful. You may experience a great deal of anger, sadness, and all the childhood, adolescent, or young adult's emotions you tucked away when you decided to shut off your emotional link to other humans. Channel these emotions. They belong to you, and they can heal you.

In addition, seek out the people who never really let you become stone-cold in their presence. There will always be one or two brave people who have tried to reach you emotionally. Stay away from the ones who try to manipulate your emotions in order to pull a reaction from you. Instead, seek out the ones who have shared their emotions, or cried in front of you, even though you made it clear that you had no emotions to share. These people were never fooled by your emotionless state, and they will not be surprised or dismayed by your process of re-opening to your emotions.

Surrounding yourself with the protection of emotionally-supportive people will protect your second chakra in the world, just as the Sentries can protect it inside your aura. With the support of other emotionally open people, the emotional vulnerability that comes with a newly opened second chakra will not be used against you.

People with healthy second chakras care about the world, their place in it, the feelings and lives of others, and the wisdom of their own reactions and emotions. As such, an open second chakra can be a real detriment in a dog-eat-dog environment. The second chakra makes you care, and our society is a perfect example of what can happen when no one really does. We're falling apart here, because people are too frightened to connect and feel. This makes room for all sorts of everyday crimes against humanity. It also creates a need for out-of-control, sponge-healing martyrs who die by the thousands without healing anyone, least of all themselves.

There are a million reasons to keep your second chakra closed and to refuse to feel or connect in healthy ways. The only reason to open it is to live as a fully human being, and not as a skew-filled reaction to the society around you. The second chakra needs permission from you, not society, in order to open up. It's *your* second chakra, *your* ability to feel, and *your* ability to connect. No one, least of all a sick society, has any business forcing you to close down your natural abilities. If you don't believe me, ask your first chakra; it has no patience with such idiocy. If you let it, it will come up into your deadened second chakra and clear out all the cobwebs, so you can open up to your emotions once again.

One of the best ways to begin to work with and to open your second chakra is to rely on water and fluidity. Hot baths and water therapy help relax the musculature, which in turn releases the skeleton, which in turn creates a more flexible, fluid walk, stance, and attitude. Fluid movements and swaying dances are especially supportive of the second chakra. I find that the simple act of allowing the hips to sway when walking or moving releases pent-up and static energy in the pelvis. This small movement in itself helps to open the second chakra.

Remember, it's okay to have issues with emotions or sexuality, but closing off your second chakra in response to those issues destabilizes your energy system and the rest of your life. If you close off the energy center that houses your emotions and your gender sexuality, you cannot move beyond your difficulties. How can you, when this basic life energy, healing ability, and information is unavailable to you? You can, however, have your emotional issues *and* a healthy second chakra. No problem.

If you are healthy and your chakras are all healthy, *and your second is still closed,* it can signal a second-chakra vacation. All chakras shut down periodically for repairs when your system is strong enough to let them do so. If you've given up sponging and are concentrating your healing, empathic energy on yourself, you can perform absolute healing miracles in your energy body. When your energy gets to a point of strength, your previously overworked second chakra may go off-line in order to remove old sponge-healer contracts and other signs of disease and imbalance. Your other chakras will watch out for your second chakra during this time. It will open back up when it is ready.

You can identify a second-chakra vacation by the health of your other chakras, the absence of your usual cast of needy hangers-on, and the sense of flow and relaxation in your pelvis and muscular body, even though your second chakra is closed for now. To support your second chakra in its time off, you can place two grounded Sentries inside your aura, at the front and back of your second chakra. These will help to guard and heal it until it comes back into service, which should be in a matter of days, or a week at most.

After a week's vacation, your second chakra should be ready to get back to work. If not, ask it why, and listen to its answer. It may need a more vital aura or Sentry system to protect it from unconscious clairsentience. It may also need you to heal your protective third chakra. Give it your support. As with any healthy chakra vacation, thank all your chakras for being well and aware enough to allow your second chakra a rest. Give them each a hello gift; they're doing a fabulous job.

TRAITS OF A HEALTHY SECOND CHAKRA

When the second chakra is open and flowing with a healthy, clear, warm orange energy, the body has a peaceful and sensual fluidity to add to the centered groundedness of the first chakra. A healthy second chakra confers an emotive, responsive connection to nature, to animals and humans, to the self, and to the spirit world. A healthy gender balance creates deeply nurturing, focused, and capable people who are also spiritually aware and emotionally responsive. People with healthy second chakras have a fluid, languid walk, like felines. They have a very deep understanding of the flow of events, and of the people around them. By connecting to their own emotions, they connect to the world.

Healthy second chakras also supply a level of internal healing that is powerful beyond belief. When the total empathy of the second chakra is brought to bear on illness, you can get to the emotional root that brought about the illness in the first place. By using the second chakra's clairsentient ability inside their own bodies, healthy clairsentients can speak to cancer cells, viruses, tissues, and diseases on their own primal level and ask them why they are living (or dying) in the body. The emotive and foundational answers within each disease are fascinating. When this information is understood and honored at a basic, feeling level, real healing can occur.

Though the emotions have long been considered lower than the intellect, people with a healthy connection to their second chakras and their own emotional state are wise beyond mere mental knowledge. They know *why* facts are true or false, not just that the facts exist. Connection to the emotional realities makes intellectual realities *meaningful*, not just factual.

THE THIRD (OR SOLAR PLEXUS) CHAKRA

This sunny yellow, expressive chakra sits right in the center of the solar plexus, directly between the navel and the sternum. The third chakra is involved in thought and intellect, and with the effect of thought on the body. It is associated with the adrenals and the pancreas. It is also the center of the psychic immune system. It will react to danger by closing down, by becoming very hot, or by spreading its energy out to protect the receptive second and fourth chakras from harm.

A gnawing stomachache that is not connected to hunger is often a sign that your third chakra is trying to close in the face of dangerous people or energy in your environment. Your third chakra will also try to close (or open far too wide) when your Sentry and aura are too dainty and ornamental to do any real work in protecting your personal territory. Beef them up!

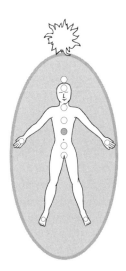

There are three body-level chakras (first through third), three spirit-level chakras (fifth through seventh), and one transitional chakra (the fourth, which acts as a bridge between the spirit and the body). The eighth chakra is the overseer of the whole system. The third chakra is the uppermost body-level chakra.

As the topmost body chakra, the third chakra is responsibile for filtering spiritual information down to the first and second chakras. This filtering and passing on of information from spirit is what keeps the bodily aspects of the body/spirit connection healthy and alive. When the third chakra and the heart chakra are healthy, the third will accept and translate the information coming down from the three spirit chakras through the heart. It will then pass this information along to the second and first chakras.

If your fourth chakra is unbalanced and the information coming from it is not clear, your third chakra may spend all its time translating garbled messages. The receipt of gibberish from an unhealthy or overused fourth chakra can leave the third chakra and you open to attack, since the translation process takes your third chakra's energy and attention away from the identification of danger in your environment. This hard-working third chakra may try to keep your body/spirit connection alive and healthy, even if your fourth chakra is not able to offer clear information. If your overworked third chakra doesn't have the time and energy to keep you safe and protected, however, you may leave your body anyway.

If your third chakra is unhealthy (for example, if you choose to stay in a dangerous relationship that forces your third chakra to remain eternally, exhaustingly vigilant), it may have to ignore all the spiritual information coming from your fourth chakra and work overtime just to keep you safe. Soon, because this normal fourth-to-third chakra communication is blocked, you will experience a body/spirit split.

The third chakra is also responsible for gathering and sending body-chakra information to the spirit chakras by way of the heart chakra. When this exchange is happening as it should, the spirit-level information and abilities of the upper chakras tend to pertain to more rational, real-world details. A good example of a working exchange of spirit/body information occurs when sensations help you to interpret a clairvoyant message, or your intuition tells you about that crick in your neck, or a food that is causing you trouble. If the third chakra is gummed up and can't channel body-level information to the upper chakras, the upper chakra's information will either be unreadable in the body, or will pertain to goofy things like the political situation in Manila (when you are not, and do not even know, a Philippine national), or the knowledge of a plane crash about which you can do nothing.

Without the support of the third chakra and the realities of the body, the upper chakras can become untethered and bring in all sorts of unrelated material. The fourth chakra may open too wide and pour all its energy away. The fifth chakra may pick up voices from all over. The sixth chakra may see unrelated, unusable visions, and the seventh chakra may channel the information of unhelpful or unaware spirits who have no real connection to your life. Maintaining a healthy third-fourth chakra connection will put a stop to such silliness.

As with a number of aspects of spirituality that have been hopelessly confused here in the West, the third chakra has been unnecessarily singled out as a less-than-perfect chakra. I really don't understand why this attitude has become so prevalent. Westerners tend to feel that the fourth chakra (the heart-love chakra) is the most important. Apparently, the "bad power" chakra (the third) keeps people out of their hearts and stuck in worldly power, and is responsible for wars, racism, money, egotism, the IRS, and clog-dancing. When we get to the section on the fourth chakra, I am going to have a little tantrum about the damage this crazy one-chakra idea has created for the poor heart chakra, but I'd also like to stand up for the beleaguered third chakra right now.

I want to make it clear that the only healthy chakra is one that is an aware, communicative member of a living, working chakra system. We've seen what can happen when the first chakra is tampered with and invited to blast upward into the other chakras for fun. A manipulated kundalini rush creates imbalance, disruptions, and an overall lack of health or useful awareness. An imbalance can also be created by shutting any one chakra down. This is what many people do when they consider the third, or power chakra, to be the root of all evil. These people are taught that the empathic, loving heart-chakra attitude is the only attitude to have—that allowing the third chakra to do its work of protection, separation, and immunity would destroy their love-in experience.

I'm here to tell you that this is completely untrue. The third chakra simply *is*. It is not good or evil, right or wrong. It performs dozens of functions, but the one that gets it into trouble is the one that allows it to control any incoming energy. If the third chakra senses a fight with another person (and you are not aware of your energy yet), it may allow you to throw a controling burst of energy at that person's third chakra, so that you can get the upper hand in the ensuing melee. Sometimes this burst will stop attackers in their tracks, so you may begin to rely on third-chakra blasting to get your way with people.

This is the extent of the crimes you can commit with the third chakra, and it is just a bad habit that can be unlearned. Turning off the entire third chakra just because it's possible to throw energy with it is extremely foolish. Besides, *all* chakras can throw energy, even the celebrated heart chakra! Without the vigilant protection of a functioning third chakra, both the fourth and the second chakra are liable to fall into damaging sponging habits of all kinds, and then all hell can break loose. From within such imbalance and chaos, your heart-love will be as powerless and confused as you are.

Without the communicative aspects of a functioning third chakra, a mind/spirit/body split is nearly assured—and we *know* that split people aren't fully functional. The bottom line is this: Don't listen to all the hooey about the "bad" third chakra, and close it down to fit in with some current ideal. Your power to protect your own energy system is absolutely essential in a healthy whole life, no matter what the current trends are in New Age thought.

A healthy third chakra is actually vital to the functioning of the heart-love fourth chakra. If the protective and communicative third chakra is turned off, the heart chakra will eventually become very large and unhealthy. All the love that it contains will pour away until its owner has none left for anyone. This unfortunate occurrence can be seen regularly in heart-love healers who burn out by the thousands as their bodies break down and their energy dissipates. Their own healing will occur when they turn their protective and energetic third chakras back on and begin to live whole lives again.

We can circumvent this sad burn-out process by keeping our third chakras healthy, open, and included in our whole lives. Third-chakra blasting will cease in a connected and aware chakra system. When the clairvoyant sixth chakra is working and overseeing the energies around it, it will alert the third chakra of any upcoming danger. In a healthy system, the third chakra will then strengthen (or ask you to strengthen) its aura, grounding, and Sentry, so that damage is less likely, and energy blasting is unnecessary.

In the physical world, there *are* dangers. Our bodies are spectacularly unprotected, in mammalian terms. We have no claws, spines, musk glands, or sharp teeth. We don't even have a protective covering. Our bodies have to deal with our dangerously exposed, defenseless state every day. If we fall into a pattern of New Age thought, and see all energy and all human encounters as safe, we will shut off our third chakras. Then we will have no protection whatsoever. None.

Without protection, we become less—not more—useful in the world. Our third chakras not only protect us, but define us and our place in world healing. Without our third chakra's self-protective support, we become less than ourselves. We become less able to function and contribute. We become filled with foreign energy, foreign messages, and foreign mindsets.

In the physical immune system, the identification of foreign bodies and foreign foods is not just a process of alarm and defense. In order to identify foreign agents, the immune system must know what its own cells look like. The immune system functions throughout the body in each moment, saying, "This is mine, that's mine, that's mine, this is mine. . . ." It can only identify a foreign or invading substance ("That is NOT mine!") if it knows its own tissues. In the healthy immune system, self-preservation comes from self-knowledge. Without such self-knowledge, autoimmune disease is certain.

The same principle holds true in the psychic, or spiritual, immune system. In a healthy, self-aware person, third-chakra energy moves through the aura and chakra system, constantly touching and monitoring the energies within. It says, "This emotion is mine, that energy is mine, this message is mine. . . ." until it comes upon a foreign substance. When it does, it alerts the sixth chakra, which studies and categorizes the energy—or it alerts the second chakra, which performs an energy-matching with the strange energy to determine its emotional content. The healthy third chakra then alerts its owner with a stomach twinge, or a shimmering in the aura. Hopefully, the owner will respond. If not, the healthy third chakra will wrap the foreign energy in a cocoon, and wait until the next healing session, when the foreign energy will (or should) be grounded out.

In an unhealthy chakra system, especially where a body/spirit split has occurred, or an all-accepting mindset is present, the third chakra will be so harried and overworked that it will often just smack people away in order to gain some sort of control. In many instances, the third chakra's alerting stomach twinges will turn into full scale digestive disturbances, ulcers, hiatal hernias, or solar-plexus fat pads. In such an unhealthy system, you will find a person with very little useful self-awareness. Their third chakra, which is so degraded and damaged by their split state or all-accepting nature, will have no time at all to identify what belongs to it. This third chakra will spend its time putting out fires, trying and failing to connect to the often runaway-healing heart chakra above it, or wondering when the next kundalini blast will hit. This third chakra may also begin to attack its owner's energy—it may exhibit a spiritual autoimmune disorder.

Such third-chakra owners may have a hard time making decisions or remembering things. They may be ungrounded and unsafe, they may often be far off-path, and they may be filled with a quiet despair that their all-accepting philosophy cannot cure. Eventually, they will become spiritually and physically ill, as would anyone with a nonfunctioning immune system.

Healing energy for these people generally arrives in the form of fits of anger. Anger, as you know, contains boundary energy. This boundary energy helps to rebuild a protective aura, thereby protecting the third chakra. Anger also loudly proclaims the existence of many unmet and ignored personal needs. When anger is channeled, and the underlying emotions of despair, depression, and fear are given their time as well, the third chakra often comes back on line in a healthy and centered way.

When your third chakra is back in business, it will ask you to protect your heart chakra, and to become aware of and responsive to your authentic human emotions ("This is mine"). With these supports, you will be able to ground and center yourself within your own life. You will learn to integrate your chakra energies with one another. When your energies are available to you, and your third chakra is self-protective and self-aware, you will no longer need to rely on the crutch of accepting everything outside of you *instead* of learning to accept everything inside.

Going outside of yourself to find inner peace is backward. It is also a diversion. Don't divert. Get your third chakra up and running, and it will teach you to accept the most important person in your world. Self-accepting people accept others, within reason. All-encompassing, other-accepting people are not rational, and soon cannot accept themselves or their own reactions. Other-accepting people become runaway, out-of-control healers who are soon incapacitated and unable to help or heal anyone. Self-accepting people maintain their spiritual health, and can easily help others, when they deem that help necessary.

OPEN OR CLOSED THIRD CHAKRA

A very wide-open third chakra needs to be resized immediately. If the nearby chakras are shut down or strangely colored, or the openness of the third chakra is accompanied by stomach, kidney, or mid-back pain, it is a sign of general chakra-system distress, or danger in your daily environment. Closing down and protecting the third chakra with Sentries and negativity-eating gift symbols is very important, but so is continuing on and healing the rest of your chakra system as soon as possible.

Because the third chakra is a center of immunity and the ability to be safely separate on an energy level, it can be affected by assaults on or imbalances in any of your other chakras. A third chakra in distress requires immediate attention, so that the rest of the chakras and the aura can function normally. The sections on chakra healings later in this book will guide you through a chakra-balancing meditation.

A very open third chakra in an otherwise healthy and aligned chakra system is a sign that the spirit and body are communicating. This third chakra is gathering energy and information in order to make a leap in the conscious aspects of thought and health. You can identify a healthy, open third chakra by the health and color of *all* the other chakras (not just the ones nearby), and by a feeling of safety and peace in your exterior environment and in your digestive tract. A chaotic exterior or interior environment signals that this opening is not a healthy leap in consciousness, but an unhealthy use of the third chakra.

Pro-heart/anti-third-chakra teachings suggest that we should be open to all energy because we are all *one*. This can lead to an unconscious and unhealthy expansion of the third chakra, where its edges may reach the very edge of the torso. Such teachings exhort us to become nonjudgmental, nondiscerning, and accepting of all energy, all experience, all people, and all circumstances. Such teachings *require* an unhealthy third chakra. Clearly, we need to examine this "all-one" idea in light of each aspect of the quaternity.

※

In spirit, we *are* all one. There is no work to be done to achieve a state of oneness in spirit. At the spirit level, we are all God's children, coming from the same place, though we will always have our individual spiritual work to do. Spiritual oneness does not require an unhealthy third chakra; therefore, spiritual oneness will have no damaging side-effects.

※

In the intellectual realm, we can work to *become* one. We can change our thoughts or expand our intellect to embrace all forms of thought. At the intellectual level, we can learn to come from the same place, though our mental processes will always be individual. Intellectual oneness does not require an unhealthy third chakra either. Other than a bit of confusion when long-cherished beliefs are shown to be insupportable, intellectual oneness will have no damaging effects.

※

In the emotional realm, it's pretty easy to become one with others. Our second chakra can open and allow another person's emotive state to come right into our bodies. This is not a perfect situation, because it relies on the bad psychic habit of sponging, but it can be done. A better method of working with another's emotions is to honor and validate them from within your own separate, individual emotional reality. This separateness (which is the opposite of sponging) is fostered and maintained by your healthy third chakra.

Emotional oneness, unlike spiritual or intellectual oneness, requires sponging. It requires the dropping of boundaries, an acceptance of foreign energy, and a lack of psychic protection. Emotional oneness *requires* an unhealthy third chakra. The damage this causes can be complicated. Not only will all the troubles related to second-chakra damage be present, but physical damage may be present as well, due to the prerequisite imbalance in the third chakra.

Such "emotionally one" people will have a very low immunity, both to the emotions of those around them, and to opportunistic infections of the body. They will suffer from recurrent colds and flus, allergies, food and chemical sensitivities, stomach and digestive problems, and will have trouble sorting out their thoughts and reactions from the thoughts and reactions of those nearby. They may also have chronic skin disorders. When emotional oneness (sponging) is attempted outside of the family sphere, and foreign energy is courted and drawn into the body, the third chakra *must* be damaged in the process.

※

Physical oneness is an impossibility. There is no way to become one and stay one with someone on a physical level. Sexuality can bond lovers for an instant, but only an instant. Longer contact is both inappropriate and ridiculous. Bodies *cannot* become one with other bodies.

※

The only person we must become one with is ourselves. The only spirit we must become one with is God. Get back to the real work of becoming one with yourself, and one with your concept of God. When you know yourself, you will know all people. Trying to know all people *instead* of yourself is backward. Gathering all experience and information in order to know God is backward, too. When you know God, you will know everything you need to know. Your healthy, normal-sized, working third chakra will remind you of this again and again if you will just listen. By reminding you of your individual goals, thoughts, tasks, reactions, emotions, health concerns, and realities, your healthy third chakra will make true and useful oneness possible. It will protect you from oneness that is unworkable, unnecessary, and inappropriate.

If your third chakra is wide open in a healthy, balanced chakra system, and you experience *none* of the symptoms of emotional oneness above, you may congratulate your chakra system on its health and awareness. It is very unusual in our day for a third chakra to be too open as a result of being healthy enough to move on to the next level of awareness. Our society, and numerous religious and spiritual teachings, degrade the third chakra's protective aspects to such an extent that I am surprised when they work at all in early readings!

Please protect and honor your healthy chakra system by placing a congratulatory hello gift in front of each of your chakras. Place at least three strongly grounded Sentry roses at the front and back of your open third chakra as a protection against any wandering energy.

Carefully monitor your open third chakra. Use your hands to close it back down to its regular three-to-five inch diameter at the end of one week, though it may want to stay open for a longer period of time. If your environment is safe and sane enough, let your healthy third chakra remain open. If not, close your third chakra back down and get yourself to a sane environment before you allow it to open back up again. In such a safe place, your third chakra, and all your other chakras, will be able to do their best work.

A constantly closed third chakra can be a sign that you are not willing to think about or question the life you are living, or that you are not willing or able to protect yourself in the face of danger. A working third chakra asks you to think about safety, right livelihood, correct thinking patterns, warm and healing environments, and peace. These are wonderful topics, unless your current life choices steer you away from all five. In opening your third chakra, you will have to ask the hard questions. Is your life safe? Are you supported and cared for? If not, why not? Opening your third chakra will give you the answers to these questions.

Your newly-opened third chakra will react to dangers in your environment. If it has been closed for a long time, and your environment is completely unsafe, your third chakra may go a little crazy with stomach distress, fears, rages, rescue scenarios, racing thoughts, and more. Please support your third chakra by moving away from your abusive environment. Blame other people all you like, but get yourself out. Use all the skills you have, reach out and ask for support, but *get out*. Your health *requires* you to live free. Your healthy third chakra will help you protect yourself long enough to get to freedom.

When I reopened my third chakra after fifteen years of closure, I had so much work to do to regain my life that I felt overwhelmed. It took fully six years of work, meditation, processing, and help to get all the way back to health, but only one minute to take back my control and regain my freedom. My freedom came back as soon as I opened my third chakra and began to protect myself. My immediate freedom required the support of a battered women's shelter, a rape crisis group, the welfare system, and my return to school after a ten-year absence. Your freedom may require less support. However far you may seem to be from your freedom, you are only a moment away. Reopen your third chakra; you'll see what I mean.

When a normally healthy third chakra is closed, and all the other chakras are working and balanced, it can mean that the third chakra is reacting to a controlling person or energy pattern in the immediate environment by becoming unavailable for a blasting fight. This kind of immediate closing in a healthy third chakra is often accompanied by a hunger pang or minor, fleeting stomach distress. Be aware of these moments of clear communication from your working third chakra, and assist it by turning the front of your body away from the offending energy. This will make blasting less likely, and it will give you a minute to put up a Sentry blanket, send free gifts, or burn a contract. Bless the person or energy pattern that shows you where your defenses are still in need of work. Thank them. They've done you a service.

As with any other chakra, *a temporarily closed third chakra* in a healthy system can be a sign that a bit of quiet study is going on. Chakras sometimes go off-line for a little while when your awareness reaches a point of balance. They heal themselves, recharge their batteries, and get rid of old patterns, while the other chakras watch out for them. If you find a closed third chakra in an otherwise healthy system, and there is no identifiable danger in your immediate environment, you may be experiencing a third-chakra vacation. You can identify this state, not only by the health and condition of your other chakras, but by a sense of relaxation and well-being in your mid-back and your digestive tract, even though your third chakra is shut down.

Congratulate all your chakras for their excellent work, and give each of them a hello gift. Place two protective Sentries inside your aura, right in front and in back of your third chakra, and go on with your reading. Your third chakra should open up on its own within a matter of days, or a week at the most. If not, ask it what help it needs from you in order to do so. It will usually ask for a brighter aura boundary and a hardier Sentry system, or more awareness of your honest emotional responses.

TRAITS OF A HEALTHY THIRD CHAKRA

When the third chakra is open and flowing with a clear, sunny yellow energy, it confers a centered intelligence to the body and spirit. When it is part of a healthy chakra system, a working third chakra adds the ability to think, discern, process, and protect to the emotive and connecting qualities of the second chakra.

The healthy third chakra also lends an ability to protect the health through work, study, meditation, and application, in addition to the first chakra's purely physical, life-force brand of healing and body maintenance. Healers with healthy third chakras have a virtual encyclopedia of information available to their clients and themselves, because true third-chakra healing is supported by knowledge *and* faith.

A healthy and communicative third chakra also makes itself known through an all-over sense of comfort about spiritual knowledge and intuitive abilities. When the third chakra is sending and receiving information freely, the body understands the spirit, and the spirit understands the body. Clairvoyant knowledge is real, valid, and useful, instead of confusing, unconnected, and ungrounded. Bodily information is heard, validated, and translated for spiritual help without mental obstruction. Self-knowledge is a simple, everyday reality for healthy-third-chakra people.

A person with a working third chakra has achieved a balance between intellect, spiritual understanding, and bodily knowledge. The three aspects don't fight one another for dominance. Instead, they communicate with and rely upon each other. Add a healthy second chakra, with its command of the emotions, and you've got a balanced quaternity—all four sides of a perfect square.

THE FOURTH (OR HEART) CHAKRA

The fourth chakra is an emerald-green, receptive energy center that resides in the center of the chest. It is called the heart chakra, but it is really centered behind the sternum. It is associated with the thymus gland.

Celebrated, courted, deified, overworked, and misunderstood, this energy center has had so much said and written about it that it's hard not to get crushed under all the weighty suppositions, or imprisoned along with it in the temple of ritual and superstition it has engendered among *old souls* and *higher beings*. Yuck. Let's start over from scratch, shall we?

The heart chakra is an emerald-green, receptive energy center

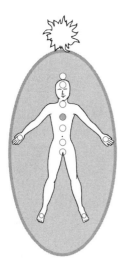

that contains the ability to love and feel compassion, both for oneself and the world outside. The heart chakra is (or should be) connected to the hand chakras. If this connection is not healthy, the ability to give, love, connect, and receive may be damaged. In any study or healing of the heart chakra, the hand chakras must be included. Please study the hands and their connection to the heart in the section on the hand chakras (page 227).

The heart chakra is the central (or transitional) chakra of the seven-chakra system. It bridges the gap between the three body chakras below it, and the three spirit chakras above. In a healthy system, the heart chakra accepts the purely spiritual information of the upper chakras (which is gathered by and sent directly from the fifth, or throat chakra) and translates it into the language of the lower chakras. It also translates the purely physical information of the lower chakras (which is gathered by and sent directly from the third chakra) into language the upper three chakras can understand.

The vital linking abilities of a healthy fourth chakra are necessary in any healing of a spirit/body split. When the fourth chakra is up and running, it works as an information collection and distribution center. It constantly facilitates and mediates between the spirit and the body. Without the support of a fit and capable heart chakra, the spirit and the body tend to career off on all sorts of mutually exclusive tangents.

Given the above information, you'd think that people involved in spiritual study would have healthier heart chakras than normal folks, but think again! Unfortunately, students in most spiritual growth and meditation classes often have the most damaged, overburdened, nonfunctional heart chakras imaginable. In most forms of spiritual study, so much emphasis is placed on the heart's ability to love others that all of its diverse and intrinsically useful auxiliary functions are essentially squashed and ignored.

Loving and forgiving others is considered the best possible spiritual behavior. The ability to give selflessly and compassionately is thought to be the paramount heart function. Certainly, these are some of the leading traits of fourth-chakra energy. They are also some of the leading traits of de-selfed, dissociated, runaway healers who do not incorporate the leading traits of the other six central chakras.

Yes, loving others is vital. It's irreplaceable. But such other-love must not be used as an excuse to de-self in the early portions of a spiritual journey. Truly loving others comes only *after* learning to love the whole self, the creepy, majestic, childish, exquisite, stupid, all-knowing self. This self-love can't flourish if all the heart energy is directed outward. None will be available for the self, or for the vital communication between spirit and body.

All the other-love and other-compassion in the universe will lead nowhere if no love or compassion is directed inward. It's just that simple. Heart-chakra energy must be brought back into the body and honored before it can be of any use in truly loving others.

Overemphasis on the heart chakra has many drawbacks. It destroys the balance and alignment of the chakra system as a whole, because the constant outpouring of heart energy leaves little space for communication between the spirit chakras and the body chakras. Overemphasis on the heart chakra also interferes with psychic and physical immunity, because the third chakra spends too much time trying to protect the exhausted heart, and not enough time protecting the physical and energetic bodies.

An outpouring heart chakra fosters an inability to ask for help and healing, because the communicative fifth chakra, above it, will be as overburdened as the third chakra, below. The fifth chakra won't be able to express the needs of the individual. Heart-chakra people continually find themselves healing in dangerous environments, completely unable to ask for support. They usually burn out, and then can't help anyone, including themselves.

Overemphasis on the attributes of the fourth chakra can also damage the chakra itself. In most cases of overuse, the fourth chakra spreads out from its healthy circular shape into a hyperextended, horizontal oblong, reaching almost to the shoulders in unprotected healers, physicians, and therapists.

One key sign of heart-chakra problems is a contention, or a split, between spirit and body. Because the heart chakra exists in the ether between the body and the spirit, living from the heart chakra assures a spirit/body split. Heart-chakra healers often vacillate wildly between purely physical needs and pursuits, and purely spiritual beliefs and actions. Neither side feels right. There is no flow and no balance between the two.

The owner of an overworked heart chakra swings between loving and understanding all beings, and stuffing their face with chocolate while having tantrums about money. They think either that they can meet their own needs and take from everyone else, or that they must be totally selfless and give every part of themselves away. There will be only black and white, with no communicative gray material in between. People who try to live from the heart chakra alone see life on this planet as an either/or proposition. Either they live in the world of the body and deal with ego, sex, and money, or they live in the world of the spirit, where they need nothing and are totally selfless. These split-apart people swing from one extreme to the other, without ever coming to a balance between the two poles.

I use a pendulum analogy to describe such people. A pendulum that has swung all the way to one extreme of its arc requires tremendous energy to remain there. Something would actually have to grasp and hold it in place in order to keep it in that position. This is totally unnatural. Pendulums only swing wildly if one puts energy into them. In their natural state, they move in gentle, circular arcs around the very center of their radius. Real pendulums live *only* in the gray area between black and white.

The antidote to extreme and unnatural swings is, of course, balance. That balance is possible even in cases of grievous heart-chakra damage. Through balancing the chakra system, you can learn to love and heal appropriately, just as you can learn to emote, think, protect, survive, communicate, know, give, and receive appropriately. Use the pendulum analogy to remind yourself that life on this planet is not an either/or proposition. We are spirits in bodies, and bodies of spirit. Neither side is better or worse, higher or lower, or richer or poorer than the other.

If you feel split in two by the needs of body and the needs of spirit, it is a clear sign that your heart chakra isn't free to do its mediation and translation work within your chakra system. Burn your contracts with the wide pendulum swings, and use your freed-up energy to heal your heart instead.

OPEN OR CLOSED FOURTH CHAKRA

In any heart-chakra difficulty, the hand chakras may also be involved. As you heal your heart-chakra issues, be aware of the connection between heart and hands. Healing this connection will help to support any heart work you do. See the section on the hand chakras (page 227) if your heart is in need of attention.

We've already talked about the reasons for and dangers of a very open or misshapen heart chakra. *If your fourth chakra is wide open* (larger than five inches in diameter) and your other chakras are out of whack, get them all healed and back into alignment as soon as you can. Make sure your heart and all your chakras stay open to a three-to-five inch diameter at the very most.

As with any other chakra, a momentarily open heart chakra is fine in an otherwise healthy and balanced chakra system. Heart chakras will open on their own when they need to move through issues relating to love, self-love, and competent spirit/body communication. If your chakras are balanced (especially chakras three and five), and your upper back and lung area are free of discomfort, let your heart chakra remain wide open. Cover it, back and front, with a few protective Sentry symbols so it can have some privacy. Check on your heart chakra twice a day. Resize it yourself if it remains wide open for more than a week.

A misshapen heart chakra is another story. No matter how well the other chakras seem to be functioning, a noncircular heart chakra is not a good thing. This shape-shifting can be a sign of a tendency toward full-blown, out-of-control heart-chakra healing, or an attempt to replace self-love with the love and approval of others. Reshape a noncircular heart chakra as soon as you find it. Use your hands to bring all its energy back into a circular form, and skip forward to the section on the hand chakras for more support.

A tiny or tightly-closed heart chakra is a sign of heart fatigue, betrayal of the heart, or distrust. Though it seems to be a protective move, the closing of the heart is self-punishing and other-punishing in actuality. A heart that closes in response to heartbreak is a heart that agrees it is unlovable. This heart does not have the background of love or trust to weather the storms of human encounters. It does not believe in fairy tales, it cannot wish for happiness, and it cannot ask for love. It also cannot give love. A closed heart chakra stops growth when it refuses to act as a mediator between the spirit chakras and the body chakras. The closed heart creates more tragedy than it alleviates.

Reopening the heart chakra is as difficult as it is imperative. The requirements are not only foolhardy bravery, but a willingness to let go of long-cherished beliefs about lovelessness. Love exists everywhere, but one has to believe in love before it can be seen or felt. A closed heart chakra doesn't believe in much of anything.

All the slathering devotion in the world, and forty perfect relationships in a row, will mean nothing if the heart and the eyes are closed to love. If both are open, love appears in startling places—in the touch of a child at the supermarket, in the eyes of a neighborhood dog, in the dressing-down from a superior at work, and in the constant intrusions from a family member. Love is a language that requires special awareness; otherwise, it can sound like garbled, meaningless noise.

When I am tempted to close my heart, I repeat this saying to myself: "Love is constant; only the names change." If I sit and think, I see that love of some kind is always available, but that my problem is in craving only romance or undying excitement. I convince myself that there is no love, when in reality, the love available is just uninteresting to me. In those moments of closed-hearted stubbornness, I see that I am listening to love in my own language, instead of listening to the language of love.

Love always provides itself, free for the taking, to people whose fourth chakras are open. All it requires is that the love be *used*, on the self or for others, and not hoarded or hidden. Love requires that the fourth chakra stay open for giving and receiving. You can have numerous love, healing, and spirit/body communication issues rumbling around inside you, but you must keep your heart chakra healthy and open if you are ever going to move forward. Your open heart does not require you to love, heal, trust, or share anything. It must be open, however, if you are going to live a whole life. Go ahead and be as unloving and unlovable as you like, but keep your fourth chakra open and healthy, okay?

If your chakra system is healthy, but your heart is closed down right now, it may have gone off-line for repairs or study. Heart chakras are very susceptible to damage, and sometimes they need to sneak off and take a private vacation. If you are able to stay in your body, and your upper back is flexible and unrestricted, your closed fourth chakra is not a problem. Congratulate your chakra system for being aware enough to perform its own healing, and give each of your other chakras a hello gift. Protect the back and front of your vacationing fourth chakra with at least four specially dedicated Sentries. These Sentries will help your heart maintain its privacy until it is ready to open up again, which should be in a matter of a week at most.

If your heart chakra is still closed after a week, it may need you to strengthen your aura boundary and Sentry system before it will agree to open up again. It may also need you to heal its neighboring chakras so that its mediation work will be easier. Ask your heart what it needs. It will tell you.

TRAITS OF A HEALTHY FOURTH CHAKRA

A healthy heart chakra in a balanced chakra system is a beautiful sight. The heart channels love and acceptance inside the body and out into the world, and the emerald-green energy inside it moves with grace and fluidity. The healthy fourth chakra is available to receive energy and information from the body and the protective third chakra, which it then invests with love and empathy before sending it on to the upper chakras. The heart also heeds and accepts energy and information from the spirit and the communicative fifth chakra, and adds compassion and emotion to it before passing it on to the body chakras.

One of the key signs of a healthy fourth chakra is a loving sense of humor about the self. The healthy heart is dedicated to instinctual self-care; it relies on the intense physical, emotional, intellectual, and protective information of the three body chakras. However, the healthy heart helps to relieve the body chakras' intensities with humor.

The three body chakras exist in an atmosphere of danger and survival during much of their lives, and, as such, don't often get a chance to relax. A healthy heart chakra is able to process the input of these three hyper-vigilant chakras in a less urgent, less survivalistic light. The heart chakra has more of an eagle-eye view than the lower three chakras; it can laugh at yet another intrusion, or more physical and emotional ailments.

The laughter of the heart chakra is not derisive or immolating. It is a warm and knowing laughter that can help the body to gain distance and perspective during trauma. The heart can help to bring a little bit of the spirit's detachment into the body—but not so much that the body's reality is dismissed. It can rub a smashed shin, and yell and laugh and channel healing energy into it, while still being present with the pain. Heart laughter reduces stress in the body by giving the body a healing break from the pain of the present moment. Heart laughter also brings a healing awareness to the upper three chakras; it reminds them that they are responsible for and connected to the body. Without the reality-based support of a functional fourth chakra, the three spirit chakras can go careening off into the blue and leave the body behind.

Sometimes, a physical-world crisis may not look like a crisis at all to the spirit. It may look like an excellent learning experience that will lead to ascendance. Without heart humor to bring it back to Earth, humor that says, "Hello? I live on the planet in real time! I have to eat and sleep and pay the rent!" spirit can leap off cliff after cliff in search of enlightenment. A healthy fourth chakra bestows humor, balance, self-love, acceptance of others, and a good fit between the spirit and body of its owner. It also brings with it an empathy for the self. This allows you to take time off, to create or choose loving environments, to seek out healing touch and healthy relationships, and to listen to your body. A properly cared-for heart chakra creates a beautiful relationship between the body and the spirit, which then creates a beautiful partnership between the emotions and the intellect.

After healing and integrating the whole self, a healthy heart chakra knows enough to heal others appropriately, as opposed to compulsively. It knows how to give without giving it all away.

THE FIFTH (OR THROAT) CHAKRA

This sapphire-blue, expressive chakra sits right above the hollow at the base of the neck, where it processes communication from the spirit and the body, and transmits it to the world. It is associated with the thyroid and the parathyroid glands.

Because of its ability to channel the information of the spirit into real, tangible expression, the fifth chakra is also the center of change and commitment. The health of the fifth chakra relates not only to the level of communication possible at the present moment, but to the capacity for making and upholding change in the inner and outer self. In many cases, illnesses or blockages in the throat and neck, or headaches that originate in the neck, relate to an unwillingness to express oneself and commit to change.

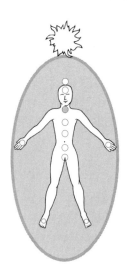

The fifth chakra is also the center of the psychic ability of *clairaudience*, or the ability to hear disembodied voices and messages from the spirit world. Clairaudience is a difficult psychic ability to balance, especially since it is viewed in the Western medical model as a clear precursor of schizophrenia and other psychiatric disorders. Since psychic abilities beyond intuition are unwelcome in the world of medicine, many unfortunate clairaudients are misdiagnosed as schizophrenic and shunted into the world of drugs and institutionalization. Hearing voices is not given even the tiny credence that is lent to seeing visions. Clairaudients are usually offered no support, and no choice but to agree that they are insane and out of control. When placed on drugs that unground them and shoot them out of their bodies, which makes uncontrolled clairaudience more likely, they usually become truly insane.

An unpleasant reality, but it's all a part of life in a society that tries to live without spirit. Life without spirit can't work. Unfortunately, the people who suffer the most are the people who have real, but unprovable, spiritual difficulties, for which there are no readily available answers. Perhaps we, the spiritually educated, can use our fifth-chakra ability to communicate the need for spiritual healing in psychiatric therapy. Perhaps we can change the dreadful legacy of zombiehood and lifelong institutionalization for humans in spiritual distress.

My frustration is that it's a snap to heal a too-open, overly clairaudient fifth chakra. You just close it up a little with your hands, and cover the back and front of it with grounded Sentries, as you renew your grounding and reform your aura. Perhaps this information could be whispered in a few mental hospitals and homeless shelters.

✳

The fifth chakra can sometimes have very distinct energy and color discrepancies between its top and bottom halves. This is due to the often separate channeling duties it provides for the fourth chakra below it, and the sixth chakra above. When the connection between the fourth and the fifth chakras is good, a person can express the needs of the body and the heart with clarity. In this instance, the energy in the lower half of the fifth chakra would be clear-blue and moving well. If the fourth-fifth connection is not good, and the energy in the lower half of the fifth chakra is dark, slow-moving, or deadened, this indicates a person who gives too much and cannot ask for help or nurturing, or speak from the heart.

When the connection between the fifth chakra and the clairvoyant sixth chakra is good, a person can share their intuitions, visions, and discerning abilities. In this instance, the energy in the top half of the fifth chakra will be clear-blue and moving well. If the connection is bad, and clairvoyance is not acceptable in or outside of the self, the top half of the fifth chakra will be dark, slow-moving, or strangely shaped.

The ability to communicate clairvoyant perceptions is generally more acceptable in men, who are often free to bring their clairvoyance into business, if they just call it discernment or horse sense. Women's sixth-chakra energy has been considered somewhat less valid and called intuition, which is just another name for guessing. Women are not usually allowed to be discerning and clairvoyant, therefore, females will oftentimes have completely darkened upper fifth and sixth chakras.

Often, a woman's ability to discern without emotion, which is a sixth chakra function, is invalidated and unused. Her empathic, emotive fourth chakra is often overused as a result, which unbalances her energy system as a whole, and her fifth chakra in particular. Because her heart chakra's empathy hasn't got the balancing support of her sixth chakra's ability to separate, discern, and look at life from above, she may lose her objectivity. This woman's fifth chakra would not be very healthy, stuck as it is between two unwell and conflicting energy centers. Men who run a lot of feminine energy will also exhibit this intuition/discernment imbalance.

Men, or women, who run a lot of masculine energy, will generally exhibit the opposite imbalance, where the unemotional, discerning sixth-chakra ability is overutilized, and the emotive, intuitive, loving qualities of the heart are underutilized. Men are allowed to know things from their clairvoyant sixth chakra, but not to love, connect, and feel things from their heart chakra. This societally approved attitude creates many men with little empathy and human warmth, and eventually a body/spirit split, as their fourth-chakra energy becomes clogged through lack of use. In this imbalance, the fifth chakra can show signs of distress, overwork, and one-sidedness, stuck, as it is, between noncommunicating fourth and sixth chakras.

Balance in both instances comes through healing the chakra system as a whole, and through being careful not to overuse (or ignore) any one chakra's abilities. As previously over-or-under-used chakras stabilize and improve their communication with one another, new and more holistic ways of functioning become possible. The old spirit/body or intellect/emotion splits become unnecessary.

I also see fifth-chakra damage among people with strict religious backgrounds, where individual spiritual knowledge and discovery are frowned upon. In these cases, a controlling image from the church or the parents is usually alive and active in the upper part of the fifth chakra. This controlling image seeks to stop any communication that is different from that of the religious group. It also helps to ensure an inability to change, or to commit to different belief styles. Burn your contracts with these controlling images if you suspect you have agreed to live your spiritual life following an iron-clad study guide.

A segmented, light-and-dark fifth chakra usually points to chakra-system imbalance, especially when an overburdened heart chakra is present. This burden can be due to the shutting off, *or* the overuse, of the heart chakra. When the damaged heart chakra is not available to channel physical-world information to the fifth chakra, or accept spiritual-world information from it, the fifth chakra has to work in halves, if it is going to work at all.

A very bright upper half of the fifth chakra usually means heart-chakra overload. In this situation, the fifth chakra still gathers spirit information from the sixth and seventh chakras, as it is supposed to do. Because it can't reliably off-load to the heart, however, it just tries to keep its upper half clean and working as best it can. In a sense, it kills off the lower part of itself (the heart connection) so that the rest of it (the sixth/seventh chakra connection) can live.

What I find in this instance is a very spiritually attuned person whose heart-love healing or heart-closure creates imbalance. Because the fourth chakra is too busy or blocked to channel physical information to its spirit chakras, there is usually a spirit/body split. This split creates a lack of bodily self-awareness. It makes the body's realities—emotions, money issues, and human relationships—seem unreal and unimportant. Such people are often quite filled with spiritual information, but, without a healthy fifth chakra, they can't channel or use it properly. They are often ill or over- or underweight due to a lack of grounding and safety in their bodies.

In people with a very bright lower half of the fifth chakra, I see psychic energy that pretty much stops at empathy. For whatever reason, these people cannot hear or accept spiritual information. They feel everyone else's pain very deeply, but cannot separate from the world around them, or see a way out of their distress. Overly empathic people do not have the guiding, eagle-eyed support of the three spirit chakras, or the energy to commit themselves to change and growth. This may be caused by an injunction against exploring spirituality in their growing years, or it may be self-created, out of a fear of what might be seen or heard in the spiritual realm.

In many cases, empaths' spirit-body splits occur when they enter into lifestyles that are at cross-purposes to their true path. Detaching from and ignoring their spiritual information allows them to stay in wrong environments with the wrong people. Detaching shuts them off from their spirit chakra's messages, chatter, and commandments, all of which could get them back on their own path again.

I see this spirit/body and fifth-chakra split very often in heart-chakra healers who live in abusive or imprisoning environments. Their sixth-chakra spiritual knowledge, if channeled, would know exactly what was going on and tell them in no uncertain terms to get out. Their sixth chakra might also get them in trouble by channeling itself down into their communicative fifth chakra, which would read the riot act, out loud, to their abusers.

We could go on forever about the causes of chakra deviations without ever healing them and getting on with life. If you have a bright half to your fifth chakra, it's a good thing. It means that your fifth chakra is alive and working to the best of its abilities right now, even if you aren't. Don't obsess about the dark half of your fifth chakra. Just get your entire chakra system into balance, and clean up the connection between the dark half of your fifth chakra and its neighboring chakras. If your fifth chakra has had the energy to keep half of itself working without your help, it won't have any trouble becoming whole when you get your act together. Be aware, however, that getting your act together, with a healthy fifth chakra, can be intimidating. The fifth chakra is about change and commitment. These are two energies that scare most people out of their minds. Change and commitment both require trust in yourself and in the universe.

Changes and commitments made from a fifth-chakra perspective are serious, courageous, life-affirming adventures. If you have dreams of a life purpose very different from your present occupation, your healthy fifth chakra will pull you out of the mud or the clouds. It will help you sign up for classes, or quit your present job and move on. One small look around you will prove that very few people in our society have healthy fifth chakras.

There is very little real support for the kind of self-affirming cliff-jumping the fifth chakra advocates. All sorts of books and television commercials exhort us to be brave and fearless, but precious few friends and business associates would support us in, say, leaving nursing to be a nature photographer, or putting all our assets into a venture providing books to children in the Kalahari. We seem to be able to support fictional or far-removed heroes, but are often unwilling to support change or commitment to true ideals in ourselves or those around us.

My suggestion for supporting your fifth chakra is to seek out and befriend brave, active, and nonconforming people. You may find them in men's and women's groups, in church outreach programs, in the healing arts or local arts council, or out in nature pursuits. You will also find unwell people, egotists, and rabid runaway healers in these same places. Every now and then, however, you'll find a gem of a person in whom love and courage are stronger than excuses. With people like this, you can speak your true feelings and share your dreams. With people like this, your fifth chakra will begin to blossom.

Don't be surprised if these brave people ask you to account for any falseness they see. Fifth-chakra people have almost no patience for whining and lies. They will not be able to support you in remaining in abusive, unhealthy environments or mindsets, no matter how convincing your arguments may be. You'll need to hang out with runaway fourth-chakra healers if you want support in continuing to hurt yourself.

Because a healthy fifth chakra is all about communication, its healing will require you to speak your truth. In general, only people with healthy fifth chakras will be able to hear your heartfelt truth, which is why it is so important to find them as you commit to yourself and your change. Without the human support of other healthy fifth-chakra people, this aspect of your spiritual journey can be an utter fiasco, especially if your life is filled with powerless, excuse-filled, and emotionally controlling people.

To the fearful and unmoving, fifth-chakra energy is jarring. It reminds them that they can change and get out of their rut if they would only commit to themselves. Such commitment means ending blame and excuses. It means accepting total responsibility for their destiny. This is terrifying. Being a victim of other people and of blind chance is a very empowering thing; it removes all personal responsibility. Inside the world of victimhood, people have no responsibility. Bad guys and bad energy control them, and there is nothing to do but give up. It's actually comfortable to see the world in this way, because it means that no action is necessary. Life is simply bad, nobody gets out alive, and if it isn't one thing, it's another.

The fifth chakra doesn't take this view. It sees abusive people and environments for what they are and either tries to change them or leaves them far behind. It doesn't waste precious days and hours in places where no growth occurs. It sees challenges as opportunities, not as life-sentences. It speaks its mind when lies are present (which can make for very uncomfortable social gatherings), and it commits itself to change and growth. This can frighten conservative people. In truth, the commitment of fifth-chakra energy is very unsettling to anyone not doing their work.

Working with your fifth chakra will shake up the psychic fabric around you. If you've forgotten the whole idea of stasis, you may be astonished at the blockages your friends and family can put in your way. They may try to terrify you out of change and movement. They may question and degrade everything you say, and everything to which you commit. Or, you may attempt to do this to yourself in response to old, entrapping messages that flourish in your fifth chakra.

The solution? Use your skills to center and ground yourself, destroy images, burn contracts, and separate from old mindsets. Your healthy and functioning fifth chakra will help you do all this by adding the energy of commitment and dedication to your cleansing and separation work.

When you work with fifth-chakra energy, you may experience throat and neck problems in response to dealing with old fears and contracts. When your body signals blockages in your fifth chakra, it is very healing to place your fingers gently on your throat and say out loud, "I can change, I can change, I can change." This can become a wry, laughter-filled action when you notice which relationships, ideas, or movements make you clear your throat, cough, or suddenly throw your neck out. Some concepts may even make you feel as if you might cough up a hairball. These are the ones that require contract burning. You can change, you can change. . . .

OPEN OR CLOSED FIFTH CHAKRA

A wide-open fifth chakra in an unbalanced chakra system must be resized immediately. Because the fifth chakra is a little-used chakra in our present-day world, it seems to attract unbalanced spiritual attention like crazy. Unbalanced others can co-opt a too-open fifth chakra, causing hearing problems, clairaudience, throat and neck problems, and an inability to communicate effectively.

Our society is in turmoil. It is unable to deal with change, communication, and commitment to higher ideals. You can separate your fifth chakra from the imbalanced society around you, however, and live your own life untainted by toxic beliefs. The fifth chakra, in this instance, should be sized back down to its healthy three-to-five-inch diameter, and covered, front and back, with grounded Sentries.

In a healthy chakra system (with a smooth-functioning heart chakra, and a very clear sixth chakra) *a temporarily open fifth chakra* is a sign that you are opening to new levels of commitment, communication, and awareness. This opening may be accompanied by neck vertebra dislocations, or a cleansing, coughing, sneezing, mucus-filled cold. In this case, place grounded Sentries at the front and back of your open fifth chakra, and see your acupuncturist, chiropractor, or massage therapist for support in clearing blockages from your body. Do not suppress your symptoms. Doing so may close your fifth chakra prematurely.

Your fifth chakra should size itself back to normal within a week or so. If it doesn't, perform a full chakra reading to ascertain whether you should resize it, or let it remain open for a few more days. Because it is the center of communication, it will have no problem in letting you know how it wants to look and what it needs to do.

A *closed fifth chakra* in an unhealthy or unbalanced chakra system is a sign of unwillingness to grow, change, listen, communicate, or be connected to spirit. This closing can occur in response to fear (especially the fear of clairaudience), or with a kind of "No one can tell me what to do!" temper-tantrum energy. There's nothing as stubborn as a person with a stubborn fifth chakra. They commit themselves to doing nothing with an energy that almost fools them into thinking they are doing their work! They usually have chronic neck or throat blockages that accessorize their chronic life blockages nicely.

Closed-fifth-chakra people are, by far, the hardest people to work with. They go a certain distance in their growth, and then trash themselves and anyone who tries to help them. Like the fifth-chakra energy they try so hard to squelch, they are focused, communicative, and committed, but unfortunately, only when it comes to protecting their position. For a person with a clogged, closed-off fifth chakra, that position is usually illness, obstruction, and justification.

I have seen suicidal people with blockages of all kinds, most of which can be released through emotional channeling.

However, I can spot a closed-fifth suicidal rage by one determining factor: the person will fight like crazy for their pain. They will actually yell and stomp off if anyone suggests that they could feel other feelings, or live life another way. They will defend their suicidal urges as a lioness would protect her cub. People with closed fifth chakras are unbelievably defensive. This stubborn temper-tantrum energy usually brings out the fifth-chakra energy of others. Confrontations ensue. Because fifth chakras can get right to the meaty center of any issue, things get pretty pointed and uncomfortable. Fifth-chakra fights can be startling in their unblinking truth, but sometimes, such fights are needed to clear out all the rubbish that builds up around a closed fifth chakra.

If your fifth chakra is closed, you can break up the blockages by sitting down and listening to yourself. Your confusion and stasis come from closing off your ability to hear. If you commit to listening to yourself, your fifth chakra will begin to come into consciousness. In a balanced chakra system, confusion occurs only rarely, because fifth-chakra energy channels spiritual truth, physical knowledge, and a commitment to balance and self-nurturance. When you are closed off, and you cannot use these fifth-chakra attributes, confusion reigns. The way to stop the confusion, besides having someone yell at you, is to sit and listen to yourself as you heal your chakras.

The constant turmoil in your life is not natural, nor is it necessary. Indeed, it is unnatural and unnecessary. Pain, drama, and turmoil are a part of life, but not the be-all and end-all of existence. You can lighten up and let your defenses and justifications go. You can live as you wish to live, and you can connect to your dreams and hopes. You can move on from limiting environments, and you can change your health picture, or at least your outlook about your health. You can dream of accomplishments and plan to change your career, and you can imagine a healing love life. You can create meaning that is specific to you, even if the world around you is meaningless. Your open fifth chakra will help you do all of this and more. These are not silly ideals.

It is a good idea to hang out with the healthy-fifth-chakra people I wrote about a few pages back if you want support in strengthening your ability to hear, speak, change, and commit to your life. These people are truly alive. They see the ugliness of life, but they don't let it stop them from creating their own meaning. They say, "Sure, life sucks, everyone blames everyone else, evil is real, and mosquitoes won't go away—but I have this really good idea for solar cars, or a wish to travel and teach, or a need to play music, so I'm going to be happy in spite of it all." People with healthy, open fifth chakras aren't happy idiots who live in a dream world. They are active, aware, and caring members of society who have fun because they live their dreams every day.

I am going to tell you this once again: you may feel free to have issues with communication, commitment, and change, but don't hurt your fifth chakra in the process. If you shut it down, you will find yourself incredibly stuck in a very short, yet excruciating, period of time. Go ahead and be as stubborn as you like, but let your fifth chakra live its life unmolested by you or anyone else.

As with any other chakra, *the fifth can close itself off and take a vacation* when the other chakras are healthy enough to let it do so. If your other chakras are up and working, and your neck, throat, and ears are clear and healthy even though your fifth chakra is closed, congratulations! You can support your fifth chakra's vacation by placing a congratulatory hello gift in front of each of your open chakras, and by placing a protective Sentry in front and in back of your closed fifth chakra. This chakra should come back on line in a week or so. If it doesn't, ask it what it needs in order to open up. Usually, your fifth chakra will require a new aura, Sentry, and grounding system to keep it safe from entrapping energies, as well as your commitment to listen to and act upon its information. Good luck.

TRAITS OF A HEALTHY FIFTH CHAKRA

People with healthy fifth chakras often say the strangest things, or hear the strangest truths in mundane conversations. Their communicative skills are highly attuned, and, even if they do not call themselves psychic, they usually are. Fifth-chakra people have a very active awareness that makes them good, communicative healers, speakers, or therapists. They are also very reliable, because, when they make a commitment, they follow through. Unlike a heart-chakra person who may commit beyond fatigue and reason, a fifth-chakra person will commit only to those things that resonate deeply for them.

Fifth-chakra people may be hard to keep up with. They may even look flaky to some, because they commit to things wholeheartedly, then leave when their commitments do not provide service, healing, or meaning. They do not leave people in the lurch, but they do follow the dictates of their own internal knowledge, which is unlike anyone else's.

Being in the life of a fifth-chakra person can be exhausting, if you try to keep up with them. But keeping up is not the point. If you tried to commit to their commitments, or believe in their beliefs, you'd be off your own path in a matter of hours. The best way to live with a fifth-chakra person is to get your own fifth chakra in shape, and to find your own dreams and beliefs with their loving (if unorthodox) support and example.

Fifth-chakra people are very insightful and supportive if you want to hear the truth—but very annoying and rude if you don't. In living with or relating to them, you must be willing to hear the truth, to speak the truth, and to live your truth. Otherwise, it's going to be a bumpy, lonely ride. If you have a fifth-chakra person in your life, stop resisting them. Bless them. They, more than anyone else (besides you, your guides, and God), will keep you honest and on your path. Let them in. They need your friendship and your love.

THE SIXTH
(OR THIRD EYE) CHAKRA

This brilliant indigo-colored, receptive chakra sits right in the center of the forehead, between the eyebrows and the hairline. It is associated with the pituitary gland. The sixth chakra is the center of *clairvoyance*, or the ability to receive energy vibrations visually. When people contact you psychically, the clairvoyant sixth chakra is often the first chakra alerted. It is usually very active and lively. The sixth chakra is also the center of discernment, unemotional judgment, and the higher brain functions of learning and information processing and retrieval.

Sixth-chakra energy confers a focused consciousness that blends nicely with the grounded, emotive, protective, empathic, and communicative chakra energies below

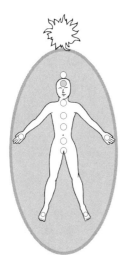

it. With the support of a healthy sixth chakra, you'll have a certainty about yourself, your path, and the needs of others. This certainty can seem cold and detached to unaware people, or to people too heavily dependent on heart-chakra attributes. Sixth chakras see things as they are—not as they pretend to be, not as they would like to be, but as they are.

Your healthy, aware sixth chakra helps you make decisions based on facts instead of hope. The sixth chakra's unemotional certainty, coupled with the decisive, committed communication and action of the healthy fifth chakra, can be unsettling to people who prefer excuses over action.

When the heart chakra looks at the pain of others or the self, it moves to empathy, care, love, and healing from a personal standpoint. The heart understands and empathizes with pain, and has limitless emotional patience. The sixth chakra looks at the pain of others or the self from a different viewpoint, seeing not just the pain, but the issues behind the pain. It sees the level of comfort the pain provides, and the length of time the pain has been allowed to be present. It sees how the pain generates the attention of family and friends, and how much work has been done to process the pain. It also questions the willingness to release the pain and move on to something else. The sixth chakra regularly asks questions that the emotive fourth chakra would consider jarring, unsupportive, or unloving.

In this time of victim consciousness and inner-child work, which is all from third- and fourth-chakra awareness, the emotionless, truth-seeking mission of the sixth chakra is not supported, courted, or appreciated. Sixth-chakra energy can be annoying and even threatening to people who need to maintain their victim status in response to their childhood traumas, or in the face of their less-than-healthy adult choices. Sixth-chakra energy has very little patience with victim consciousness.

In response, most people shut off their own sixth chakras so they don't have to know the truth—about themselves, or about the people they allow into their lives. Shutting off the sixth chakra also obscures information about true life path and purpose. People with closed sixth chakras don't have to think about their work and relationship responsibilities either. This can make for a rather relaxing time, because shutting down the questing, truth-at-all-costs sixth chakra can provide a little bit of peace and quiet.

The problem with shutting down the sixth chakra is that it also holds the ability to discern properly in everyday situations, and to process and qualify the information coming into the brain. People whose sixth chakras have been shuttered for a period of months or years tend not to have a clue, not just about the big spiritual questions, but about mundane things as well.

They choose strange relationships, and go-nowhere jobs. They don't know what they want to do, or how they feel about things. They move from place to place and from idea to idea, with no logical thread. They don't have tangible dreams of purpose, or even of a better life. They often have a number of brain dysfunctions to go along with their dysfunctional lives. People with closed sixth chakras may be forgetful and undependable. They may have difficulties processing information. They may have trouble reading or writing, and they may experience sudden thought-or-word loss and periodic stuttering, all of which will diminish when their sixth chakra is up and running again.

✳

Reopening the sixth chakra requires personal bravery. When the sixth chakra has been closed for a period of time, one tends to career off-path. When it re-opens, it immediately asks the hard questions: "What are we doing here? Why does our body look and feel like this? What happened to our art and our dreams? Who are all these strange people, and *what the hell* is going on here?" If you have no excuses, explanations, or answers, congratulate yourself. It means you're on your way home.

The beautiful thing (or the horrible thing, depending on your attitude) about sixth-chakra questions is that they require no answer—only acceptance, processing, and action. Sixth-chakra questions and remarks often leave people dumbfounded and speechless. The sixth may look at a searing pain in someone's arm or low back and ask, "When did you first want to strangle your mother?" or, "How many people rely on you to do all their emotional work for them?"

The information from the sixth chakra is often startling, yet it provides a strange comfort in its own way, because it sees through all nonsense. If you like your nonsense more than your health, you won't want sixth-chakra energy in yourself or anyone around you. If you are committed to your health and happiness, no matter what, sixth-chakra energy will be your new best friend.

OPEN OR CLOSED SIXTH CHAKRA

A wide open (anything larger than five inches in diameter) sixth chakra in an unbalanced chakra system can cause myriad problems, from an onslaught of visions and vivid dreams, to a brain full of racing and contradictory thoughts. Wide-open sixth chakras can also bring so much energy into the brain that its synapses fire wildly in response, creating tics, shooting pains, migraines, and seizures. The eyes can also become blurry, tired, or allergic when too much uncontrolled energy is present in the sixth chakra. A wide-open sixth can also make the room in your head jangly and uninhabitable.

Usually, the sixth chakra will open too wide when other chakras are off-kilter. When the second chakra is uncentered and sponging energy from others, the sixth will often open to provide discerning energy to the essentially nondiscerning second chakra. Sponging is so ungrounding, however, that the sixth chakra will soon be off-kilter as well.

When the third chakra is not protecting the aura and the body, the sixth will open wide. It will try to work as a psychic first-defense system by clairvoyantly deciding who is safe and who is not. Without the protection of the third chakra, however, the sixth will often get smacked and blasted by people who would rather not be looked at quite so closely.

When the fourth chakra is pouring all the heart energy out of the body in runaway healing, the sixth will often open wide to provide the same discernment it offers to a sponge-happy second. Since the heart is unavailable to connect body and spirit, the entire system soon becomes unstable and ungrounded. In addition, the unhealthy heart will often fight the sixth chakra for dominance (my healing is better than yours!), which squashes the poor fifth chakra between two warring nations.

As I write this, I want to remind you that your chakras are symbols of your awareness, and that your awareness directs their actions. If you've got a war between your fourth and sixth chakras, you have personally created a conflict between your empathic abilities and your discerning abilities. Your chakras are only illuminating this conflict for you, not acting as free agents. They are following your lead. You can heal them and regain control of all your previously warring aspects. When you do, your healthy chakra system will support you, as much as it can, in maintaining your new balance.

Close an unbalanced and open sixth chakra as soon as you can, and perform a complete chakra system healing. With an open sixth chakra, you can expect to see imbalances throughout your system. Thank your sixth chakra for trying to keep you alive in spite of yourself. Also, remember that your sixth chakra is often a first-contact chakra for psychic communication. People will very often try to tune into your sixth chakra in order to get to know you, or to get information from you.

If your sixth chakra is wide open, unprotected, and existing in an unbalanced chakra system, these psychic contacts can be very disconcerting. You may have frontal-lobe headaches, visions, trouble concentrating or thinking, and trouble sleeping, because so much foreign energy is inside your sixth chakra. Cover your sixth chakra, even after you perform a complete chakra system healing, with at least six or seven grounded Sentries, front and back. This will help your sixth chakra to remain centered when previously welcome people and energy come knocking again. The special gift facial technique (see page 110) taught in the section on Advanced Techniques will be very helpful in pulling energy off the face, the eyes, and out of the sixth chakra. Try it.

In a healthy, grounded chakra system, the sixth chakra will open to accept new information about your life path and your intuitive abilities. The sixth will also open to allow a spiritual healing of brain and vision dysfunctions. I suggest that you watch a healthy, wide-open sixth chakra carefully from the room in your head. Even in a robust system, a wide-open sixth chakra can attract too much attention from the psychic fabric around you. The healthy opening of the sixth chakra is a very exciting and evolutionary process that your friends and family may want to share with you. Though they all mean well, their attention and focus can affect you, spiritually and physically.

Because the sixth chakra is directly inside the brain, its energy-attracting openness can affect not only your clairvoyant abilities, but your thought-processing abilities as well. I would allow it to stay wide open for two to three days at the very most, unless you have a hermitage available. If you do not have a place where you can have long stretches of peace and solitude, resize it within three days. Use your hands to mold it into its normal three-to-five-inch diameter, or envision it closing as a camera shutter does.

If you have a peaceful, solitary place to stay, go there and let your sixth stay open for a week or so. Without a barrage of people around you, it will be safer to be a totally open and receptive clairvoyant. In either case, place a protective Sentry in front of each of your chakras, and at least six grounded Sentries directly in front and in back of your sixth, until you get it back to size.

A *closed sixth chakra* in an unbalanced system is a sign of closing off the clairvoyant spiritual information, and the more normal discerning, processing intelligence. As you can imagine, this makes a conscious life nearly impossible. It does, however, make an unconsciously suicidal, off-path life more bearable. For a while.

This is my open sixth chakra talking: Any path that is not your own is dangerous to you. Any relationship, job, choice, or idea that does not feed you eats off of you. Happiness can only come when you are truly and unashamedly yourself. You must live your life as yourself and stop making excuses, or you will live and die in pain that has no meaning.

Ouch! My empathic fourth chakra is going crazy over that one! It's doing back flips to make allowances for all the off-path and de-selfed positions we have to take every day. But my sixth chakra sticks by its information.

This is an interesting example of the kind of communication that goes on in a connected chakra system. As each chakra wakes up, its information is added to the whole. Sometimes the information makes sense to the other chakras, sometimes it doesn't. Our job is to balance the system in the midst of what may seem to be conflicting information.

In truth, the fourth and the sixth chakras are doing the same work. The fourth chakra is not less-evolved, or less intelligent. It knows that the unflinching information of the sixth is true, but, from the almost-body, almost-spirit position it inhabits, it can see physical reality, which is not as cut-and-dried as spiritual reality. It sees the pain humans go through in trying to become whole, and it has empathy for that struggle. The fourth sees where humans are heading, which is toward spiritual certainty, but it also knows the difficult reality of life on this planet. It has more patience than the spirit-centered sixth chakra.

When the fourth and sixth chakras can communicate freely (through a healthy, unsegmented fifth chakra), the fourth will spend less time making excuses for off-path behavior. The sixth will then lighten up and offer guidance in a more gentle way. This balance can only be achieved if the sixth is allowed to open up and live again.

At first, the communication from a previously shut-off sixth chakra will be somewhat strident. With frequent healings and work with the grounding cord, the aura, and the separation tools, however, it will attain a place of balance within the whole.

Here is the sixth-chakra message above from a more balanced perspective: Any path that is not your own can be dangerous if you forget who you are, but all paths have meaning and lessons if you remain aware. Any relationship, job, choice, or idea that does not feed you eats off of you, and sometimes, what is eaten lightens your load and frees you for the next step in your journey. Happiness can only come when you are truly and unashamedly yourself, which takes time, support, study, trust, and love. You must live your life as yourself and stop making excuses, for yourself or anyone else, or you will die without ever having lived.

✳

Opening the sixth chakra after a period of darkness may require a few days off from your life and responsibilities. Successfully opening the sixth chakra may also require you to change that life and amend those responsibilities. The support of healthy-fifth-chakra people may be needed, because this is not a fun process to follow all by yourself. You may require people around you who honor dreams, individuality, and spiritual purpose. If you cannot find such people in your life, visit a book store or a library. Let your sixth chakra choose some supportive and empowering books on healing, career changes, conscious relationships, religious or spiritual teachings, and love. Don't pick up any victim-consciousness books, though. Your sixth chakra will become grumpy if you try to wallow in helplessness and blame right now.

Your sixth chakra likes to look inside and ahead of you, at your heart, your dreams, and your connection to God. It does not like to spend its time outside and behind you with perpetrators, past injuries, and old stories. Open your sixth chakra and point it at yourself. Let it help to lead you back home.

As with any other chakra, *the healthy sixth can close off and take a vacation* when the chakra system as a whole is in balance. A closed sixth chakra in a healthy system also signals a fairly healthy exterior life. Because the sixth is so vigilant and responsible (bossy, even), it won't usually close off if there is any possibility of danger in your environment. When you find a closed sixth in a healthy chakra system, congratulate not only your other chakras, but yourself as well. You've placed yourself in a supportive, conscious, and healing environment. You've been doing your work!

You can tell that your sixth chakra is taking a healthy vacation by the condition of your other chakras, and specifically by the health of the upper portion of your fifth chakra, which should be bright blue and moving well. You will also be free of headaches, eyestrain and confusion, and you will be able to stay in the room in your head, even though your sixth chakra is closed for now. Your sixth chakra will close when it needs to review its information, reconnect with the pure spiritual information of the seventh chakra, or remove contracts and old clairvoyant relating patterns that unground the body.

While your sixth chakra is healing itself, please give each of your other chakras and yourself a congratulatory hello gift, and cover your aura with a blanket of strongly grounded Sentries. Place a grounded Sentry in front and in back of your sixth chakra, and let it stay closed for up to a week if it likes. Because it is so vigilant and responsible, your sixth chakra will not usually stay closed for more than a few days. If your life is safe enough, however, it may be able to stay closed for a longer period.

To support your vacationing sixth chakra, stay in the room in your head and keep an eye on it until the week is up. If it has not re-opened by the end of the seventh day, ask it what it needs from you. It may require a material change in your life, the release of certain relationships, a dedication to specific goals, or a strengthening of your separation skills. Be prepared. When your sixth chakra re-opens for business, your life will be excitingly different.

TRAITS OF A HEALTHY SIXTH CHAKRA

People with active sixth chakras have access to amazing amounts of information. If their sixth chakra is active in response to the inactivity of their other chakras, the information will often be about other people and other events. If their sixth chakra is a part of a healthy, active, and balanced chakra system, the information will refer more specifically to themselves, their health and wellness, and their own life path.

This is an important distinction. Many gifted psychics have extremely active sixth chakras that allow them to access information about and for their clients. These same psychics often need tremendous support in order to keep their own lives on track. Like runaway fourth-chakra healers who cannot make time for themselves, runaway sixth-chakra clairvoyants cannot find truth for themselves. All their clairvoyant energy is used on and for others. In a healthy chakra system, sixth-chakra energy is honored, protected, and used primarily on and for the self, so it's easy to stay on track and on path.

When people have a healthy and balanced sixth chakra, they are naturally clairvoyant, which means that their clairvoyance is not flamboyant and dramatic. Natural clairvoyants don't see lotto numbers and plane crashes in the Andes; they see things that are useful in their own lives. They find antique truck parts for their friends, or vital information at a strange bookstore in a strange town. Healthy clairvoyance is just as magical and inexplicable as the more lurid or thrilling clairvoyance of famous psychics, but, because it has more to do with quiet, inner reality, it gets less attention.

A healthy clairvoyant does not have a lot of unanswered questions, or a deep need for money, fame, and external security. The very act of being on path, whatever that path is, creates support and comfort for healthy clairvoyants, even if it doesn't look that way from the outside. Their paths may take them into unfamiliar areas: into poverty, into conflicts, or away from everything that is familiar, but still they feel secure.

The life paths of healthy sixth-chakra people are clear, though difficult. They are able to find support for their paths in unusual ways that seem perfectly normal to them. They are able to process lessons and information with ease and speed, and they are often treasured counsellors for people who want to live spiritually attuned lives. Sixth-chakra people are often separate from the people around them—just as sixth-chakra energy is separate from our everyday world. If the fact of their uniqueness does not separate these people from the masses, their blinding honesty usually will. They can find true comradeship only with other healthy sixth-chakra people. In the company of unbalanced or less attuned people, they will always be separate—treasured, perhaps, but separate nevertheless.

If you are fortunate enough to have balanced sixth-chakra people in your life, love them, include them in your life, and soon you will see that they are not strange or otherworldly. They are just doing their work. So can you.

THE SEVENTH (OR CROWN) CHAKRA

This purple/violet-colored, expressive chakra sits above the very top of the head, almost floating over the body. It is the only central chakra that is outside of the body. The seventh chakra is the center of our bodily connection to pure spiritual energy and information, whether that be our own higher spiritual energy, the energy and information of our spirit guides and angels, the energy of other, unrelated beings not currently in bodies, or the energy and information of God. The seventh chakra is associated with the pineal gland.

The seventh chakra contains the blueprint (or violetprint, in this case) of spiritual purpose we agreed upon before we en-

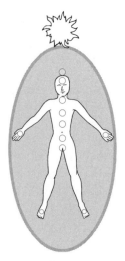

tered our bodies and our usually confusing and unspiritual lives. Because so much of our lives is spent in confusion between spirit and body, pure seventh-chakra energy is often ignored, shut off, corded, squashed, and damaged. If you think it's hard to live from the pure commitment of the fifth chakra, or from the pure knowledge of the sixth chakra in this world of trivia and violence, you ain't seen nothing yet. The seventh chakra contains absolute certainty and absolute purpose. It is pure spirit. And living from the seventh chakra on this planet can be pure hell.

The seventh chakra, because it is not centered inside the body, has very little connection to the mundane aspects of real life. Though its information on direction, purpose, spiritual journeys, soul mates, and right livelihood is vital, the seventh chakra speaks from a place little understood by 98 percent of the humans on this planet. It is as if the seventh chakra speaks a dead language that only scholars can interpret. In an unbalanced chakra system, it doesn't even speak of the time-space continuum. Its spiritual information, though often valid, will have no real application to a human who needs to know *when* to make a move, *how* to get there, *where* to get the money, and *who* to contact.

In a very balanced and aware chakra system, the information from the seventh can be filtered and communicated to the body through the intellectual sixth, the communicative fifth, and the empathic heart, but even then, its information is often strange and otherworldly. When the chakras are balanced and active, and the energy body is grounded, cleaned out, and centered inside a protected aura, the information from the seventh chakra provides clear (but not always comforting) direction.

When the energy is balanced after a long, confused, abuse-filled fallow period, the information from the seventh chakra can be terrifying. The seventh chakra knows with certainty that much work must be done to get back to the correct path. This path is very often out of reach for people who have been living in abuse and despair. You may be living in the Midwest with four children and an abusive spouse when your seventh chakra points out that your true destiny lies in Cambodia, or in an alternative doctoral program. It's easy to see why seventh-chakra information is generally ignored on this planet. It's just not practical.

Here's a strident message from my seventh chakra: Not *practical*? Is it practical to incarnate with a specific life purpose, only to forget it once puberty hits? Is it practical to stay on Earth plane for ten to twenty lifetimes because you keep forgetting why you came to Earth in the first place? Is it practical to scrabble around like a little pack rat, gathering this pointless item or that pointless experience, instead of living to the limit of your being and your essence?

All beings have purpose and meaning, and the ability to heal themselves and their particular portion of the world, but no one seems to care. Seventh-chakra energy encourages the study of Chinese medicine or homeopathy, and is answered with excuses about finances, time, and logistics, while people who don't need to live and die in pain do so by the thousands.

Seventh-chakra energy advocates the creation of art and music, but is rebuffed with lame excuses about the lack of talent, courage, or finances, while children's minds and hearts lie fallow and the majesty of art is used for vodka ads. It exhorts people to reach out to one another, but is squelched while people die alone of "unacceptable" diseases, or live out their poverty, retardation, psychiatric distress, or old age in places no sane or practical person would ever call a home.

Seventh-chakra information is not impractical. The people on this planet are impractical, precisely because this spiritual information is dishonored. For every problem on this planet, spirit has placed ten thousand living people who are able to help—ten thousand individuals who have a specific, practical part in healing the difficulties of Earth, and in helping the humans, animals, plants, and mineral beings who live here. Do even 10 percent of these ten thousand people help, or do they surround themselves with ten thousand excuses about how hard everything is? Do they even recycle their *garbage*, for Spirit's sake? No. They just recycle their excuses, and say that spirituality is impractical, while the beautiful Earth struggles under the killing weight of all their practicality. End of sermon.

OPEN OR CLOSED SEVENTH CHAKRA

A very open (anything larger than five inches in diameter) seventh chakra in an unbalanced system is often a sign of a spirit gasping for air in a very unspiritual life. When the seventh is wide open, its owner is often seeking tremendous support from the spiritual plane in order to survive an ungrounded, unprotected daily life. In such a case, the body/spirit skew is often extreme.

The first order of business when the seventh chakra is wide open and overburdened is to create a room in the head that is grounded and securely anchored. In cases of seventh-chakra malfunction, I often see floating rooms, rooms with no walls or ceiling, or hazy and indistinct rooms that cannot be used. These must be dealt with immediately. Though grounding the body is just as important as keeping a usable room in the head, a very open seventh chakra tends to keep people out of their bodies completely, which makes grounding impossible. Getting the attention into the head is an easier first step than grounding in these instances, because it centers awareness fairly close to the seventh chakra. When the room in the head can be used and grounded, the spirit tends to settle itself back into the body, so that first- or foot-chakra grounding is possible.

Closing up a wide-open seventh chakra requires that you wake up the rest of the chakras, specifically the body-centered lower three. You may need to start over at the beginning of this book, or perform a complete chakra reading/healing. A wide-open seventh chakra needs complete attention, because it can create difficulties with grounding and living in the body.

A wide-open seventh in an unbalanced chakra system is as serious a call for help as a kundalini rush from an unbalanced first chakra. A wide-open first chakra is a defense system for the body that ensures survival in the face of danger. A wide-open seventh chakra is a defense system for the spirit that ensures survival in the face of an anti-spiritual life. Heal this chakra and you can get back to the work of living your life.

In a healthy and balanced chakra system, especially one where the heart fosters an excellent connection between body and spirit, *the seventh chakra will open up* in order to renew and rededicate its connection to the spiritual realm and God. In some cases, it will open to collect new orders when life purpose has been achieved and it is not yet time for the body to die, or when life-and-lesson contracts have been burnt sufficiently to allow new information to flow down from the overseeing eighth chakra. When the seventh chakra opens, it always signals exciting new direction, information, and purpose. Get ready!

When your seventh chakra is open, remember to protect it and all your other chakras with grounded Sentries, front and back. Close this chakra by the end of a week, unless it specifically asks to stay open for a longer period of time. If your chakra system is balanced, your seventh chakra will know what physical time means, and it will be able to tell you when it will return to its normal size. Protect it while it's open, and use this time to get your daily life in order. You may soon have new travel plans.

A tightly closed or very small (anything smaller than three inches in diameter) *seventh chakra* in an unbalanced chakra system is a sign of a refusal to listen to spirit, to believe in the spiritual world, or to communicate with God. Closed and damaged seventh chakras are very common these days, especially among intellectuals, religionists, and cult members. In the latter two cases, seventh-chakra damage comes from without, from an often punishing or closed-minded experience of God. The chakra damage usually involves controlling images or contracts from church or cult leaders.

In the case of intellectuals, the damage to the seventh chakra comes from within, from an unwillingness to fall for the supposed idiocy of blind faith. Intellectual groups such as collegiate or atheistic societies can make contracts with the seventh chakras of their members to assure that nothing but the prescribed and agreed-upon information gets through. Burn those contracts.

When the seventh chakra is closed, life becomes a temporal experience—an experience of the five senses only. The intuitive skills of the other chakras become dull, average, and unmagical. The sixth chakra's clairvoyance becomes horse sense, discernment, and plain old lucky guessing. The fifth chakra's clairaudience becomes a little birdie, or common sense. Everything becomes commonplace, rational, explainable, and tedious. Wonderful experiences of spiritual synchronicity are seen as coincidences, or examples of random chance. Healing pilgrimages to Lourdes are seen as prime examples of mass hysteria. Every bit of magic or divine talent is brought down to the mundane level of human understanding, or the understanding agreed upon by one's church or group.

Opening the seventh chakra in the face of group pressure or intellectual prejudice requires courage, but it also requires a certain silliness. In the early stages of opening, it may even require that you see every common thing as magical, whereas before, every magical thing was seen as commonplace. When you walk, you may see the movement of your body as magical (How does your foot know to move itself?). When you eat, you may see the transfer from matter to energy as magical (How do your cells know to break your dinner into nutrients?). Your television and car and computer become absolute wonders undreamed of just one hundred years ago. Powerful emperors of the not-so-distant past would have given everything to have your clean running water and the use of your toilet on special ceremonial occasions! Think about it!

This world, every second of every day, is magical, spiritual, and inexplicably complex. We think religion and intellect can bring the whole planet into some sort of rational order, but they can't. If you've ever met a true holy person, or a real genius, you know that they are absolutely filled with childlike wonder and millions of unanswerable questions. Top-level scientists and religious leaders can explain a lot, but they know that they can't possibly explain it all. They don't even want to, because they're too busy exploring, testing, asking, experiencing, and living to presume to know the whole story of the universe, or the whole mind of God. Those of vast intellect and spirituality are not separate from simple magic and wonders. Nor should any of us be.

If your seventh chakra is closed off for any reason, you may long for rationality, but closing off is not the way to find it. Rationality requires meaning, connection, and purpose, or the facts, figures, and information gathered rationally will never gel into anything. Even fourth-rate scientists know that, without a working theory, experimentation and fact-finding are useless. When you close (or allow any group to close) your seventh chakra, you sever your access to the meaning, connection, and purpose of your spirit. Any fact-finding endeavor undertaken with a closed seventh chakra, especially one that attempts to

explain the meaning of life or God, will have no meaning. It will
have no rational construct. Each of us can only find the meaning
of life, and the love of God, through the channel set up specifically for that purpose. That channel is our own working seventh
chakra.

I am not in any way saying that religions and intellectual pursuits are wrong, or even damaging. Right now, we are talking
specifically about an injured chakra. When the seventh chakra is
open and healthy, religious study and group pursuits have their
healing place. There is nothing intrinsically wrong with group
experience, unless the group requires seventh-chakra damage in
order to remain a cohesive unit. If group communication or any
relationship requires chakras or auras or personalities to be damaged or truncated, they're bad. If not, they're good. You can figure the rest out for yourself.

Though your seventh chakra's spiritual path and information
may not look right at a dinner party or church social, and may
not be scientifically provable, they may be completely rational to
you. Only your own spiritual information will work in your life,
although sometimes the teachings of Jesus or Buddha or
Whomever will strike a very deep note in your healthy spirit.
Follow that music, keep all your chakras open and healthy, and
listen.

In a healthy chakra system, the seventh chakra will close if it needs
to shake off its dust and any old controlling messages or contracts. You can identify a healthy-seventh-chakra vacation by the
health of all the other chakras, especially the body/spirit-
connecting fourth, and the clairvoyant sixth. You will also have a
lack of tension in your skull, you'll be able to stay in the room in
your head, and your aura and grounding cord will be strong and
whole, even though your seventh chakra is currently closed.
Give each of your chakras a congratulatory hello gift for doing
such a good job that the seventh can take a rest. Place at least
seven strongly grounded Sentries in front and in back of your
seventh chakra as protection. You may allow your seventh to stay
closed for up to a week. If it wants to stay off-line for a longer
period of time, ask it why.

Your seventh chakra will often need you to go through and examine your spiritual beliefs to see what fits and what doesn't. It is helpful, at this point, to burn a number of contracts with your spiritual or religious beliefs. After you perform a spiritual housecleaning, check in with your seventh chakra once again, and see if it is willing to open. If not, you may also need to strengthen the upper portion of your aura. Place a number of grounded Sentries in front of your seventh chakra as protection against invalid belief systems.

When any chakra refuses to open back up, it can be a sign that someone in your life is still contractually connected to it. Sit and listen to your cautiously closed, yet healthy seventh chakra. Perform a complete chakra healing, and burn that contract!

TRAITS OF A HEALTHY SEVENTH CHAKRA

The seventh chakra contains the specific life purpose, spiritual path, healing information, and God-connection for each being. When seventh-chakra energy is allowed to flow, the highest level of spiritual knowledge, which is the knowledge of the self, is reached. When you truly know and honor yourself, honor is conferred on all nearby. Honor is given to life and to God. Honor is accorded to thoughts and to emotions, in their own time and in their own languages. The body and its needs are honored, and all parts of life are accepted as intrinsic to spiritual purpose.

When the seventh chakra is open in an unbalanced system, its energy can separate individuals from normal human interactions, but when it is open in a healthy and nonskewed system, it makes one very much a part of life. Healthy seventh-chakra people can work, have money and children, drive a car, and eat, all while maintaining a spiritual path. They live in the world and in their bodies, but they maintain constant consciousness while they do so. They have difficulties, because this is a difficult planet to live on. They get grumpy, they get sick, they stomp and whine, but they stay on path, and they keep doing their work. They make wonderful friends and lovers for people who want to do their own work, but, because their very presence tends to shake up the psychic fabric around them, they often spend their lives alone.

In a balanced seventh-chakra person, we see conflicting thoughts, strong emotions, healthy sexuality, a sense of humor, strong intuitive abilities, silliness, and divinity. In an unbalanced-seventh-chakra person, we would often see only the intuitive abilities and the divinity. This lack of balance trips over itself eventually, but usually only after hundreds or thousands of followers try to live the unbalanced life themselves, while their leader decays in some dramatic way.

You see, it's all about balance. Seventh-chakra energy is very important, but if you try to have it all by itself, without the support of all the other chakra energies, you'll get into ungrounded, unsafe, inhuman trouble.

While you live in a body, you have real-time, real-life work to do. This work requires the support of all your skills, all your awareness, and all your chakras. The addition of healthy seventh-chakra energy in a healthy, imperfect human body will make your real work beautiful, meaningful, funny, and possible. You will be spiritual *and* human. It can be done.

THE EIGHTH
(OR GOLD SUN) CHAKRA

Your eighth chakra is a golden, Sun-like energy center located above and outside of your aura. The Gold Sun chakra is not so much a gauge or container of specific abilities as it is an energy resource. Its function is to oversee the energies in your aura and your life. Your Gold Sun oversees all of your aspects, which include your spiritual, mental, and emotional bodies, your physical body, your past, your present, and your future.

The eighth chakra and the first chakra are not associated with any particular gland. Instead, the eighth chakra acts, in cooperation with the first chakra, as the spiritual or cosmic energy regulator of the endocrine system. The first and eighth chakras function as energetic "bookends" of the endocrine system. The eighth chakra provides clean and neutral energy to the glandular system, energy which is stored in, and regulated by, the first chakra. If the first chakra is damaged, or the Gold Sun energy is not accessed, the chakric and endocrine systems may fall into imbalance. See the Troubleshooting Guide for information on endocrine imbalance (page 269).

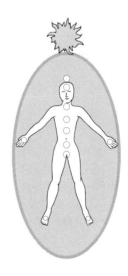

Your Gold Sun's specific function is to cleanse and redirect energy. It acts as a beacon for your own energy, which it cleanses of any attachments before making it available to you. Your Gold Sun also sorts the foreign energy you have picked up in images, messages, and contracts. It can identify and cleanse foreign energy, if you take responsibility and ground the energy out of you.

Your Gold Sun is like a guardian angel or coach in your spiritual growth process. If you will trust it and rely on it, your Gold Sun can help you address any difficulty. By providing you with constantly available, cleansed energy, it can help you find the answer to any question. Your Gold Sun's energy can help you find the solution to any problem. It can also provide you with the energy to hurt yourself or others, if that is what you choose to do. Your Gold Sun chakra is an energy storehouse and an energy clearinghouse. What you do with the energy it provides is your decision.

Because your Gold Sun lives outside of your aura, it is separate from your particular story and drama. It is dispassionate, unbiased, and neutral. It won't withhold energy from you as a punishment, and it won't make more energy available as a reward. If you learn to manage your spiritual life in responsible ways, you will have more energy available. If you choose to squander your energy in attachments and addictions, you will have less energy. The condition of your Gold Sun chakra depends on you—on your treatment of yourself and others, and on your commitment to responsible spiritual communication.

The Gold Sun chakra exists in every person on the planet. Everyone has the opportunity to experience the flow of abundant, clean, and healing energy. Most people don't realize this opportunity exists.

※

I worked with the Gold Sun symbol for fifteen years before realizing it was the eighth chakra. I first thought it was just a nice visualization and centering device, but when I began to see the Gold Sun above all people, I knew it was real. Because of its neutrality, I guessed that it had something to do with spirit guides. I thought it was a representation of each person's guiding information, but the golden energy surrounding it remained a puzzle.

Golden energy has always symbolized Christ energy, whether the Christ-being is Jesus, Buddha, Allah, or Horus. Over the years, I began to piece the puzzle together.

The Gold Sun chakra *is* Christ energy, spirit-guide energy, and personal energy. It is the energetic container created for each of us by God. It is the superconscious, and it is the unconscious. When we call our energy back to us, or ground energy out of our auras, our bodies, our images, or our contracts, our Gold Sun chakra goes to work. It acts as a beacon, and a purifier for energy. The Gold Sun is the best chakra for this task, because it lives outside of the aura and the body. If any of the lower chakras attempted to pull stuck or foreign energies inside themselves, there would be trouble.

When unhealthy hand and heart chakras vacuum energy, it can cause chest, arm, hand, and neck pain. A third chakra that tries to vacuum up energy will create stomach distress first, and numerous problems later. A sponging second chakra can even lead the body into cancers and reproductive diseases. Too-receptive first or foot chakras will interfere with grounding, and may lead to uncontrolled kundalini rushes. None of the lower chakras have the time or space to cleanse and purify foreign energy. A vacuuming heart chakra leads to runaway healing, and possible problems with the heart and lungs. An overly receptive fifth chakra can lead to schizophrenia, while an overly receptive sixth chakra can become exhausted by unending clairvoyant visions. An overly receptive seventh chakra can lead to brain dysfunctions and seizure disorders.

None of the body-linked chakras should vacuum energy. They're just not set up for it. The Gold Sun chakra can and does vacuum energy, because it was provided to us for that specific purpose. It is our prayer bank, our energy clearinghouse, our link to Christ energy, and our all-purpose energetic cleansing tool. The Gold Sun chakra is the energy that makes all the other chakras function. It is the energy that keeps us alive. When we perform our Gold Sun Healing, we are accessing this chakra's highest purpose.

OPEN OR CLOSED EIGHTH CHAKRA

I have never seen a closed Gold Sun. I don't think it's possible to close it. Our body-linked chakras are *supposed* to react to our strengths and our weaknesses. This is how we grow and learn. The Gold Sun chakra, however, has to remain available to us at all times.

We can and do ignore our eighth chakras, but they always appear if we ask them to. I've seen less shiny Suns in people who throw their energy away, but I've never seen a closed-down Gold Sun. Gold Suns are always open.

TRAITS OF A HEALTHY EIGHTH CHAKRA

I think this section should be called "Traits of a Person who Pays Attention to His Gold Sun." The Gold Sun chakra, even when it's pretty dim, can brighten up in minutes when people sit and ground. There's no real trick to healing a Gold Sun chakra. You just have to pay attention to it!

If you stay in contact with your Gold Sun chakra, you will have all the knowledge you need. You'll have all the healing information, all the laughter, all the self-love, all the forgiveness, all the emotions, and everything else. When you are connected to the wealth of your Gold Sun, you'll have more energy than you can ever use, more true riches than you can ever dream of, and more opportunities than you can possibly undertake. With this kind of backup, it's a cinch to be healthy and to be of service to the world. With this kind of backup, your service will be inestimable.

THE HAND CHAKRAS

In the center of each of your palms are your hand chakras. They can be either expressive or receptive, depending on the circumstance. During a healing or artistic expression, your hand chakras channel energy from within your body or from a healing guide, and send it out into the world. During intense study, love-making, or meditation, your hands can channel external energy and information into your body.

If you have lost one or both of your hands, this information still pertains to you. Though your physical hands may be gone, your energetic hands, and your hand chakras, are still alive and active. Read on.

The hand chakras are not exactly like the seven major chakras. They are naturally smaller in size (about two to three inches in diameter, when open), they open and close more often than the major chakras, and they do not have a particular color. The hand chakras are more like channels through which any energy can flow than they are like specific storehouses of specific energy. Your hand chakras are connected to your heart chakra, and their general condition shows where you are in your ability to give, receive, and create in the world.

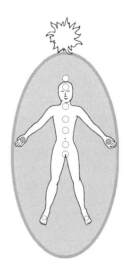

Your heart chakra's condition relates to your ability to channel internal love and artistic information throughout your body and spirit, whereas your hand chakra's condition speaks to your ability to channel these things in the external world. When your hands and heart are properly connected, the outward flow of heart-chakra energy can be controlled by your hands. With this proper connection, runaway healing is far less likely. A method for connecting your heart and hands is included in this section.

In interpersonal healing, lovemaking, or deep creative expression, the heart chakra sends its energy through the arms and out the hand chakras. This can feel wonderful and healing, unless the heart chakra is overstimulated or unaware, and spends too much time draining itself in this fashion. Without a conscious connection from the heart to the hands, however, the heart chakra may become misshapen as it tries to pour itself out and down the arms. As with the kundalini rush, a little bit of overflowing heart-chakra energy goes a long way. Reading and healing the heart chakra pulls its energy back to center once again, as does connecting the hands and heart in a conscious manner.

The hand chakras are used most actively by massage therapists and intuitive healers who, in many cases, don't know how to keep their hand chakras healthy. I see many cases of hand, wrist, elbow, and shoulder problems in such people. This can, of course, be attributed to overwork, or to an improper use of the muscles. It can also be a sign that the healers are allowing their client's energy to flow into their hands and up into their bodies.

Healers are not the only people who have this hand-chakra problem. House cleaners, executive secretaries, elementary school teachers, and counselors of all kinds will very often vacuum up the distress around them as they clean up, or type memos, or place their hands on people. Symptoms of hand-chakra vacuuming include hand and arm pain, shoulder stiffness, weakness in the arms and upper back, and pain in the region of the heart.

Your body doesn't like to be filled with other people's energy, attention, problems, and wishes. It will react with pain and dysfunction, because it knows that its own needs are always ignored when other people's problems are brought inside it. If you have learned the bad habit of empathetic hand-chakra sponging (see the section on the second chakra), your body has probably been complaining about it for a while. Apologize, learn the correct method of heart-to-hand connection, and break the habit.

OPEN OR CLOSED HAND CHAKRAS

The hand chakras open and close all the time, and change their degree of openness in each moment. They are very much more active, in this respect, than the seven central chakras. If your chakra system is fairly aligned and healthy, but your hand chakras are wide open or tightly shut, rub your hands together and check their chakras for changes. Rubbing your hands together brings energy to these chakras and often calls them to attention. During a reading or Chakra Check, your hands should be open to two or three inches in diameter and ready to work. If they're not ready or willing to open to your specifications, read on.

Constantly open hand chakras in an unhealthy chakra system can affect the joints and muscles of the hands. This can make them weaker than usual, or unable to grasp and hold on to things. All the energy that should be in the hands pours out of them, weakening them. People with clumsy hands, or hands that are constantly being bumped, scraped, banged, or burned, generally have their hand chakras far too open for health or safety. This weakened state of the hands often accompanies a wide-open, runaway-healing heart chakra.

Open hand chakras are necessary during specific tasks, such as healing or creating art, but you must be able to close them back down when necessary. If your training has placed an overemphasis on the heart-chakra attributes of healing and the giving of unconditional love, your hand chakras may be open and pouring out heart-chakra energy twenty-four hours a day. If this is the case, your heart chakra will usually be flattened out into a horizontal oblong shape instead of maintaining a healthy, rounded circle. The heart chakra, in this situation, actually looks like it's starting to drain out into the arms.

We've talked about closing down a runaway heart chakra. Working with the hand chakras is vitally supportive in bringing the heart back to a place of balance. Closing the hand chakras, which you can do simply by making a fist, blocks off a traditional avenue of heart energy drainage. When your hand chakras are closed, your heart energy has to stay in your body. This may be uncomfortable at first, especially if your sense of self is based on your ability to love and heal others. You may not know what to do with your own healing energy. You may not know how to give to yourself. You may not even want to. Do it anyway.

Give to yourself by taking it easy, by feeding yourself handmade foods, by taking time for yourself, by saying no to half of the demands on your time, and by caring for the room in your head. Set aside a time each day to do whatever you like to do, no matter how silly it may be. Color in a coloring book, buy a goofy shirt, play with a puppy, or go to the zoo. Lighten up and have a little fun, and place your hands right over your heart when you feel the need to ignore yourself and plunge headlong into a one-sided healing relationship. Take your life into your own hands, literally.

Open hand chakras can also be in the vacuum, as opposed to the draining, mode. When the hand chakras are vacuuming energy into the body, the heart chakra will not be spread out and elongated. The heart chakra, in this case, will usually be rather small and bright. It may have squared-off, as opposed to rounded, edges. In any chakra, squared-off outer edges often signal distress. You will find corners and angles on chakras that are trying to keep their energy protected from incorrect energies, or belief systems that damage their functioning.

A squared-off or polygonal chakra is trying to deflect incoming energy by presenting sharp angles instead of welcoming curves. A heart that is trapped between two unaware, vacuuming hand chakras will become defended, as well it should. Physical symptoms may include upper-back pain or distress, breathing problems, and all sorts of digestive disturbances, as the third chakra tries to step in and protect the heart.

A vacuuming-hand-chakra healer will also experience burn-out during or after his healing, cleaning, organizing, or counseling sessions. He will require a great deal of rest. Essentially, a vacuuming-hand-chakra healer is a sponge healer who will soon break down. Fortunately, the correct heart-to-hand connection technique taught in this section can help heal such healers.

Tightly closed hand chakras can stiffen and swell the joints and muscles of the hands. This is a sign that the ability to give and create is stunted and somewhat arthritic. If your hand chakras are shut tight, the normal flow of energy through your body may be negatively affected. You'll be "clogged up." If you can't paint a little picture or play chopsticks on the piano, please find some other way to create a flow in your hands. Our society places such impossible requirements on artistic and creative expression that it is a wonder anyone gets out there to love and paint, dance or create. But you don't have to meet society's requirements. You can bake or cook something by hand, clean and restore a piece of furniture or automotive gear, give someone a shoulder rub or a haircut, do Tai Chi or Yoga, or spend some time petting an animal. Concentrate on learning to connect your heart and your hands in healthy ways, and get your energy flowing again. If your hand chakras have been closed, perform the heart-to-hand healing at least twice a day, until you reestablish their flow.

Hand chakras can also take healthy-chakra vacations, but, because they are in use so much of the time, it is highly unusual for them to go off-line for more than a day or two. You can identify a healthy hand-chakra vacation by the health and circular shape of your heart chakra, and by the feeling of relaxation and grace in your arms, hands, and fingers, even though your hand chakras are closed.

Hand chakras go off-line when new information about appropriate healing and self-love is being processed. Your hands will close off in order to keep your heart-chakra energy in your body, and to help you step out of the healer-giver role for a while. Hand chakras, however, need to be available to you, so check in on them two or three times a day while they are closed, and give all your other chakras, especially your heart chakra, congratulatory hello gifts. Let each of your chakras know that you appreciate the balance and communication skills that have granted your hands this vacation.

For the hands themselves, cover them with a glove of grounded Sentries, and ask them to show you what energy support they need to open again. They will usually describe it manually. Watch and learn.

CONNECTING YOUR HAND CHAKRAS
TO YOUR HEART CHAKRA

The hands and heart are usually connected in most people, but it is always a good idea to examine the quality of the connection, especially in cases where the heart chakra is troubled or mis-shapen, or the hands and arms are stiff, cramped, or accident-prone.

The connection between the hands and the heart begins with a healthy heart chakra, so the healing of the heart is the first step in this process. When you are centered and in your head, please envision your heart chakra as a circular, emerald-green energy center, three to five inches in diameter. Now, envision each of your hand chakras in the center of the rounded depression in your palms as circular and open as well. Your open hand chakras should be two to three inches in diameter, so they fit comfortably in the center of your palms.

As you remain seated behind your eyes, envision a portion of the emerald energy in your heart chakra moving up toward each of your shoulders. Be sure that your heart chakra remains circular and normally sized. Know that you are not draining the energy out of your heart, but simply redirecting some of its abundant supply. See the emerald energy of your heart chakra moving up into your shoulders and then down into each of your arms. Feel your heart-chakra energy as it moves gently through the bone marrow of your upper arms to your elbows and lower arms. Watch from inside your head as your heart-chakra energy moves down through your wrists and flows out of each of your hand chakras, pushing any energy blockages in front of it.

When your hand chakras are connected to your heart chakra, you should be able to feel an increased heat or pressure in your hands. If you can't, you may have a clog somewhere in your arms or hands. To release the clog, bring your palms together and rub them briskly, until you can feel heat inside both of your hands. Now, let your arms hang down and feel their tingling heaviness. This is what you should feel when your heart energy flows into your hand chakras.

Bring your hands together and rub them briskly again. When they are warm, use them to move your heart-chakra energy out into your arms. Place your right hand a few inches in front of your heart chakra, and describe a small circle over it, as if to stir the heart chakra's energy. Use your right hand to bring some of the heart's emerald energy out and up to your left shoulder. Gently move a portion of your heart-chakra energy out and down your left arm. When you get to your left palm, use your right hand to describe a circle around that hand chakra. See your left hand's chakra fill with flowing green heart energy.

When your left-hand connection is made, drop your right hand, and use your left to bring your heart-chakra energy into your right hand. You may need to establish this connection a few times each day if you are an unconscious vacuum healer, but the connection will soon begin to flow on its own.

Move your hands and arms around. Open and close your palms and feel the difference in heart-energy flow as you do. Place your open hands onto any uncomfortable place on your body, and you can perform a small heart-chakra healing on yourself. Place your open hands over your heart chakra, and you can close the energy circuit and give love to yourself when your heart falls out of balance.

Maintain this heart-hand connection at all times, but be aware: If runaway healing is part of your past, don't allow heart energy to rush out of your hands in unconscious ways. Don't start vacuuming up the energy around you, either. When your heart is connected consciously to your hands, and you have control and awareness of your heart energy, runaway healing and hand-sponging is far less likely to occur. It's still a hazard, however. Reread the warning signals of too-open hand chakras, and the section on the sponge-healing second chakra if you fall backward into old relating styles.

If you have trouble keeping your healing energy in your own body, place your open hands over your heart each morning and evening for about a month. If you feel your heart going out to another person who has not specifically asked you for a healing, place your hands over your heart immediately. Remind yourself that everyone has their own healing energy. You don't have to heal the world right now; you have to heal yourself first.

Now that you know how to connect heart and hands, look in on their connection each time you do a Chakra Check or reading, and every time you perform a Gold Sun Healing. Be aware that your heart chakra should not flatten into a horizontal oblong as it tries to pour itself down your arms. The hand-connected heart chakra should remain healthy and circular, just as the first chakra remains healthy and circular even though a portion of its energy is directed downward as a grounding cord. Don't allow your hands to vacuum energy in unconscious ways. This will only create havoc in your heart chakra and the rest of your chakra system. Stop hurting yourself.

TRAITS OF HEALTHY HAND CHAKRAS

People with healthy hand chakras can translate the information of their healthy chakra system out into the world. They are naturally (as opposed to compulsively) giving and caring, but they have an extra dimension: they can also receive. They can receive help, compliments, gifts, and loving advice, without losing their center. And, they can give all these things to others without creating indebtedness, guilt, or recriminations.

Healthy hand chakras confer a natural creativity on their owners. The creativity of these people flows. They don't suffer from dramatic artistic blocks or fallow, muse-free periods. They have a flair for dressing, cooking, home decoration, car restoration—whatever makes them happy. They don't need to rely on teachers or institutions to validate their artistic expression. They have a comfortable give-and-take relationship with the world and the people around them. They also have a comfortable give-and-take relationship with their own energy, and are able to protect their giving nature by closing off their heart-to-hand connection in the presence of habitually needy people.

THE FOOT CHAKRAS

Each foot has a chakra in the center of its arch. Like the hand chakras, your foot chakras can be both expressive or receptive in turn. During grounding and exercise, your foot chakras help your body to channel energy downward into the Earth. During walking meditations or nature excursions, your foot chakras will open to allow Earth energy to come up and cleanse your body.

If you are missing one or both of your feet, this information still applies to you. Though your physical feet may be gone, your energy body still has legs, feet, and foot chakras. Keep reading.

The health of your foot chakras relates, not just to your ability

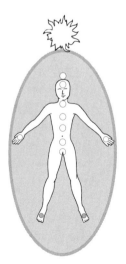

to be in your body and grounded, but to your ability to act on the planet in real time as a grounded spirit. This is an important distinction. It is quite possible to be in your head and grounded from your first chakra without really connecting to the Earth, especially if your third, fourth, and fifth chakras are not able to communicate with one another.

If the important spirit/body communication is blocked in chakras three, four, or five, the spirit and body will not have a clean connection. The grounding abilities, which are a sign of spirit/body agreement, will be more of an intellectual ideal than a hands-on (or feet-on) reality. By looking at your foot chakras and their connection to your first chakra, you can find out if your grounding is as strong as it can be.

The foot chakras, like the hand chakras, open and close at will in response to the need for earth connection or earth energy in the body. They, too, are smaller than the central chakras, two-to-three inches in diameter when open. The foot chakras do not have a specific color. They are often shades of brown, like the brownish tinge of earth energy, or red, if they are connected to the energy of the first chakra.

When grounding and body-connection are strong in an individual, some first-chakra energy may flow down the center of the legs (inside the marrow, usually) and out through the foot chakras. This flow means that the first chakra is healthy, and that its grounding functions are not conceptual, but actual. When the heart energy flows properly from the hands, you see concrete examples of self- and other-love and healing. When first chakra energy flows properly from the feet, you see concrete examples of grounding, earthiness, and a healthy spirit-body connection.

Healthy foot chakras create and nourish a connection to the wise, calm energy that lives inside the Earth. Your foot chakras connect you to nature by allowing earth energy into your body. This energy will cleanse, center, and ground you. Your foot chakras also give you the chance to off-load any stress, fatigue, or disharmony in your body, by allowing energy to drain out of you and into the accepting, cleansing soil.

If your foot chakras are healthy, any lower-body movement is grounding. Walking, dancing, skating, and pushing a shopping cart all become spiritual grounding exercises when your feet are allowed to maintain a constant, give-and-take connection with the Earth.

OPEN OR CLOSED FOOT CHAKRAS

Very open foot chakras in an unhealthy system are an emergency grounding tool. If you are out of balance and ungrounded, and your feet try to keep you connected to earth energy by staying

wide open, consider yourself lucky. Though it's important to heal
and align all of your chakras as soon as you can, it is also important to congratulate your open foot chakras for doing the right
thing! If your foot chakras try to keep you grounded, even when
you're not helping, you've got a very evolved and responsible
body. Treat it with love and care. Evolved bodies have a difficult
time in our noisy, chaotic society, especially if their owner (you)
ignores them!

As you go through a full chakra healing in response to your
too-open foot chakras, pay special attention to the connections
between your third, fourth, and fifth chakras. Their body/spirit
agreements or arguments are usually mitigating factors in any
grounding blockages. When you get to your first chakra, see a
portion of its ruby-red energy flowing down the center of the
bones in your legs and straight through to your foot chakras
(more on that later in this section). This connection will help
calm and resize your foot chakras so that they can relax a little. If
you need a bit of visual help in resizing these chakras, envision
the closing mechanism of a camera shutter.

At the end of your full chakra healing, spend some extra time
in the Gold Sun Healing for Chakras, described at the end of this
book. Establish a flow of golden energy throughout your pelvis,
hips, thighs, knees, calves, ankles, and feet. These areas may
need extra attention for a while. It would be wise to do a Gold
Sun Healing daily, until the flow of energy from your first chakra
to your foot chakras is easy to maintain.

Unhealthy, open foot chakras can create physical problems,
such as clumsiness, constant toe-stubbing, or the tendency to
sprain ankles and knees. Once the healing flow of energy is
reestablished, and the foot chakras are reattached to conscious
awareness, these difficulties should subside.

Wide-open foot chakras in a healthy chakra system are a sign that
the body is reacquainting itself with the wisdom and healing of
earth energy. Though many people feel that true guidance comes
only from above—from the cosmic, spiritual realm—the fact is
that real wisdom comes from a balance of earth energy *and* cosmic energy. Cosmic energy makes for a well-balanced spirit, and

earth energy makes for a well-balanced body in which the spirit can live. Physical balance is vital in these ungrounded times. Wide-open foot chakras in a healthy chakra system are gathering wisdom and guidance on how to attune the body to the rhythms, cycles, and energies of the planet. This information brings healing insight to each of the central chakras.

Though you'll usually want any wide-open chakra closed within a week, the foot chakras and earth energy may need more time to establish their healing connection. Since the Earth works in cycles, seasons, and real time, it may need more real time to fully involve your body in a particular lesson or healing modality. Let it.

Maintain the health and alignment of your central chakras, and meditate regularly to support them, as your foot chakras participate in this earthy healing. Sit and practice your meditation and healing at the same time and in the same place each day. Earth energy is very responsive to time, place, and stability. When you center yourself on a regular and dedicated schedule, the earth energy will be able to align itself to your schedule, and offer healing information to you as you meditate. Listen and learn. Earth energy is infinitely healing and infinitely wise.

Closed foot chakras in an unhealthy system are signs of an unwillingness to connect with the Earth, or a symptom of the feet's response to first-chakra damage. The foot chakras can also close when the body is not getting enough gentle, reasonable daily exercise to keep its energy flowing. I say gentle and reasonable because many exercise addicts have closed foot chakras and are prone to constant foot, leg, and lower-body injuries.

Compulsive exercising is a very ungrounding act, because it ignores normal bodily signals, such as pain, hunger, fatigue, and plain old common sense. If you are a no-pain, no-gain type of macho workout person with grounding trouble and closed foot chakras, lighten up. You don't have to stop exercising, but you do have to learn to listen to your body instead of forcing it to do so many miles or reps or whatever. Getting into contact with your body and your foot chakras will help enormously.

Closed foot chakras can affect the feet and legs by making them very tight, inflexible, and possibly arthritic. The feet and legs may even show signs of vascular insufficiency, because energy is not flowing through them. There may also be wide temperature swings in the feet, as the body tries to respond to the lack of energy within them.

I often see closed foot chakras in people I call *seventh-chakra fairies* (myself, at times, included). Seventh-chakra fairies are people whose body/spirit skew is decidedly spirit-inclined. They are often filled with spiritual information, intuition, and guidance, but their bodies, their homes, and their relationships are usually in a complete shambles. Interestingly, many spiritual teachings have downplayed the importance of the physical world (calling it an illusion), precisely because so few of their spirit-skewed disciples could function within it.

Let's not kid ourselves. We are spirits in bodies, and our whole purpose in incarnating is to learn to live in and communicate with our bodies and the physical world. Astral travel, higher guidance, communing with the spirits, and so forth are nice, but without grounding, these activities can create or intensify a whopping body/spirit split.

When seventh-chakra fairies ask me for spiritual guidance, or astral travel tricks, I ask them how their legs feel. I ask them about their hair, their stomach, their car, and their finances. I get disjointed and unsure answers, because common, everyday life is uncomfortable, and even unknown, to these people. They often have no idea about how they feel, what they want, where they're going in the world, or how to get there. But they want to do more astral travel.

I will tell you what I tell them: As soon as you fall asleep, you can astral travel to your heart's delight. As soon as you die, you will be one with all the spirits. While you are awake and alive, be awake and alive. Get into your body. You can only ascend to spirit after you do your work on this planet properly, which means in an in-body way. If you overbalance to the spiritual side of life and ignore your body, no matter how exalted you become, you'll have to come back into another body, because you didn't take care of this one.

When you get into your body and get grounded, your spirituality will have a depth of meaning unavailable to seventh-chakra fairies. When you allow your foot chakras to connect you to the Earth and all its incredible wisdom, your body will become, not only a healthy, aware organism, but a true temple of spirit as well.

As with other healthy chakras, your foot chakras can close off for a vacation. You will know this vacation by the health of your first and second chakras, and by a loose, relaxed, and lively feeling in your pelvis, legs, and feet, even though your foot chakras are closed.

Your foot chakras will go off-line, usually for no more than a day or two, when new information about grounding and earth-connection is being processed. If they stay closed for more than two days, their absence could create imbalances in grounding. It is wise to check in on them throughout their vacation days, and to enclose your feet in grounded Sentry socks.

If your foot chakras are still on vacation after two days, perform a complete chakra reading. Reestablish the flow of energy from your first chakra down to your foot chakras, using the connection technique below. Ask your foot chakras what energy or real-life support they require to reopen. Often, they will ask you to commit to daily leg movement, such as walking or biking. Do it.

CONNECTING THE FOOT CHAKRAS TO THE FIRST CHAKRA

In naturally grounded people, the foot chakras connect themselves to the healing energy of the Earth without any assistance. In split people, the foot chakras are generally cut off from the healing energy of the Earth. This makes grounding, and living, very difficult.

When first-chakra energy can be channeled through the legs and down to the foot chakras, the legs themselves become a grounding tool. Connecting the first chakra and the foot chakras

makes walking and exercising a meditative process. Each time
your legs move and your feet touch the ground, your connection
to the Earth is reestablished. When your foot chakras are connected and healthy, simple movements of your body will provide
grounding.

Your first-foot connection begins with a healthy first chakra.
By this time, your first chakra should be fairly healthy, if you
have maintained your regular grounding cord. If it is not healthy,
study any deviations it may have, and heal it before you attempt
to connect it to your foot chakras. If your first-chakra energy is
blasting upward, skip to the Kundalini Healing in the Troubleshooting Guide, then perform an entire chakra system healing
before you come back here.

✴

When you are centered and in your head, envision your first
chakra as a healthy, circular, ruby-red energy center. See the clear
and strong attachment between it and your grounding cord.
Now, envision the chakras in the insteps of each of your feet as
open and circular.

From inside your head, allow a portion of your red first-
chakra energy to flow out and through each of your thighs. See
the ruby energy traveling from each side of your still-circular first
chakra down through the marrow of your thighs. Watch the energy continue down through your knees and calves, and know
that you are not draining your first chakra, just redirecting some
of its inexhaustible energy.

Stay centered and in your head. Watch your red first-chakra
energy travel down into your ankles and then out of the chakras
in the insteps of each of your feet. Feel the energy moving
through your legs and down into the Earth.

If the feeling of being connected to the Earth is very unusual,
or if your legs feel hot or heavy, you can bet that your foot
chakras were not previously in use. If you experience only slight
changes, your foot chakras were probably working well on their
own. Now, attach a grounding cord to each of your foot chakras,
and you're done!

If you're having a lot of trouble making this connection, use your heart-connected hands to help move the first-chakra energy down into your legs. When you get to each of your feet, use your hands to describe circles over your foot chakras, and feel yourself stirring up their energy. This will often wake them up and get them ready to work.

You may need to use your hands to move the energy from your first chakra to your foot chakras a number of times. This is a normal occurrence at first, but in time, your first-to-foot connection will be effortless.

Maintain a constant awareness of the connection between your first chakra and your foot chakras, especially if you have had trouble grounding in the past. This connection will help to clear out the energy trapped in your lower body, which will make grounding easier. From this point on, check in on this connection every time you perform a Chakra Check, a chakra reading, or a Gold Sun Healing.

Many students find that this first-to-foot connection can be substituted for the first-chakra grounding cord. If you can maintain your grounding better this way, please feel free to drop your first-chakra grounding cord, and ground through your feet instead. It's actually a more natural way to ground, once you've gotten your first chakra cleared out and revitalized.

TRAITS OF HEALTHY FOOT CHAKRAS

When your foot chakras are healthy, they make grounding second nature. They connect you to the information, energy, and healing qualities of the Earth, and help your body feel more real. Self-respecting, reasonable exercise, proper diet, peaceful living and working situations, and intelligent health-building are all external signs of a close and healing internal connection with the planet.

Healthy foot chakras confer a centered, stable, grounded, yet deeply spiritual energy to their owners, very much like the energy of nature-centered tribal people. When the body holds its honorable position as the arbiter between earth and sky, all its movements on the planet are a part of the movement of spirit, and vice versa. Healthy foot chakras, and the planetary connection they provide, help to make this interconnectedness possible.

Sometimes, healthy foot chakras can make the body feel almost sluggish, as if gravity were exerting more force on it than on other people's bodies. This happens when people with healthy foot chakras head toward a spirit/body split. The heaviness in the feet is in direct proportion to the overemphasis on cosmically centered spiritual information. When your legs or pelvis begin to feel dragged down, it doesn't mean you are grounding *too much*. It means that you are heading for a spirit/body split again, and are, most likely, grounding *too little*. Pay attention to this feeling, get back into your body, and reconnect your feet to your first chakra. With your help, your body and your spirit will communicate effortlessly.

READING
YOUR CHAKRAS

After you've done a Chakra Check and are in a clear, grounded, in-your-head meditative state, you can revisit each chakra, starting at the seventh chakra and working your way down. Reading your chakras, now that you know the Chakra-Check norm, is a simple procedure of direction and reception.

During your chakra reading, first place an image of an ideal chakra over your own, to become aware of any changes your chakra shows you. After you put up your picture of what your ideal chakra *should* look like, you can make room for what it *does* look like.

This is the technique most good psychics use to clear their thoughts and release their preconceptions: they place an image of what they think should happen, or what they think they know about their client, and then sit and wait for changes. When the changes are received, the reading begins. Psychics who cannot be honest about their preconceptions usually give readings tainted with their own personal issues. Many beginning psychics tell me, "I can't get the hang of this! My seventh chakra doesn't look anything like it should. I give up!" They think real psychics know everything right away, and are all powerful. Wrong!

Good psychics aren't cocky know-it-alls. They go into readings ready to find out what they *don't* know. The confused and upset trainees in my classes are already well on their way to competence—they don't know anything yet! Their chakras don't respond to Chakra Check images because they are ready to be healed immediately. These chakras don't waste any time.

The changes chakras exhibit can be dramatic in terms of shape, size, and color, or they can be very minor, such as the chakra showing you a lighter shade of the color you placed there during your Chakra Check. Do not consider yourself unintuitive if you perceive no changes. You may have a very healthy set of chakras that don't show any signs of damage or disruption. Perhaps your simple Chakra Check was all they needed to get back on track. Good. In your case, all you really need to do is to go on to the Gold Sun Healing for Chakras in the next section, and you're done!

THE CHAKRA READING

Start your reading at your seventh (or crown) chakra and work your way down to your first chakra. Read your hand chakras along with your heart chakra, and read your foot chakras along with your first chakra.

To read your chakras, place a Chakra Check picture of how you think each chakra should look, and then be open to any changes you may perceive. If you find changes and deviations from the Chakra-Check norm, look up the possible meanings below, or let your chakra tell you what's wrong with it.

As you read each of your central chakras, note their size and shape. They should have circular edges and be three to five inches in diameter. Check their size and alignment in relation to one another. They should all be roughly the same size and in a straight line up the front of the body. Note the purity of their color. Their colors should be clear and distinct from one another. Examine the completeness of their edges. These should be free of tears, holes, bulges, or thin spots. Each chakra's energy should be moving freely.

As you check in with your hand and foot chakras, be aware that their normal size is two to three inches in diameter, and that they have no regular color. Your foot chakras can be red, if they are connected to the energy of your first chakra, or brownish-green, if they are connected to the Earth. Your hand chakras may be heart-chakra green, if they are connected to your heart, but they can be other colors as well. Both the hand and foot chakras should be circular, with distinct edges free of holes, tears, or hazy sections.

After you read each chakra, send it another Chakra Check picture of itself at its healthiest, and move down to the next chakra. If you need to, you can use your hands to mold your chakras into the correct size and shape, and to stir their energy with your fingers before you move on. When all of your chakras have been read and attended to, and your hands and feet are attached to their respective central chakras, you're done. Then, all that's left is to perform the special Gold Sun Healing for Chakras described in the next section.

This chakra-healing series may seem time-consuming. It certainly can be, if your chakras need a lot of attention. Once you've gotten them aligned and connected, your chakras will maintain their balance, and this reading may take as little as five minutes from start to finish. At first, you may want to heal your chakras every day. Later, you'll be much more lax, as you should be. I probably perform a major chakra healing three or four times a year, but I do a Chakra Check every couple of days or weeks, just to check in.

WHAT TO DO ABOUT PROBLEMS
IN YOUR CHAKRAS

Though we are now going to take a look at the meanings of chakra deviations, all chakra problems can be addressed by placing a Chakra-Check picture of each chakra at its healthiest over the injured chakra. Anything that does not immediately respond to your Chakra-Check suggestion may simply need to be there for a while. Don't pour grunting, sweating effort over your chakra's problems. Each chakra is alive and aware. Chakras naturally know what they are doing. If you simply allow them to communicate with each other, they'll pull themselves together.

The most healing thing you can do for your chakras is to be aware of and responsive to their messages. Keep your meditation and healing skills alive and active so that your energy body is in general good health most of the time. Chakras do not need you to obsess and fret over them. They only need gentle attention and a little direction. If an injured chakra does not respond to your suggestions, just cover it with a Chakra Check picture of it at its healthiest, and go on to the next chakra. After you finish reading all of your chakras, the Gold Sun Healing for Chakras will help your chakras come into alignment and into present time. This will supply all the healing energy they need. Do another full reading in a day or two, and you will see the changes your chakra system has made on its own. However, if your system is just as injured as before, with no changes whatsoever, that may be a sign of a need to burn contracts, attend to your endocrine system, or release drug damage.

If you are at all serious about becoming spiritually aware, clean the drugs out of your body and give your poor energy tools a rest. Drugs create chaos in your chakras, but the damage can be alleviated if you clean out now. A good acupuncturist/herbalist can not only help you detoxify, but can help rebalance your energy field so that you can work with it again. Otherwise, you'll just spend all your healing and meditation time putting out the fires that drugs cause, instead of moving forward in ability, awareness, and strength.

CHAKRA DEVIATIONS

ALIGNMENT: The seven central chakras should be lined up, both vertically and laterally, and should face forward from the centerline of the body. When the chakras are out of alignment, they are also out of contact with one another.

Sometimes, the chakras will edge away from centerline if the system as a whole is filled with unhealthy and unworkable information. The chakras will try to move away from the main channel of energy so that they can function on their own to some extent. This left- or right-sided deviation can be healed easily in the special Gold Sun Healing for Chakras, but it is also good to check in on left/right deviations in a philosophical way.

For some people, the aspects particular to each chakra exist in one gender only. Women can be fourth-chakra empathic, but men can't. Men can be first-chakra sexual, but women aren't allowed. Women can have sixth-chakra intuition, but men can only have facts, and so on. We know that all of this is nonsense, but check it out. Are your receptive "feminine" chakras (second, fourth, sixth, and eighth) drifting to the left while your expressive "masculine" chakras (first, third, fifth, and seventh) drift to the right? If they do, take another look at the section on the second chakra and gender skews and pull your chakras back to center.

In another alignment deviation, the chakras may line up vertically, but may not face forward as they should. Instead, they may face up, down, left, or right. This deviation usually occurs in people with long-standing, ungrounded body/spirit splits. These people's chakras may face downward to seek grounding and Earth energy, or they may face upward, seeking spiritual information and guidance. Or, they may look off to the left or right, if they are depending on the teachings of an authority figure or guru for their sense of well-being. Because these troubled chakras cannot rely on their owner for safety and information, they may try to reach out and connect themselves with someone or something else.

In all cases of misalignment, the chakras need to be gently moved back to center and faced forward. This can be accomplished in the Gold Sun Healing for Chakras. The earlier skills of grounding, staying in the center of the head, and defining the aura, however, must also be revisited.

COLOR: When you find a different color in your chakra than the one you placed there in your Chakra Check, it is a message. To help you decipher that message, I refer you to the small color guide found on page 123. I warn you again, however, that colors are completely subjective, and that your interpretations of their meaning are *always* better than mine.

There is a very specific color deviation (I call it an *assist*) which should be understood first. If you find the color of another chakra in the one you are currently reading, congratulate yourself. You are the owner of a communicative chakra system! Sometimes, when one chakra closes down or becomes unhealthy, and your chakra system is aligned and aware, a nearby, healthy chakra will lend a part of its energy to the ailing chakra. Unlike a kundalini rush, in which the first chakra rather ham-handedly blasts its energy through all the upper chakras, an assist is a very directed, partial or complete color wash that is specific to the injured chakra.

For instance: If a man is having a terrible time communicating his psychic knowledge, the connection between his clairvoyant sixth chakra and his communicative fifth chakra may weaken. His fifth chakra may even lose energy and threaten to close or go dark as his communication skills decay. Often, his third, fourth, or seventh chakras may become aware of the problem. They may send a portion of their own energy into his ailing throat chakra, to keep it going until the crisis is over. I call this an assist, and it usually means that the sending chakra is healthy, and that the chakra system is fairly well-balanced, aware, and inventive. In a healthy system, the chakras communicate with and look out for one another.

When I find a color assist, I always congratulate the person and each of their chakras for doing such good work. I then ask them to ground the assisting color out of the ailing chakra, and place the correct color in. It doesn't take a lot of work. As I said, a chakra system that is aware enough to perform an assist is healthy enough to get back into shape with only a minimum of spiritual healing.

In general, an assist is a good sign, unless the assisting chakra is more than three chakras away from the unhealthy one. If I see red first-chakra energy in an ailing heart chakra, I want to know why the second and third chakras didn't notice the problem, and what is going on with them. Or, if I see violet seventh-chakra energy in an ailing second chakra, I want to know what chakras three through six have been doing in their spare time.

An assist should be done by a nearby chakra. If it's not, the chakra system may not be aligned or healthy. It can signal that only one or two chakras are functioning, and that the few strong chakras are being overburdened by taking responsibility for the weak ones. You can identify this situation if you find one chakra's color in more than two of your other chakras. In this case, a complete chakra reading/healing is called for, with specific emphasis on alignment and size matching, and special attention to the Gold Sun Healing for Chakras. Be aware, however, that bits or splashes of colors are not the same as an assist, which shows up as either a complete or a partial wash of another chakra's color in the chakra you are reading.

In all cases, shade and energy are more important than color itself. If you have a fifth chakra that is all blue, don't think you're done reading. Is the blue pastel? If so, it can mean that your communication skills are pastel and washed-out as well. Is the violet in your seventh chakra very dark? Then your spirituality may be very dark and rigid. Is the emerald energy in your fourth chakra like stagnant water? Then the love you have is not as fluidly available as it could be. Does the orange energy in your second chakra career around like a pinball? Then your emotions may need to be channeled. If you sit with your chakras and let them speak to you, their colors will become only a portion of what you read. There are other things to see and feel.

EDGES: The edges of each of your chakras should be complete and well-delineated from the energy outside and inside of them. I like to see chakra edges that are a darker or more vibrant shade than the color of the chakra itself. This helps the chakra to remember who it is and where its energy is supposed to be. A pastel or indistinct edge creates a pastel and indistinct energy delineation; chakra problems may follow.

The deviations seen in chakra boundaries are like the ones seen in aura boundaries (see the section on Reading Your Aura), except that the information is more succinct. A spiky aura boundary means that you are taking in too much energy and information, and that your aura can't cope. A spiky second-chakra boundary means that you are specifically taking in too much emotional or sexual energy. You can fix that. A dent in your aura means that something outside of you is crowding and invalidating you. A dent in your third chakra means that something is crowding and invalidating your thought process or your ability to create personal safety and power. That's much more specific. It's easy to look at, and easy to explore and heal.

To know what your chakra-edge problems mean, skip back to the section on aura boundary deviations in Reading Your Aura, and apply those definitions to your specific chakra's abilities and functions. Otherwise, re-form the circular edge of each of your chakras by visualizing them as whole, healthy, and vibrant in color and energy. You can use your hands to gently reshape your chakras if your visualizations aren't strong enough yet.

If your chakric edge problems are constant, you may not be quite centered and in your body yet. Revisit all your early healing and meditation skills, as well as the Gold Sun Healing for Chakras.

ENERGY FLOW: Each of your chakras should be filled, not only with color, but with a sense of flow or movement. Depending on the day or moment, your chakra energy can swirl in circular patterns, bubble up and percolate, careen around and bounce off its edges like a billiard ball, or flow in eddies and waves. Your own energy flow will tell you what is going on, or what emotional component is guiding each chakra. In most cases, a constantly moving, medium-to-slow, circular flow is best, but your chakras may have different ideas at different times on how fast, or in what pattern, their energy should move.

The only real imperative of chakric flow is that it be present. A completely still chakra, or a chakra made of glass or crystal, is a stuck chakra. If your chakra is perfectly colored, perfectly delineated, and perfectly shaped, but completely still, it is not yet healthy. Each chakra's energy must have movement and flow within it, or it will not be able to change, grow, and react appropriately to the energies in the world around it. I see glass, crystal, and absolutely still chakras in intuitive beginners who become trapped in myths of spiritual perfection. Their chakras are perfect in every way, but framed and slip-covered to keep the dust out. I remind them that perfection, at least in its current definition, is static, and therefore not alive or vital.

Wholeness, on the other hand, is lively, messy, and healthy. Unmoving and unchangeable chakras cannot function (or help their owners to function) in the turbulent, living world. Chakras must be allowed to move with and react to the energies they encounter. If you find no movement in one or more of your chakras, whether or not they are otherwise healthy, place your fingers inside them and stir their energy around in a circular pattern. Try a clockwise pattern first, but reverse it if clockwise feels wrong to you. Remind yourself that the whole of life has flow, and a whole and healthy chakra system flows enough to roll with the punches.

During your Gold Sun Healing for Chakras (see page 256), pay particular attention to running your golden energy through each of your chakras, stirring as you go. This will help them break out of the perfection trap.

IMAGES: In some chakras, you may find images of people, places, magical beings, and more. You may hear sounds, perceive aromas, or feel transported in time and space. People who find images are usually voracious readers or dreamers whose minds and imaginations are very active. These are the storytellers and hidden mystics among us. Their mental and emotive aspects may need a whole beautiful story to explain the function or malfunction of a chakra, while a more pragmatic person may experience the process in a simpler and more straightforward way. Both methods are correct.

Images and visions inside a chakra are often messages from the spiritual world, either from your own spirit-self, your spirit guides and angels, or God. Try to see them, not only at face value, but on a deeper and more symbolic level as well. For instance, one student saw her seventh chakra as a beach where one small boat sat waiting. She interpreted this to mean that her spirituality was vast, but that her vehicle for exploring it was small. She went on to heal the rest of her chakras, then came back to her seventh. She expected to see a bigger boat, or a smaller body of water, but this time, her seventh chakra showed her a picture of a monk tending a large field of flowers, while young animals cavorted around him. She took this as a message about the incongruity between her forgotten childhood love of nature and her current lifestyle, which was lived indoors, in front of computers. She suddenly found a major piece for the puzzle of her adult life.

Images are necessary for some lessons, but not for all. If you find images everywhere, you may just be an image-centered thinker. If you are very pragmatic, however, and are beset by images, you could be living off-path. Your less-fluid thinking style may require a barrage of images before awareness emerges. Generally, more images will come forward before or during times of great turmoil and transition. Watch and learn.

SHAPE: All chakras are healthiest when they are circular, but chakras will transform themselves into bizarre shapes, either because they are damaged, or because they are stepping into unknown territory. A quick way to determine if a strange shape is a healthy one is to look at the color and the edge of the chakra. If the color is correct for the chakra, and the edge is strong and unbroken, your chakra may just be opening to unusual information.

For instance, a new health regime that makes sense but goes against your schooling may cause your otherwise healthy third chakra to do a squashy contortion until it digests the new information. Or, a previously abused and out-pouring heart chakra may distort itself in a number of ways as you bring it back to a healthy, balanced, circular shape. These distortions signal that you and your chakra have been off track, but that it is willing to ingest and accept your new, even contradictory information in order to get back into balance.

When your chakras are healthy but strangely shaped, you can ask them what's going on, but trust that they will bring themselves back to shape in time. If they are strangely colored or have compromised edges, however, they need to be healed right away. Misshapen and unhealthy chakras are signs of psychic injury, either from an unsupported, too-quick opening of the chakra, or from abuse. Abuse includes consenting to numerous contracts, refusing to acknowledge the ability of the injured chakra, or that old devil, recreational drug use. All abuses can end, and all chakra deviations can be healed.

If your chakras are unhealthy and misshapen, revisit all the aura-boundary definition skills in Parts I and II, and study the section on the Gold Sun Healing for Chakras. As you rededicate your energy and the energy of your injured chakras, make sure to use your hands in reshaping and healing them. If your sick and neglected chakras know you care, they will heal very quickly.

THE GOLD SUN HEALING
FOR CHAKRAS

Your Gold Sun chakra contains the overseeing energies for your aura, your body, and your other chakras. Now that you can work with your chakra system, your Gold Sun Healing should include your chakras, both individually, and as members of a working, connected system.

The following technique is a quick addition to your regular Gold Sun Healing, and a very simple way to bring your chakras into alignment. When they are aligned, your chakras can maintain a healthy, flowing communication with one another. Once your chakras are lined up, you will see them giving color assists to one another in times of stress. This is a hundred times better than having one close down and the others open too much in response. You should perform this special chakra healing after any meditation and healing session, Chakra Check, or chakra reading.

HEALING YOUR CHAKRAS
WITH GOLD SUN ENERGY

To align your chakras with Gold Sun energy, get grounded and centered. Envision your Gold Sun, channel it through your aura, and breathe it into your body in the usual way (see the section on the Gold Sun Healing).

Create a solid ribbon (at least five inches wide) of golden energy from your Sun, and bring it down through your seventh chakra, turning it from purple-violet to gold. See the ribbon entering your head and going through your sixth chakra, turning it from indigo to gold, then traveling through your skull to your throat chakra, turning it from blue to gold. See the ribbon traveling down to your heart chakra, turning it from green to gold. Stay in your head.

If you need to, you can use your hands to grasp the ribbon. You can pull it down and guide it through each of your chakras. Feel the ribbon passing through your chest and into your third chakra at the solar plexus, turning it from yellow to gold. Feel the ribbon pass through your second chakra, turning it from orange to gold, then moving down to your first chakra, turning it from red to gold. See the golden ribbon continuing all the way down your grounding cord to the center of the planet.

When the ribbon reaches the center of the planet, allow gravity to tug on the ribbon and straighten it. Envision an absolutely straight path from your Sun chakra, down through all of your central chakras, and on down through your grounding cord to the center of the planet. This straight-up-and-down alignment will help your chakras pass energy and information to one another, and it will help to keep them all balanced and running at essentially the same size and speed.

Let this gold ribbon swirl healing, present-time energy through each of your chakras for at least a minute, or longer if it feels right. Fill all of your chakras with flowing golden energy, and bring them up to date with your present-time healing information and abilities. During this healing, allow golden energy to flow out of your heart and down to your hand chakras, then out of your first chakra and down to your foot chakras. This will clear out your arm and leg channels and bring your hand and foot chakras into present-time as well.

When you are done, thank your Gold Sun, close off the top of your head, close off the top of your aura, and let the gold energy drain out of you, if it wants to go. Bend over and touch the ground. Let your head hang down, and let your hands and feet come into contact with the Earth after this spiritual healing. You may feel excess energy draining out of you, or you may not. Your body, aura, and chakras may want to keep all the gold, so don't worry if you don't feel any draining at all. Stand back up, and you're done.

※

This Gold Sun Healing for Chakras can now replace your simpler Gold Sun Healing. It should be used at the end of any sit-down meditation and healing session. This alignment and chakra-feeding technique will create flow and balance. It will maintain the health of your chakra system, thereby relieving you of the need for extended chakra readings and healings.

PART IV

The Troubleshooting Guide

THE TROUBLESHOOTING GUIDE

I love new books and ideas, but I hate having questions about them, because it's almost impossible to contact authors. Even if I get through, I usually receive an impersonal, generic reply or a costly newsletter subscription. Not acceptable.

I deliberated for many years before writing a book containing so many energy techniques. Too many people will skim lightly over a new set of techniques and try them without much thought. I have healed dozens of people who astral-traveled but couldn't get all the way back into their bodies, and I have turned off numerous kundalini rushes in first chakras whose owners couldn't center long enough to do it themselves. I think the unexamined attitudes and expectations found in many self-help books create more questions than they can possibly answer, while other books are so unbending in their dogma that many readers neglect to ask enough questions before they embark on a new regime.

My solution is twofold. I offer this alphabetized Troubleshooting Guide, similar to one you'd find in a computer or electronics manual. I want you to be able to thumb through this portion of the book and find concrete answers if you get stuck. In addition, I am including a way to actually contact me if your awareness levels start taking you into areas I haven't covered. If you need more help, please write and we will work together to find your answers. I promise not to send you an autographed photo, a newsletter, or a list of promotional items you can buy. Good luck.

Karla McLaren, P.O. Box 1155, Columbia, CA, 95310-1155

ANGER: Anger is a sign that boundaries have been crossed without permission. Though this may also bring up fear, sadness, depression, or diminishment, it is anger that both signals the injury and creates new boundaries after any damaging incident. Because of this usual layer of emotion right under anger, anger is often misrepresented as a second-hand emotion. This leads people to see anger as unimportant or counterfeit. This is a mistake. Anger is just as important as sadness, fear, joy, or desire. It is a real and irreplaceable emotional state that offers protection and requires action. For an overview of the usefulness of emotion in concise spiritual communication, see the section on "Channeling Your Emotions," page 89.

ANXIETY: As with any other emotion, anxiety holds specific healing energy. Often, the only clue an otherwise aware person will have that anything is at all wrong will be a gnawing anxiety. There will be fear of going out or of making movement, fear of natural disasters or attack, severe reactions to certain stimuli, or a generalized dread of people. Dealing with anxiety from a psychological viewpoint can help, because it can bring the shadowy causes of anxiety out into the open. Talk-and-desensitization therapy for specific anxiety-causing events makes the anxiety real, and therefore curable. Desensitizing individuals symptomatically, however, can be too much of a quick-fix. It can overemphasize the fear of heights or going outside, but fail to address the underlying imbalance that brought the current anxious symptoms to consciousness. When channeled in the body and throughout the energy tools, anxiety becomes very clear, concise, and useful. Its action-oriented, protective energy helps create real solutions and real change. See *Fear*, *Panic Attacks*, and *Terror*, and the section on "Channeling Your Emotions," (page 89) for help in working with your anxiety.

AURA: An area around any living organism, best described as its energetic territory or spiritual skin. The aura is often seen as a halo or aureole of colored energy emanating from the body. The aura is a protective energetic boundary; auric damage affects the entire organism. For general information on auric awareness and healing, see the section on "Defining Your Aura" (page 27). For an in-depth look at auric reading and healing techniques, see the section on "Reading Your Aura" (page 121).

AURA COLORS: People with the psychic talent of clairvoyance can see colors in auras with the help of their sixth chakras. Though colors can have specific meanings, the meanings usually vary from individual to individual. In addition, auras change colors often throughout the day in response to spiritual communication, health issues, emotional states, and thought processes—any color seen can be expected to change within seconds. General color interpretations can be found in the section on "Reading Your Aura," (page 121), but a much more useful gauge of auric health is found in its size, shape, and condition. These topics are covered in the same section.

AURA HEALING: Auras can easily be healed in meditations taught in this book. Simple self-definition of the aura, as taught in "Defining Your Aura" (page 27) is a healing in and of itself. For a more advanced healing, see the section on "Reading Your Aura" (page 121).

AURA PROBLEMS: Chronic and serious aura damage or insufficiency is usually caused by damage from the environment, such as abusive and unhealthy living or working situations. Though aura problems can be disconcerting, they are both instructive and eminently fixable. If the aura is aware enough to break down in response to exterior stress, it is on its way to a new life, which it will seek out by alerting its owner to what does and doesn't feel good. See the sections on "Defining Your Aura" (page 27) and "Reading Your Aura" (page 121).

   A warning: Auras can also break down if the body is heading toward a serious illness, or in response to drug and alcohol abuse. Stop the drug abuse immediately, and see your health worker if your aura is breaking down around specific areas of your body.

AURA READING: Auras contain and process a tremendous amount of information, much of which can be accessed during the simple meditation and reading session outlined in the section on "Reading Your Aura" (page 121).

AURA VACUUM: A grounding exercise to cleanse and redefine an injured or indistinct aura. See the section on "Defining Your Aura" (page 27).

BURNING CONTRACTS: When people enter into relationships, they often set up a series of postures, behaviors, actions, and reactions that can allow the relationship to take over their lives completely. When such relationships and relating styles can be imagined as actual contracts, they can be brought to light and amended—or destroyed. See the section on "Burning Contracts" (page 77).

CHAKRAS: Chakras are a series of energy centers in and outside of the physical body. They can be considered the energetic glands or organs, just as the aura can be considered the energetic skin. Each chakra represents a different aspect of the entire being, and each can be read, healed, cleansed of injuries, and brought into conscious awareness. See all the sections on chakras in Part III.

CHAKRA ALIGNMENT: The seven major chakras, which stack up in a line from the genitals to the top of the head, work best when they are vertically aligned. Aligning the chakras is a simple part of the special Gold Sun Healing for Chakras, outlined in the section of the same name.

CHAKRA COLORS: The seven major chakras have specific colors that run up the vibrational spectrum, from red in the first chakra to purple/violet in the seventh. These colors, as opposed to the often subjective colors in the aura, have specific purpose, meaning, and interpretations. See the section on "Reading Your Chakras" (page 245).

CHAKRA HEALING: The chakras can easily be read, healed, aligned, and cleansed. See the sections on "Reading Your Chakras" (page 245) and "The Gold Sun Healing for Chakras" (page 256).

CHAKRA PROBLEMS: Problems in the chakras usually appear as shape and color deviations. These can be seen or felt in chakra readings and healings. Chronic chakra problems can signal health, mental-health, or endocrine imbalances, drug damage, a long-standing acceptance of energy-diminishing contracts (see *Burning Contracts*), or a refusal to work with the leading energy of the damaged chakra. See the section on "Reading Your Chakras" (page 245).

CHAKRA READING: This is a healing technique for listening to the information in each of the chakras. See all the sections in Part III on chakras.

CHANNELING THE EMOTIONS: Though ignored, de-meaned, and devalued, emotions are actually valuable messages from deep within the wisdom of the soul. When an inescapable emotional state is reached, channeling the emotion through the body, aura, and grounding cord can bring absolute clarity and healing. See the section on "Channeling Your Emotions" (page 89).

CLAIRAUDIENCE: The ability to hear psychic vibrations through the fifth, or throat, chakra. Often, clairaudience, or hearing voices, is misdiagnosed as a sign of schizophrenia. See *Ears* and *Ringing in the Ears,* and the section on the fifth chakra (page 192).

CLAIRSENTIENCE: The ability to receive psychic vibrations emotionally or empathically through the second chakra. Clairsentience can be a hazardous healing method if it is used on people outside of the immediate family. See the section on second chakra (page 158).

CLAIRVOYANCE: The ability to see psychic vibrations through the sixth chakra, or third eye. See *Visions,* and the section on the sixth chakra (page 204).

CLUMSINESS: Clumsiness that is not caused by inner-ear or limbic-system imbalance is often a sign of trouble in your grounding or your chakra system. Tripping and stumbling can relate to problems with your grounding, or in your first chakra and foot chakras. Loss of balance can also relate to problems with the room in your head, or in your fifth and sixth chakras. Clumsiness in your hands and arms can relate to trouble in your hand or heart chakras. Please see the sections related to your area of concern.

COLORS: Colors are often valuable tools in readings, healings, and other psychic communications, but their meaning is very subjective. See the color guide in the section on "Reading Your Aura" (page 121).

CONTRACTS: See *Burning Contracts,* and the section on "Burning Contracts" (page 77).

CROWN CHAKRA: Another name for the seventh chakra, which is an energy center located just above the head. See the section on the seventh chakra (page 214).

CRYING: Sadness is a wonderful way to restore the tempering influence of water to an arid system. Sadness allows the body to relax into itself after a period of rigidity or self-sacrifice. Sometimes, however, sadness and crying become unmanageable. This is a sign of imbalance throughout the system, and a call for an emotional channeling session. See *Sadness* and *Despair,* and the section on "Channeling Your Emotions" (page 89).

DEPRESSION: Depressions are funny things. I don't even know if I can call them emotions, because they either mask all feeling, or trap people in a constantly repeating emotion that doesn't ever go anywhere. It is very hard to remember to channel your emotions during a depression, because the depression sucks way all your energy, leaving you uninterested in work of any kind. *This is a clue.*

Remember to see depressions as vital warning signs that your energy is leaking away *and you are not calling it back.* Your body is evolved enough to stop all your forward movement at such times. Why? Usually, because your energy is stuck in a painful relationship, or a painful past-time event. Your body knows that no real forward movement is possible—so why should it pretend that all is well?

Thank your body and your emotions for their unwillingness to lie to you. Get grounded, and seek out the painful contracts you've forged with old, unworkable energies. Drain your aura and your body, burn your contracts with your despairing memories, and explode your images of your past injuries. Fill yourself up with your Gold Sun energy and get on with the work of living—and healing—in the present.

If these steps do not relieve the depression, and you still have no energy, seek out a Bach Flower Remedy practitioner and ask for the remedies Mustard, Gorse, Sweet Chestnut, or Wild Rose. Often, a body experiencing depression will need bolstering before its owner can get back in and resume the work of clearing energy and healing. When the depression has cleared, revisit the skills of aura definition, contract burning, image destroying, and chakra healing. See also *Despair* and *Suicidal Urges,* and the section on "Channeling Your Emotions" (page 89).

DESPAIR: Despair and despondency are signs of a long-ignored sadness that has become an unworkable, prevalent emotional state. Any deep, unrelenting emotion is a call for awareness, and each one has a specific and almost magical healing property tucked inside it. Through channeling despair in the body like any other energy, you can finally see what it has been trying to tell you. See *Grief, Sadness,* and *Suicidal Urges,* and the section on "Channeling Your Emotions" (page 89).

DISORIENTATION: Disoriented forgetfulness is usually a sign of being out of the body. Grounding and working through the beginning meditative processes will help to heal body/spirit splits that can lead to disorientation. See *Kundalini* and *Kundalini Healing*, and the sections on "A Room of Your Own" (page 9) and "Getting Grounded" (page 14).

Special topic: If you are in your body and you are still disoriented, you may have placed the room in your head too high, centered directly behind your clairvoyant, vision-receiving sixth chakra. Destroy your room and create a new one, anchoring it below your eyes, so that its ceiling is no higher than your eyebrows. This should help to center you.

DIZZINESS: Dizziness can signal all sorts of medical imbalances that should be looked into. However, dizziness can also stem from being ungrounded, out of the body, and out of the room in the center of the head. See *Kundalini* and *Kundalini Healing*, and the sections on "A Room of Your Own" (page 9) and "Getting Grounded" (page 14).

EARS: The ears are psychically connected to the fifth chakra, and can sometimes pick up audible psychic transmissions. These can take the form of ringing or tinnitus, chronic ear infections, a constant need to pop and clear the ears, or hearing voices. The psychic skill of clairaudience (hearing voices) is a difficult one to master, and, since it is one of the leading symptoms of schizophrenia, it is also a difficult one to share with health professionals.

Without competent help or useful information, many clairaudients begin to perceive the voices they hear as directive—as if the information from the voices were their own, or God's, and should be acted upon. If untrained clairaudients hook up with unbalanced people or beings, and believe the perceived information to be an aspect of their own personalities, chaos usually ensues.

All clairaudients require psychic training, specifically with regard to separating from the psychic information being received. This book can be used by clairaudients to center and separate from disturbing or uncontrolled psychic receptions. See *Insanity* and *Ringing in the Ears*, and the section on the fifth chakra (page 192).

EMOTIONS: Emotions carry messages from the emotional body to the physical, mental, and spiritual bodies. Each emotion has its own purpose, voice, and character, along with specific healing information that can easily be accessed. The trick is not to express emotions all over the exterior world, or lock them away and ignore them as they fester, but to use them as healing energies. See the section on "Channeling Your Emotions" (page 89).

ENDOCRINE IMBALANCE: The endocrine (or glandular-hormonal) system is connected to the chakra system. Imbalance in either system can interfere with the balance of the other system. And, as with the chakra system, disturbances in individual glands can pull the entire hormonal system into disarray. Often, a hormonal-endocrine imbalance will benefit from a chakra-system healing, and a chakra imbalance will benefit from an endocrine system healing. Please see the sections on the chakras in Part III of this book, and refer to the book, *Healthy Healing* by Linda Rector-Page (see bibliography) for comprehensive and masterful information about healing the endocrine system and the rest of the body.

EXHILARATION: Though celebrated the world over as the emotion of choice, unending exhilaration brings as much trouble as unending sadness, anger, fear, or grief. Exhilaration is especially damaging if it is seduced into existence and then imprisoned by those who want only to see the bright, "up," and happy side of life. Sadness is ignored, fear is explained away, anger is shamed, and grief is repressed while all the life is strangled out of the exhilaration.

In essence, exhilaration is often used as a drug, and abused so that real life and true emotions can be skimmed over. Imbalances in any emotion bring about turmoil, but the dramas of exhilaration-mongers are often the most tragic, because they usually involve large groups of people. Exhilarated, endlessly joyful people often draw many followers. They live an overwhelmingly seductive lie that says one can be happy and joyful at all times, as if that one emotion were enough. And, when difficulties inevitably arise, personalities clash, and money gets tight, the group of happiness-addicts often cannibalizes itself.

Happiness addicts have no idea how to channel their "bad" emotions. Their anger becomes unconscious, passive-aggressive rage; their fear becomes anxiety and paranoia; their sadness becomes unmanageable depression and sleep disorders; and their grief seeks the death of the group—or the exhilaration-guru.

Like any real emotion, exhilaration has it honorable place in the pantheon of feelings. The trick is to see it as a part of the whole, and to accept it for what it is when it comes forward. Exhilaration lets people know that they have just completed a vital (and often wrenching) series of learning experiences. If naturally joyous people try to stay in the exhilaration, they will not have the emotional arsenal to enable them to go on to the next set of difficult and emotionally involved lessons.

Joy and exhilaration give people a moment to see themselves as wonderful, powerful, and at one with the universe. Then, it's time to move on and get back to the real work that will lead inevitably back to the real joy. Healthy joy is meant to be as fleeting as healthy anger, grief, fear, or any other strong emotional state. It was never meant to be imprisoned and used to gain prestige in an emotionally stunted world. See the section on "Channeling Your Emotions" (page 89).

FEAR: All forms of fear are protective mechanisms that should never be ignored. Without fear, people would not survive. They would have no sense of self-preservation whatsoever. Fear, like any other emotion, contains vital information when it is simply allowed to be itself. Fear should not be ignored or pandered to, but channeled appropriately. See *Terror* and *Panic Attacks,* and the section on "Channeling Your Emotions" (page 89).

FURY: Fury is anger with fire, or anger getting an assist from the powerful energy of the first chakra. If used in the emotional work described in the section on "Channeling Your Emotions" (page 89), fury can be extremely useful in creating real separations from old relationships and restrictive energy patterns. However, fury also signals a boundary violation that is life-threatening, and a generalized inability to protect the body or the energy field.

The living environment of a furious person needs to be examined. It may have been time to leave such an environment a very long time ago. Uncontrollable bouts of fury can also stem from organic causes, or brain-chemical and endocrine imbalances, so a visit to an acupuncturist or other energy-aware physician would be well-advised.

GOLD SUN: This is the eighth chakra, and the symbol used to depict the unlimited amount of energy available to each person on the planet. The Gold Sun is used to rededicate the energy after a healing, to bring the body and all the energy tools into conscious, present-time awareness, and to heal the body. See the section on "The Gold Sun Healing" (page 65).

GOLD SUN HEALING: See the section of the same name (page 65).

GOLD SUN HEALING FOR CHAKRAS: An advanced but simple healing technique that cleanses and aligns the chakras. See the section of the same name (page 256).

GRIEF: Grief is a beautiful, languid, and poetic emotion that helps us to feel human. Spirit has no grief, because it sees no death and no loss. Spirit sees the continuum of all energy and all beings. Body, on the other hand, knows of loss. Humans experience death and sorrow. They can no longer touch or speak to the dead, yet they can still feel the embrace of a lost lover, or hear the laughter of a long-dead child. Bodies miss lost limbs and remember pain. Bodies live here, on the planet. They experience the reality of injury, loss, separation, and death every day.

Grief is natural to the body, and channeling grief helps the body to mourn real injury and real loss. Spirit can't really understand grief, and the intellect likes to whisk it away in a whorl of explanations, but bodies know grief. Channeling grief—and honoring the reality of the body and the emotions—helps the intellect and the spirit to integrate and mature. See *Sadness*, and the section on "Channeling Your Emotions" (page 89).

GROUNDING: An energy technique that helps to center the spirit in the body by centering the body on the planet. See the sections on "Getting Grounded" (page 14) and "Advanced Techniques" (page 101).

GROUNDING PROBLEMS: Difficulties in grounding are common. Topics covered throughout this book aim to address the many possible reasons, and offer many possible solutions. See the sections on "Getting Grounded" (page 14), "Burning Contracts" (page 77), and "Advanced Techniques" (page 101). For a specific look at grounding problems involving damage to the first chakra, see the sections on the first chakra (page 151) and the connected foot chakras (page 236).

GROUNDING RULES: Grounding is a primary step in this spiritual growth process, and with growth comes responsibility. See the section on specific grounding rules in "Advanced Techniques" (page 101).

GROUNDING VACUUM: Grounding cords used for centering can be turned into energy vacuums used for cleansing. Grounding vacuums are discussed in the sections on "Defining Your Aura" (page 27) and "Getting Grounded" (page 14).

HARA: Also known as the second chakra, the hara is the center of the musculature, the emotions, gender sexuality, and the psychic skill of clairsentience. See *Clairsentience*, and the section on the second chakra (page 158).

HATRED: Hatred, or a complete aversion to a person, place, or situation, is a sign of a chronic lack of clear boundaries, the presence of unintegrated shadow material, and possibly of life-threatening boundary violations. Hatred, like any fiery emotion, is difficult to survive or to use in any rational way. When hatred is channeled and used in energy separations (such as destroying images or burning contracts), it lends tremendous strength, certainty, and resolve. Do not express hatred in the world, or turn it on yourself. Instead, see *Anger*, and read the section on "Channeling Your Emotions" (page 89).

HEADACHES: Beyond all the physical reasons, such as illness, hunger, electrolyte and chemical imbalances, and tumors, headaches can be a sign of being ungrounded and out of your body. See *Kundalini,* and the section on "Getting Grounded" (page 14). Headaches can also mean that you're not in the room in your head (see page 9, the section on "A Room of Your Own"), or that you're out of contact with your sixth and seventh chakras (see the sections on these chakras, pages 204 and 214).

HEARING PROBLEMS: See *Ears,* above, and the section on the fifth chakra (page 192).

HEART CHAKRA: Also known as the fourth chakra, the heart chakra is the energy center of empathic healing, spirit/body communication, and love of the self and others. See the section on the fourth chakra (page 184).

INSANITY: Beyond the more mundane, chemical-imbalance-induced model of psychiatric disorder is the concept of spiritual imbalance. Psychiatric treatment modes do not even consider the possibility of clairaudience in schizophrenics, trance-mediumship and kundalini problems in aphasics and seizure-prone individuals, and second/third-chakra breakdown in depressives. One thing is certain: drug modalities and institutionalization have never proved worthy of the inexplicably hallowed place they hold in treatment of the disordered.

This is part of the legacy of Western medicine, which aims to find perfectly beautiful names for diseases without ever looking at the breakdown in life-force that causes them. Holistic mind-body-emotion awareness is making inroads into modern medicine, but the spiritual/emotional aspects of disease are still ignored.

Don't misunderstand me. Naming an illness is important, and Western medicine triumphs in that regard, but after a while, being the bipolar depressive in Ward Two, or the myocardial infarction on the table is limiting to the spirit. Knowing the name of a disease and treating specific symptoms is but a first step on the journey. It is not the end of healing.

There are no simple cures for psychiatric disorders, but nutritional imbalances and psychic injuries should always be explored. In addition, teaching psychiatrically disturbed people to ground, center, meditate, and heal their chakras and aura will be invaluable. I have never seen a mentally disturbed person with a balanced energy body. Drug therapies and institutionalization may be necessary at times, but once the symptoms have calmed down a bit, correct body care and competent spiritual grounding may help such people to explore and heal whatever it was that caused them to leave the "normal" world in the first place. My suggestion for emotional disorders in the context of this book is to spend extra time and energy on all the early skills in Parts I and II, as well as on aura healing and chakra alignment.

INSOMNIA: When children can't or won't sleep, it is usually because they fear missing out on something. It is the same with adults. Sleeplessness that is not caused by health or environmental disturbances generally stems from a gnawing lack of completeness or closure in situations or relationships. The body can't relax and let go, because the day isn't really finished. In instances of sleeplessness, it is always good to ask, "What is still undone?" as you ground and get centered. The issue will usually pop right up, and the techniques of image destruction and contract burning will help to release energy from it. See *Sleeplessness*, and the sections on "Destroying Images" (page 56) and "Burning Contracts" (page 77).

Special topic: If your insomnia is of long duration, and you are edgy, uncentered, and ungrounded after a spiritual experience, you may have blasting kundalini energy that needs to be put back into your first chakra. See *Kundalini Healing*, and read the section on the first chakra (page 151).

JOY: See *Exhilaration.*

JUMPINESS: Jumping, jerking, and starting (whether triggered by loud sounds or not) are often signs of ungroundedness (see the section on "Getting Grounded" on page 14). If the startle reaction seems to emanate from or affect a particular chakra, it can mean that the aura has broken down, and that the chakra is unprotected. See *Aura Problems, Chakra Problems,* and *Grounding Problems.*

KUNDALINI: This is the Sanskrit word for the energy of the first chakra, which is a fiery red energy that sometimes blasts upward into the other chakras during meditation, or in situations of immediate threat. Many spiritual practices encourage and manipulate these kundalini blasts, but if students are not advanced and centered, there can be difficulties. See *Kundalini Healing,* and the sections on the first chakra (page 151) and the connected foot chakras (page 236).

KUNDALINI HEALING: When the energy of the first chakra blasts upward, it does so to clean out the other chakras momentarily, or to lend power to the body in situations of immediate threat. Kundalini energy is the energy in the fight-or-flight reaction, and the energy that allows 110-pound mothers to lift cars, trucks, or heavy machinery off their children. It's powerful. It's also very damaging if it is left blasting for too long.

Too much kundalini can blast out the entire chakra system, burn holes in the aura, and shoot a person right out of her body. If too much kundalini is in place for too long, the body can even become damaged. Symptoms include dizziness and lack of appetite, insomnia, photophobia, waking dreams and visions, burn-like rashes, and tics and twitches that resemble St. Vitus' Dance. For general kundalini information, see the section on the first chakra.

For specific help in calming a blasting kundalini, perform this Kundalini Healing: (*Caveat:* I am not presupposing a knowledge of any technique in this book as we go into this healing, but I strongly suggest going back to the very beginning and starting over if you haven't any experience in grounding, getting in your head, or defining your aura. Without these basic tools, you may not be aware enough to keep your first chakra, or any other chakra, safe from kundalini rushes.)

Sit upright in a chair. Keep your feet uncrossed and flat on the floor, and your hands uncrossed and upturned on your knees. Breathe normally and keep your eyes open. This will help to keep you centered, whereas closing your eyes could make you feel dizzy. Envision or sense the energy in your body and aura right now. It may be hot and fast-moving. It may have a red-orange color or a ringing sound. You may even be able to feel the energy as a blast of heat or fire. This is your first-chakra energy, or your kundalini.

Now envision a cool blue moon about a foot or two above your head (see figure 12, page 277). See its color and texture, feel its calm coolness, and attune yourself to its gentle, relaxing energy. Bathe in the peace of its quiet blue moonlight. Envision your kundalini fire as a column that originates in your genitals and blasts up in a straight line through the center of your body and out the top of your head. The energy coming out of your head may look like a flame, a snake ready to strike, or a flame-thrower. It may even look like fireworks.

When you can easily envision the kundalini shaft and the blue moon (remember, these are both made up of your own energy, which means you are in charge of how they look and what they do), allow the blue moon to shine a shaft of light downward, directly into the fire coming out of the top of your head. See the shaft of blue light cooling and calming the fire, and pushing the fire before itself and back down into your body.

See this cool blue energy pushing the kundalini fire down into your head, down under your eyes, down into your jaw and throat, and down into your chest. Feel the calm coolness that has replaced the heat of the fire above your chest. Keep the blue energy moving, down through your sternum, and let it push the kundalini fire down under your solar plexus, down under your navel, and on down to your pubic bone. Feel the coolness in your body as the red-orange fire abates.

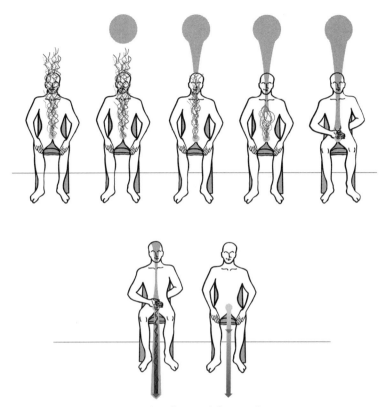

Figure 12. The Kundalini Healing

Now, with the blue moon still shining down in a shaft, center the kundalini fire in your first chakra. Place your right hand on top of your pubic bone and your left at the base of your coccyx, and massage downward as you envision holding the fiery energy in place with your hands. Watch as the energy begins to center itself and swirl inside your first chakra.

Ground yourself by allowing some of this fiery first-chakra energy to travel downward to the center of the planet in a solid red-orange cord. Grounding will help to anchor your kundalini energy in your first chakra. As you learned in the section on the first chakra, the first is completely willing to do anything you ask. All you have to do is communicate with it clearly. Once it knows what you want, it will settle itself in and stop blasting upward.

Thank your blue moon and let it disappear. Allow the shaft of blue energy in your body to exit through your new first-chakra grounding cord. Grounding out this cool energy will further help to keep your first chakra centered and grounded.

When you feel ready, skip back to the section on "Reading Your Chakras" (page 245). After a kundalini healing, you will need to heal all the other chakras, specifically in regard to getting them back to their correct size, shape, and color. In a kundalini rush, all chakras are essentially forced to work at the vibrational level of the first chakra, which is very disconcerting and often damaging to them. After a kundalini healing, you will need to maintain awareness of your first chakra and the connected foot chakras while you heal and balance your chakra system as a whole.

LIGHTHEADEDNESS: See *Disorientation,* and *Dizziness.*

PAIN: Pain is the body's way of signaling trouble or imbalance. Pain requires awareness and assistance if its message is to be deciphered. Running from, drugging, or ignoring pain heightens it, and can set the stage for serious illness. As pain is a message from the body, those with past spirit/body splits would do well to listen. Grounding the painful area is an excellent way to release the message within the discomfort. See the section on "Getting Grounded" (page 23) for a specific pain-relieving exercise.

PANIC ATTACKS: Panic attacks are fear messages from deep within the subconscious, messages that have been suppressed or ignored for years or even decades. Their energy, however, is still quite usable in emotional channeling sessions. See *Fear* and *Terror,* and the section on "Channeling Your Emotions" (page 89).

Panic attacks can cause (or stem from) organic imbalances, so a trip to the acupuncturist or homeopath would be well-advised. Also, certain Bach Flower remedies—Rock Rose, Aspen, Cherry Plum, or Rescue Remedy—will help to balance you.

RAGE: Rage is anger with kundalini fire attached. It is not going to let anyone tell it what to do, where to go, how to feel, or how to live. Rage is wonderful healing energy if channeled and used in separation work, but pretty nasty energy when dumped onto others or repressed. Repressed rage often turns into suicidal feelings (see *Suicidal Urges*), but, even then, it can be channeled and used in healing and self-awareness. See *Anger* and *Fury*, and the section on "Channeling Your Emotions" (page 89).

RINGING IN THE EARS: Ringing in the ears, or tinnitus, can have physical origins such as an electrical imbalance or a misplaced vertebra. It can even be caused by metal dental fillings that receive radio or television transmissions. Ringing in the ears can also be a sign that spiritual communication is being received and translated by the fifth, or throat, chakra. See *Ears* and *Clairaudience*, and the section on the fifth chakra (page 192). Pay special attention to contract burning in the fifth and sixth chakras, and follow the protective healing suggestions for an open, unhealthy fifth chakra.

ROOM IN THE HEAD: A meditative sanctuary created behind the eyes, specifically for people who have maintained a long-standing spirit/body split. See the section on "A Room of Your Own" (page 9). If staying in the room in your head is difficult, make sure your room is centered below your sixth chakra (see *Disorientation* and *Dizziness*), and that your Sentry and aura boundary systems are strong enough to allow you some privacy. See the sections on "Defining Your Aura" (page 27) and "Advanced Techniques" (page 101).

SADNESS: Sadness is a beautiful, watery energy that can bring stability to an overwrought emotional body. Sadness asks us to slow down, feel the losses of life, and mourn them properly. However, sadness can become chronic when it is ignored or suppressed. See *Crying* and *Despair*, and the section on "Channeling Your Emotions" (page 89).

SCHIZOPHRENIA: An incurable psychiatric disorder in the Western medical model, often linked to the misunderstood fifth-chakra ability of *clairaudience*, or hearing voices. Uncontrolled clairaudience is easily curable through the psychic healing techniques taught throughout this book, especially grounding, creating a room in your head, reading and healing the chakras, and burning contracts. See *Ears, Clairaudience*, and *Insanity*, and the section on the fifth chakra (page 192).

SLEEPLESSNESS: After all the physical causes are examined and discarded, sleeplessness can be seen as an unwillingness to doze off while things are left undone and issues go unresolved. Sleeplessness is a good thing, if it can be seen as the sign of a heightened awareness that will not allow you to go unconscious any longer. A sleepless body, however, needs help. See *Insomnia*, and the sections on "Destroying Images" (page 56) and "Burning Contracts" (page 77) for help in releasing the energy that keeps you awake and activated.

SPACINESS: See *Disorientation* and *Dizziness*.

STARTLE RESPONSE: See *Jumpiness*.

STOMACH PAIN: Fleeting stomach pain can often be a signal from your aura and your third chakra about unhealthy energy in that area. A revitalized aura boundary and a sturdier Sentry are often called for when your body gets involved in your spiritual defense mechanisms. If your stomach distress is of long duration, and includes hiatal hernias, ulcers, or colon and bowel distress, you may have a chronic case of poor self-preservation and an injured third chakra. Please pay specific attention to the Sentry and aura work throughout this book, and check the sections on "Reading Your Aura" (page 121), "Advanced Techniques" (page 101), and the sections on the second and third chakras (pages 158 and 171).

SUICIDAL URGES: Often a sign of repressed anger, rage, and fury, suicidal feelings have a power that can easily overwhelm you—not to mention your friends, family, support group, or therapist (no kidding!). When they can be rededicated and channeled, suicidal feelings can bring complete certainty to long-standing emotional confusions or muddled and obscure relationships. Suicidal urges can also be channeled into swift and decisive action in situations where one might otherwise be paralyzed by indecision.

The energy of suicide requires a death, *but not the death of the central being!* Suicidal feelings say, "Give me liberty, or give me death!" If you ask your suicidal urge what you should kill, it will tell you in no uncertain terms: "This weakness, this relationship, these flashbacks, this poverty, this feeling of worthlessness, this discomfort in the world, this depression, this situation. . . ." It will tell you what part of your life is unlivable, and, if you let it, it will help you kill off the life-aspect that is tormenting you. In essence, you can channel your suicidal feelings into your image destroying, your contract burning, and your separation processes. Your suicidal energy will help you liberate yourself on an energy level, and this inner liberation will help you become free in the world.

This is a repetition of the information in "Channeling Your Emotions," but it bears repeating if you live in terror of your own suicidal urges. Nothing exists in your life or your psyche unless it is meant to be there. All parts of you have healing attributes *and* destructive attributes. Each illness, wellness, triumph, and catastrophe has its place in your wholeness. Each will move you along in consciousness, if you will only be aware of its message and of the necessity of its presence. Everything in your psyche has been placed there specifically, by you, or by your choices in life. Every part of you is a double-edged sword that can protect and heal you, or slice you to bits. Suicidal urges are no exception to this rule.

Sometimes, suicidal feelings are the only ones that offer any hope of escape. They can be very comforting in that way. They offer an end to the drama and the possibility of a rest. We know, however, that expressing suicidal urges will end our lives, while repressing them will drive us out of our minds and our bodies. As with the channeling of any other strong emotional state, channeling suicidal urges can bring about remarkable healing changes, and, along with them, a cessation of uncontrollable suicidal mood swings. When suicidal urges are neither expressed nor repressed, but *channeled* instead, their exquisite arsenal can be used to help kill off old, unworkable aspects of our lives.

The current model of talking suicide urges away with beautiful tales of the inherent meaning of life—or drugging them to sleep—does not in any way address their reality. Suicidal urges require *death*, and often violent death at that. All the sweetness and light in the world are a total lie to the suicidal urge. Peppiness only serves to degrade and ignore the brilliant, integral message of the urge.

Suicide says it will have freedom or cease to exist. It is that serious about the issues it has come to address. Suicide does not ask for lithium or Prozac, nor does it want to be lulled by pretty songs. *It wants to kill.* If you use its energy to blast images to smithereens, and torch contracts in huge pyres, it will have its kill, and will then abate, as it was meant to. In a healthy system, emotions are fleeting. They arrive, they conquer the issue, and then they leave. Even suicidal urges, if properly channeled, will go away until another death is required. If you maintain emotional awareness, such requirements arise less frequently.

In our society, though, emotions are tragically and fatally misunderstood. We label each one as positive or negative. We strangle the life out of the positive ones by trying to have them at all times, no matter what is happening in our lives. We stuff and ignore the negative ones, or bury them in a pile of pseudo-spiritual psycho-babble, and we go quietly insane in the process. Then we wonder why we can't make decisions, why our lives have no meaning, and why we feel completely powerless—disconnected from body *and* spirit.

Let's go over this one again: true wellness is *wholeness*, not perfection. True wellness includes the body and all its knowledge, the mind and all its data, the spirit and all its information, and the emotions and all their messages. Balance comes when all four parts of the quaternity are working together. It's not easy to balance mind, spirit, body, and emotion; it's just imperative.

If you have experienced suicidal urges, go back and reread the section on "Channeling Your Emotions" (page 89). Remember that calling up any emotion to practice channeling is counterfeit. If you are feeling suicidal right now, your emotions are signaling that it is time for you to channel. If you are just reading this topic for fun, and you are not currently experiencing suicidal urges, DO NOT CHANNEL THEM! If you're alive in today's culture, you already have too much practice in playing with, devaluing, and faking your emotions. Don't do it now. Your emotions have had enough of that nonsense.

As with other deep emotional states, suicidal urges may call for a balancing Bach Flower Remedy. I've experienced excellent and long-lasting results with the remedies Cherry Plum, Gorse, Mustard, Sweet Chestnut, Star of Bethlehem, and Walnut.

TERROR: Terror is fear gone wild, and a sign that normal levels of fear have long been ignored and belittled. This hot, intense, get-me-the-hell-out-of-here energy signals a tremendous life-threatening danger in the inner or outer environment. As such, terror must be dealt with immediately, and not coddled or reasoned back into shallower, more manageable levels of fear and trepidation. As with any strong emotion, an underlying physical imbalance may be the cause. A trip to the acupuncturist is well-advised. Channeling the emotion of terror, however, will often light up the root cause more effectively. See *Anxiety*, *Fear*, and *Panic Attacks*, and the sections on the protective third chakra (page 171), and "Channeling Your Emotions" (page 89).

THIRD EYE: Also known as the sixth chakra, the third eye is the energy center of clairvoyance and discernment. See *Visions*, and the section on the sixth chakra (page 204).

THROAT CHAKRA: Also known as the fifth chakra, the throat chakra is the energy center of communication and clairaudience, commitment, and the ability to change. See *Ears*, *Ringing in the Ears*, and the section on the fifth chakra (page 192).

VISIONS: Visions are signs of activity in your sixth chakra, or third eye. If the visions are reasonably connected to your life, enjoy them. If they are confusing or disconnected, your sixth chakra, and most likely your chakra system as a whole, is not healthy. Work through the sections on the chakras, and learn to read, heal, protect, and align your entire chakra system.

Special topic: If you have created a room in your head, and the visions started soon after, you have probably placed your room too high, and are sitting behind your clairvoyant, vision-receiving sixth chakra instead of behind your eyes. Destroy your room and create a new one with the ceiling no higher than your eyebrows.

WEEPINESS: See *Crying*, *Despair*, and *Sadness*.

BIBLIOGRAPHY

Bly, Robert. *A Little Book on the Human Shadow*. San Francisco: HarperSanFrancisco, 1988.

———. *Iron John*. New York: Vintage Books, 1990.

———. *The Sibling Society*. New York: Addison-Wesley, 1996.

De Becker, Gavin. *The Gift of Fear: Survival Signals that Protect Us From Violence*. Boston: Little, Brown, 1997.

Estes, Clarissa Pinkola. *Women Who Run With the Wolves*. New York: Ballantine, 1992.

Gawain, Shakti. *The Path of Transformation*. Mill Valley, CA: Nataraj, 1993.

Grant, Joan. *The Eyes of Horus*. Columbus, OH: Ariel Press, 1988.

Hillman, James. *The Soul's Code: In Search of Character and Calling*. New York: Random, 1996.

Hillman, James and Michael Ventura. *We've Had a Hundred Years of Psychotherapy, and the World's Getting Worse*. San Francisco: HarperSanFrancisco, 1992.

Jeffers, Susan. *Feel the Fear and Do It Anyway*. New York: Harcourt Brace, 1987.

Johnson, Robert. *He: Understanding Masculine Psychology*. New York: Harper Perennial, 1977.

———. *She: Understanding Feminine Psychology*. New York: Harper Perennial, 1977.

———. *Owning Your Own Shadow*. San Francisco: HarperSanFrancisco, 1993.

Kopp, Sheldon B. *If You Meet the Buddha on the Road, Kill Him!* New York: Bantam, 1972.

McLaren, Karla. *Rebuilding the Garden: Healing the Spiritual Wounds of Childhood Sexual Assault*. Columbia, CA: Laughing Tree Press, 1997.

Meade, Michael. *Men and the Water of Life*. San Francisco: HarperSanFrancisco, 1993.

Myss, Caroline. *Energy Anatomy*. Six-tape audio series: Sounds True, 1995. Boulder, CO (800) 333-9185.

———. *Spiritual Madness*. Audiotape: Sounds True, 1996. Boulder, CO. (800) 333-9185.

Rector-Page, Linda. *Healthy Healing: A Guide to Self Healing for Everyone*. Palm Beach, FL: Healthy Healing Publications, 1996.

Roberts, Jane. *The Education of Oversoul Seven*. Englewood Cliffs, NJ: Prentice Hall, 1973.

Scheffer, Mechthild. *Bach Flower Therapy: Theory and Practice*. Rochester, VT: Healing Arts Press, 1988.

Sher, Barbara. *Wishcraft: How to Get What You Really Want*. New York: Ballantine, 1979.

Vonnegut, Kurt. *Cats Cradle*. New York: Holt, Rinehart and Winston, 1963.

Wing, R.L.. *The I Ching Workbook*. New York: Doubleday, 1979.

Yutan, Lin. *The Importance of Living*. New York: John Day, 1937.

Zweig, Connie and Jeremiah Abrams. *Meeting the Shadow: The Hidden Power of the Dark Side of Human Nature*. New York: Tarcher/Putnam, 1991.

Zweig, Connie and Steve Wolf. *Romancing the Shadow: Illuminating the Dark Side of the Soul*. New York: Ballantine Books, 1997.

INDEX

In her nearly thirty years of spiritual study, Karla McLaren has explored many forms of healing, but found that she could only apply herself in areas of real need. She has focused her practice for the last fifteen years on survivors of dissociative trauma (molestation, imprisonment, psychotic breaks, violent crime, and torture). These survivors had received, on average, five years of traditional therapy and yet had not fully recovered. Determined to offer an alternative, McLaren found a swift, sure, and loving way to help such survivors out of their traumas and back into the present. Her first two books, written for molestation survivors, *Rebuilding the Garden* and *Further Into the Garden* (Laughing Tree Press, 1997) are chronicles of that process. After seeing firsthand the incredible confusion and damage caused by ungrounded, immature, and unsafe spiritual practices, she now writes to provide the same sort of no-nonsense spiritual information for everyone. McLaren lectures and teaches nationwide. Karla and her family live with an ever-expanding mob of stray cats in the foothills of California's Sierra Nevada.

Photo credit: Sue Sparks